M000106060

BREAKING
WITH
TRADITION

THE SHIFT TO COMPETENCY-BASED LEARNING IN PLCS AT WORK™

Brian M. Stack **Jonathan G. Vander Els**

WITH A FOREWORD BY CHRIS STURGIS

Solution Tree | Press

a division of
Solution Tree

555 North Morton Street
Bloomington, IN 47404
800.733.6786 (toll free) / 812.336.7700
FAX: 812.336.7790

email: info@SolutionTree.com
SolutionTree.com

Visit **go.SolutionTree.com/PLCbooks** to download the free reproducibles in this book.

Printed in the United States of America

21   20   19   18   3   4   5

Library of Congress Cataloging-in-Publication Data
Names: Stack, Brian M., author. | Vander Els, Jonathan G.. author.
Title: Breaking with tradition : the shift to competency-based learning in
    PLCs at WorkTM / Brian M. Stack and Jonathan G. Vander Els.
Description: Bloomington, IN : Solution Tree Press, [2018] | Includes
    bibliographical references and index.
Identifiers: LCCN 2017017773 | ISBN 9781943874897 (perfect bound)
Subjects: LCSH: Competency-based education. | Professional learning
    communities. | Teachers--In-service training. | Teaching--Methodology. |
    Educational change.
Classification: LCC LC1031 .S73 2018 | DDC 370.71/1--dc23 LC record available at https://
lccn.loc.gov/2017017773

Solution Tree
Jeffrey C. Jones, CEO
Edmund M. Ackerman, President

Solution Tree Press
President and Publisher: Douglas M. Rife
Editorial Director: Sarah Payne-Mills
Art Director: Rian Anderson
Managing Production Editor: Caroline Cascio
Senior Production Editor: Suzanne Kraszewski
Senior Editor: Amy Rubenstein
Copy Editor: Evie Madsen
Proofreader: Miranda Addonizio
Cover Designer: Rian Anderson
Editorial Assistants: Jessi Finn and Kendra Slayton

ACKNOWLEDGMENTS

Breaking With Tradition: The Shift to Competency-Based Learning in PLCs at Work™ represents the synthesis of our professional work as school leaders. Since 2006, we have worked together as part of a highly functioning and dynamic school leadership team in the Sanborn Regional School District in New Hampshire. In addition, the connections and partnerships we have developed over the years with other individuals and organizations similarly engaged in this important work also shape this book.

We are forever indebted to our editors, Amy Rubenstein and Suzanne Kraszewski, and the incredible team at Solution Tree, especially Evie Madsen, Miranda Addonizio, and Rian Anderson, who helped guide and shape our work, as well as to Douglas Rife for believing in our vision. The influence of many Solution Tree authors is evident throughout this book. We thank all of you, none more so than Rick and Becky DuFour, for the tremendous work you have done in helping educators throughout the world understand ways to better support students and teachers everywhere.

To our school leadership team at Sanborn, we could not have developed our understanding and experiences as school leaders around competency-based learning without the team's collaborative efforts and willingness to "jump into the deep end of the pool." Our schools' transformations are a reflection of everyone's hard work and dedication. We would like to thank Brian Blake for his resolute leadership over the years as well as our team members Deb Bamforth, Brian Buckley, Michelle Catena, Carol Coppola, Bob Ficker, Jodi Gutterman, Ann Hadwen, Ellen Hume-Howard, Donna Johnson, Vicki Parady-Guay, Jennifer Pomykato, Annie Rutherford, Sandy Rutherford, Michael Shore, and Michael Turmelle. Additionally, to the incredible Sanborn educators who we have had the honor and pleasure to work with in our schools: thank you. You are an inspiration and exemplars for always putting students and learning first, and for being willing to travel down an unpaved road knowing that there must be a better way to support students.

We owe gratitude to countless professionals who work on competency-based learning nationally for taking time to contribute, inform, and guide us through the development of this book, including Chris Sturgis and Susan Patrick of CompetencyWorks (www.competencyworks.org) and the International Association for K–12 Online Learning (www.inacol.org), New Hampshire Department of Education Deputy Commissioner Paul Leather, and national competency-based learning specialist Rose Colby—for not only her mentorship since the beginning of our journey but also for her ongoing feedback and support as we worked through the writing process.

We would like to thank our many local, state, and national colleagues and partners who continue to strive to make learning experiences better for all students. Your hard work, dedication, and effort are inspiring. We would also like to thank our many colleagues who have reviewed our work and provided valuable insight as professional practitioners. A special thank-you goes to Mike Hopkins and Kyle Repucci, superintendent and assistant superintendent of Rochester School Department (New Hampshire); Kathleen Murphy, special education coordinator of Allenstown School District (New Hampshire); Karen Perry and Aaryn Schmuhl of Henry County Schools (Georgia); Jeff Heyck-Williams of Two Rivers Public Charter School (Washington, DC); Mary Hastings of Great Schools Partnership (Maine); Brian Pickering, former principal of ConVal Regional High School (New Hampshire); Dr. David M. Richards, superintendent of Fraser Public Schools (Michigan); Robert Scully, principal of Souhegan High School (New Hampshire); John Freeman, superintendent of Pittsfield School District SAU#51 (New Hampshire); Dan French of the Center for Collaborative Education (http://cce.org); and Virgel Hammonds, chief learning officer of KnowledgeWorks (www.knowledgeworks.org).

Last, and most important, we could not have undertaken the monumental task of putting our thoughts on paper without the endless support of our families and friends.

To my beautiful wife, Erica, you are and always will be my biggest cheerleader, my rock, and my best friend. To my children Brady, Cameron, Liam, Owen, and Zoey, dream the impossible and always remember that if you put your mind to it, you can accomplish anything. To my parents, Michael and Maria, thank you for your continual support, love, and inspiration along the way.

—Brian

Thank you, with love and gratitude, to my amazing wife, Stephanie. I am forever grateful to you for your love, support, and belief in me. And to Grace, Garrett, and Will, for being the beautiful and wonderful people you are. You each inspire me to be the best person I can be, and I am blessed to learn from and grow with each of you every day. Thank you, as well, to my mom, Linda, my sisters, Wendy and Amy, and to Brian, Nathaniel, James, and Judith for your unending support and love. And to Dad, who still guides me and always will.

—Jon

Solution Tree Press would like to thank the following reviewers:

Rick Bell
Assistant Principal
New Prague Middle School
New Prague, Minnesota

Paul Cone Jr.
Middle School Principal
Canisteo-Greenwood Central School
Canisteo, New York

Julie Delaney
Principal
St. Paul the Apostle Catholic School
Davenport, Iowa

Tim Garcia
Principal
McCook Elementary School
McCook, Nebraska

Brig Leane
Principal
Fruita Middle School
Fruita, Colorado

Michael Roberts
Principal
Desert View Elementary
Hermiston, Oregon

Ryan Rydstrom
Associate Principal
Prairie Point Middle School and Ninth-Grade Academy
Cedar Rapids, Iowa

Justin Syroka
Principal
Cheshire Elementary School
Delaware, Ohio

Cindy Washinowski
Principal
West Middle School
Sioux City, Iowa

Visit **go.SolutionTree.com/PLCbooks** to download the free reproducibles in this book.

TABLE OF CONTENTS

Reproducible pages are in italics.

ABOUT THE AUTHORS

 **Brian M. Stack, MEd,** is principal of Sanborn Regional High School in Kingston, New Hampshire. He is the former assistant principal and curriculum director for the school. Since 2010, Brian has been a member of the research, design, and implementation team for Sanborn Regional School District's nationally recognized K–12 competency-based learning system. Brian, an educator since 2001, is a former high school mathematics teacher, high school administrator, and school board member for three different school districts in New Hampshire and Massachusetts. Brian has also worked as a consultant and expert coach for a number of schools, school districts, and organizations engaged in personalized and competency-based learning across the United States.

Brian is a member of the New Hampshire Association of School Principals (NHASP) and recipient of the 2017 Charles A. Napoli New Hampshire Secondary School Principal of the Year award. In 2010 and again in 2013, he received the NHASP Outstanding Role Model award. Brian is a strong advocate of personalized learning, competency-based learning systems, and high school redesign for the 21st century. He has presented his education reform and redesign work in workshops and conferences all over the United States.

Brian received bachelor's degrees in mathematics and mathematics education from Boston University and a master's degree in education administration from the University of Massachusetts Lowell. He lives with his wife, Erica, and their five children, Brady, Cameron, Liam, Owen, and Zoey, in the New Hampshire Seacoast.

To learn more about Brian's work, visit his blog at http://srhsprincipalsblog.blogspot.com or follow @Bstackbu on Twitter.

Jonathan G. Vander Els, MEd, is director of innovative projects for the New Hampshire Learning Initiative (https://nhlearninginitiative.org), an organization dedicated to seeding and supporting innovation and personalized learning in New Hampshire schools. Formerly, Jonathan was principal of Memorial Elementary School in Sanborn Regional School District in New Hampshire. Under his leadership, Memorial became a nationally recognized model professional learning community (PLC) on AllThingsPLC (www.allthingsplc.info) and competency-based learning elementary school.

Jonathan has consulted, coached, and presented throughout the United States on building highly effective PLCs, implementing competency-based learning, and developing rigorous performance assessments. He is involved in the New Hampshire Performance Assessment of Competency Education, a first-of-its-kind accountability and assessment waiver granted by the U.S. Department of Education. Jonathan has also led the State of New Hampshire's efforts around integrating skills and dispositions into classroom curriculum, instruction, and assessment.

Jonathan has an education specialist degree from the University of New Hampshire in educational administration and supervision, a master's in elementary education, and a bachelor's in history. He is certified as a superintendent, principal, and teacher. Jonathan lives with his wife and three children in the New Hampshire Seacoast.

To learn more about Jonathan's work, visit his blog at https://jonvanderels .wordpress.com or follow @jvanderels on Twitter.

To book Brian M. Stack or Jonathan G. Vander Els for professional development, contact pd@SolutionTree.com.

FOREWORD

By Chris Sturgis, Cofounder, CompetencyWorks

The journey to competency-based education often starts when educators ask themselves a few powerful questions, such as, Are we doing what's best for our students? and What is preventing us from doing better for them? Once educators begin asking these questions, it becomes easier to understand how the United States's antiquated education system, now over 150 years old, can actually get in the way of learning. The next question they ask, of course, is What do we need to do differently? In *Breaking With Tradition: The Shift to Competency-Based Learning in PLCs at Work*, authors Brian M. Stack and Jonathan G. Vander Els serve up an in-depth exploration of how districts are redesigning their education systems to address those questions.

I became acquainted with Brian and Jon's work at the Sanborn Regional School District in Kingston, New Hampshire, soon after the launch of CompetencyWorks. Brian and Jon were—and are—risk-takers. They were willing to dive headfirst into competency education at a time when there were few models and a sparse amount of literature on the topic. They also took a different kind of risk when they publicly shared their learning along their journey as contributing authors at CompetencyWorks. They shared when things seemed to be working and when things didn't work out as well as they had hoped. In so doing, Brian and Jon embody the values of competency-based education, where learning is the ultimate goal and mistakes are simply opportunities to learn more.

Brian, Jon, and the Sanborn leadership team balanced their drive toward innovation with deep attention to execution. Before taking steps forward, they learned as much as they could. They sought to understand the activities or processes that made up the load-bearing walls of the new system and then ensured those activities and processes were fully resourced. They understood that in designing a new system, the pieces had to fit together. Designing the new system required attention to fidelity. With their commitment to innovation and execution, the authors will be the first to tell you that they never stopped learning.

Brian and Jon taught me that competency education is not just about focusing on student learning; it is equally about supporting the learning of the adults in the system. During my visit to Sanborn in 2014, Jon, then principal of its Memorial Elementary, showed me what the school called the "writing wall," where teachers were collaboratively learning about helping students to write. Taped along the entire hallway were examples of student work for each performance level with stickers showing by grade level how many students were at each level. Teachers used the wall to build a shared understanding of what it really means to be proficient at a grade level and to exchange ideas about how to help students build their skills. What Brian and Jon showed me is that the trick to building a competency-based system is to begin with investing in strong professional learning communities (PLCs). Competency-based education requires investing in teachers and their learning.

Breaking With Tradition is written by educators for educators who want to learn about competency-based education. In this book, you will find an in-depth exploration of the five-part definition of competency-based education that one hundred innovators developed in 2011 at the first national Competency-Based Learning Summit. Brian and Jon describe how the PLC process is the foundation on which the five elements rest to form a new education system. They also tackle the issues that often befuddle districts converting to competency education, including assessment, grading, and identifying the necessary schoolwide support structures.

Breaking With Tradition is a powerful resource for educators who are learning about competency education if they take the time to use the reflection questions and rubrics to spark dialogue and challenge their assumptions. Competency-based education isn't just a technical reform. It requires a cultural shift to the belief that everyone can learn if he or she receives the resources and time to do so. Find others to read Breaking With Tradition along with you, or create opportunities in your school for collaborative learning. Your first steps toward creating a system where every student is learning and progressing can start right now. Brian Stack and Jonathan Vander Els will be wonderful guides for your journey.

INTRODUCTION

Now is the most exciting time to be an educator in the United States because competency-based learning has the potential to provide students with opportunities that have never before existed in American schools. In this model, learning is a true measure of what a student knows and is able to do, and teachers work collaboratively in an environment that is both personalized and student centered, two of the defining characteristics of this model. With competency-based learning, educators can effect tremendous change and leverage opportunities for students to have choice and voice in their learning in new and exciting ways.

The federal Every Student Succeeds Act (ESSA), signed into law by President Obama in 2015, is impacting policy changes at the state level that are allowing competency-based learning models to take hold in schools across the United States, as educators have come to recognize that the American education system is broken. This trend is also apparent internationally. There are currently sixty-five countries making use of the Programme for International Student Assessment (PISA) to answer the fundamental question, What is important for citizens to know and be able to do? The highest achieving countries on this exam share many qualities with the competency-based learning model. They integrate curriculum, instruction, and assessment and use performance tasks to measure mastery of learning and the development of critical work study practices. We have spent too much time and too many resources testing students in an effort to prove whether our schools are effective. We have endlessly debated how we should change the way we evaluate teachers and school administrators. We have introduced countless programs and initiatives that we believed would provide students with better opportunities in school and beyond. Prior to the advent of competency-based learning, our shortfall was that we spent too much time focused on system-centered, not learning-centered approaches to education. Somewhere in our efforts to hold people accountable and uphold the ideals of a free and appropriate education for all, we lost sight of what the real purpose of schools *should* be: learning for all, whatever it takes (DuFour, DuFour, Eaker, Many, & Mattos, 2016). Competency-based learning focuses on that goal.

Building-level school leaders, administrators, and teacher leaders—those who are in the trenches leading their schools from traditional to competency-based learning models and those who are looking to support schools through the change process—will find this book useful. *Breaking With Tradition* makes a strong correlation between the professional learning community (PLC) framework and competency-based learning, but note that this book will not only help practicing PLCs but also schools that need to further develop or begin implementation of their collaborative structures. Regardless of where a school is on its PLC journey, this book assists the reader in finding growth areas in his or her school.

Each chapter will help school leaders understand how to sustain the change process in their schools; how to support educators in their efforts to develop the curriculum, instruction, and assessment processes that will guide them on their competency-based learning journey; and how the PLC model supports the overall work of a competency-based learning school. A summary of each chapter follows.

- ▶ Chapter 1 provides a foundation by outlining a five-part definition for competency-based learning.

- ▶ Chapter 2 focuses on the role of the PLC framework in schools implementing competency-based learning. Readers learn the components of successful PLCs and how to leverage the PLC framework to support competency-based learning design principles in schools.

- ▶ Chapter 3 focuses on the first critical question of a PLC in the context of a competency-based learning model: What knowledge, skills, and dispositions should every student acquire as a result of this unit, this course, or this grade level (DuFour et al., 2016)? Educators answer this question through the development of effective competency statements. Readers learn how to develop schoolwide and course-specific competencies that include explicit, measurable, transferable learning objectives to empower all students.

- ▶ Chapter 4 looks at changing traditional grading practices. Readers learn how teams within a PLC support competency-friendly grading practices for both academic skills and academic behaviors.

- ▶ Chapter 5 looks at assessment development, specifically in the context of the second critical question of a PLC: How will we know when each student has acquired the essential knowledge and skills (DuFour et al., 2016)?

Readers learn how teams within a PLC develop systems of comprehensive assessment to formatively and summatively assess students' competency and growth.

- ▸ Chapter 6 focuses on schoolwide support structures as they relate to the third and fourth critical questions of a PLC: How will we respond when some students do not learn and how will we extend the learning for students who are already proficient? (DuFour et al., 2016)? Readers learn how in a competency-based school, individual teachers, teams, and the school as a whole respond when students need interventions or extensions.

- ▸ Chapter 7 focuses on change management in the school setting. Readers learn how to sustain the change process in their schools as they begin to evolve from a traditional to a competency-based learning philosophy.

Embedded throughout the book are real-world examples of competency-based learning from schools and districts throughout the United States. These stories offer a practitioner perspective on how to turn theory into practice. Although not specifically highlighted as practitioner perspectives in this book, readers may also learn from several international examples of competency-based learning. Countries that score high on the PISA and that have made a commitment to a competency-based approach include Finland, Sweden, Canada, and New Zealand (Bristow & Patrick, 2014).

As you undertake the work of implementing a competency-based learning model, you may find it to be some of the hardest work of your career; however, you will also find it to be some of the most rewarding because your school will truly become laser focused on student learning. Student engagement, ownership of learning, and career and college readiness will be the ultimate, tangible outcomes of this work.

CHAPTER 1

Understanding the Components of an Effective Competency-Based Learning System

Think back to when you first learned to drive a car. Knowing what you know now as a more experienced driver, would you change anything about the way you first learned to drive? Brian's experience with learning how to drive a car happened like this.

As a sixteen-year-old teenager in New Hampshire, Brian, along with his father, spent every day backing in and out of driveways while Brian delivered newspapers in the neighborhood. Brian's father would take him to shopping malls after hours to practice parking. He eventually brought Brian to a point where he could drive on quiet streets in town as he started to learn the rules of the road.

Then, Brian started a formal driver education program. Like many programs, it consisted of both classroom instruction and actual driving on the road with an instructor. To this day, Brian doesn't remember a single thing about the instruction he received in those thirty classroom hours, but he does know that the class culminated with him memorizing a lot of arbitrary facts and figures so that he would pass the written driving exam, an exam which would contain twenty-five multiple-choice questions based on information in the *State of New Hampshire Driver's Manual*. This test never caused anxiety for Brian because he already knew how to "play that game of school" from other experiences. He was very good at cramming for multiple-choice tests, knowing what sorts of random facts and figures his teachers would likely quiz him on. The driver education manual made it easy; the real driving test would just be a subset of the one-hundred–question practice test in the back of the book.

What did scare Brian as a young teen and soon-to-be driver was not the written test, but rather the time he would have to spend in a car with an instructor, and, even more so, the actual driving test with someone from the Department of Motor Vehicles. Brian knew his skills, or lack thereof, would be on full display during the driving instruction sessions and test. He had to perform. Knowing that one false move with a car could spell disaster, there was little, if any, room for error.

As Brian reflects back on his driver education experience, a few things stand out to him that are rarely seen in our schools, such as the following.

▸ In driver education, all students are working toward the same explicit and measurable learning goal of being able to safely and effectively drive a car in any condition or setting.

▸ To a certain extent, driver education allows students to move at their own pace. Students progress from skill to skill when they are ready through their driving practice. There is no set maximum amount of time students should spend learning a particular driving skill, and students are encouraged to practice with family members on their own time to become secure with their skills.

▸ Driver education can adapt to individual student needs. Those who need more practice with a skill like parking or highway driving can get differentiated support either from their driving instructor or others (in Brian's case, his father).

▸ The true test of whether or not a student has mastered driver education is performance based; the student must drive a car while an outsider evaluates his or her performance against a specific set of driving standards.

> ▸ Driver education is not the final step toward mastery of the road; it is just the beginning. The longer you drive a car, the better you get at driving. Driver education serves as an initial base to help students apply their new driving skills and develop better habits and dispositions for a lifetime of effective driving.

Driver education is an excellent way to introduce the topic of competency-based learning for two reasons: (1) it is an education program that many Americans experience at one point in their lifetime, and (2) driver education has many of the hallmarks and characteristics of a competency-based learning model. The concept of competency-based learning is often interpreted differently from school to school and, in some cases, from state to state. This chapter provides the reader with a framework and a foundation for the rest of the book by outlining a five-part definition for competency-based learning.

A Definition of Competency-Based Learning

Competency-based learning has become a common term in education reform. The model is born from the notion that seat time and Carnegie units (credit hours) cannot confine elementary schools, secondary schools, and institutions of higher education when organizing how students will progress through learning. In a system of competency-based learning, a student's ability to transfer knowledge and apply skills across content areas organizes his or her learning. *Transfer* means that students are able to take what they have learned (the skills and content within a course) and apply this skill and knowledge across other disciplines to solve unfamiliar problems. Students refine their skills based on the feedback they receive through formative assessment (assessment *for* learning) and, when they are ready, demonstrate their understanding through summative assessment (assessment *of* learning; Stiggins, 2005). Competency-based learning meets each learner where he or she is and allows the student to progress at his or her own speed along a developmental continuum. Chris Sturgis (2015) provides a clear and concise five-part working definition of competency-based learning:

In a system of competency-based learning, a student's ability to transfer knowledge and apply skills across content areas organizes his or her learning.

> › Students advance upon demonstrated mastery;
> › Competencies include explicit, measurable, and transferable learning objectives that empower students;

> › Assessment is meaningful and a positive learning experience for students;

> › Students receive timely, differentiated support based on their individual learning needs; and

> › Learning outcomes emphasize competencies that include application and creation of knowledge, along with the development of important skills and dispositions. (p. 8)

Organizations like the International Association for K–12 Online Learning (iNACOL; www.inacol.org/about) use Sturgis's (2015) definition as a basis for much of their policy advocacy and learning systems transformation work. In the pages that follow, we expand on this definition and provide context for school leaders.

Students Advance Upon Demonstrated Mastery

Fred Bramante and Rose Colby (2012) write extensively about how educators should imagine a school without clocks, and think about what it would look like to move the standard measure of learning from seat time to mastery of learning objectives. Secondary schools and colleges have used time as the standard measure of learning since the American industrialist and steel mogul Andrew Carnegie first proposed the idea in the early 1900s. The Carnegie unit was introduced as a way to award academic credit based on the amount of time students spent in direct contact with a teacher or professor. The standard Carnegie unit has long since been defined as 120 hours of contact time with an instructor, an amount roughly equivalent to one hour of instruction a day, five days a week, for twenty-four weeks or 7,200 minutes of instructional time over the course of an academic year. At the time of its inception, the Carnegie unit helped bring a level of standardization that the American education system had never seen. It provided for the education model what the dollar first provided for our financial system: a common language and a common unit of measure that could be quantified, assessed, and traded (Silva, White, & Toch, 2015).

Education reformers like Bramante and Colby have challenged Carnegie's industrialist model for measuring learning. They believe there are more effective ways to measure student learning, but it hasn't been until the mid-2000s to present that these reformers had the opportunity to challenge the model at a systemic level through policy changes at the state level in states such as New Hampshire that have been early adopters of the model. Bramante and Colby (2012) write:

> That opportunity to reimagine public education is before us today. At no other time in public education have we been so challenged by the constraints of the economy, the public outcry for changes in financing personnel and resources, and the demand for accountability through testing. (p. 2)

Bramante and Colby (2012) call for moving from a system that measures learning by the minutes a student sits in front of a teacher to one based on mastery of learning objectives. Their work challenges the organizational structure of most American schools. If schools no longer use seat time to measure student learning, how will that impact schools of the future?

Both school and education policy leaders use the following arguments to support why the Carnegie unit should *not* be removed from American schools. We add our own counterarguments that support the removal of the Carnegie unit to each argument as well.

- ▸ **Argument:** Without the Carnegie unit and a nationally defined and mandated curriculum, Americans will lose the level of standardization schools have to measure learning.

    Counterargument: We argue that there are better ways to provide a standard measure for learning in schools. The Common Core State Standards (CCSS) Initiative (www.corestandards.org) and state and local standards provide the ruler sticks for which schools could and should measure student learning.

- ▸ **Argument:** If schools remove all time requirements, they run the risk that students will advance through grade levels at a pace that exceeds their social maturity.

    Counterargument: If schools use a student mastery model, then they must develop quality instruction for each of the standards and student learning objectives they will measure. Good instruction takes time; it is unlikely that a student would advance through multiple grade levels too quickly, although the notion of students moving on when ready does highlight other considerations schools must balance, which leads to the next argument.

- ▸ **Argument:** Without time as the constant, schools will move away from grade levels, which will require a whole new organizational structure in schools, impacting everything from staffing and funding to the organization of grade levels and school calendars.

    Counterargument: This is a very valid point; however, rather than use it as a reason not to move forward with competency-based learning, it should be seen as the rallying point that will define a brave new world of American schools that are flexible enough to grow and adapt with students, providing them with a level of personalization and differentiation that is unparalleled in traditional school systems.

In competency-based learning schools, standards are the true measure of learning. With carefully crafted assessments tied to standards and rubrics that can measure to what degree students have mastered a concept or skill, it is possible to create a structure whereby students can advance to mastery. The simplest way to imagine this model in action is to look at successful online schools. Unbound by the organizational structures of traditional calendars, bell schedules, and staffing patterns, many online schools have developed successful competency-based "move when ready" systems. Here are two examples.

The Virtual Learning Academy Charter School (VLACS; http://vlacs.org) is the largest charter school in New Hampshire. Each year, thousands of middle and high school students enroll in VLACS programming, either as full- or part-time students looking to supplement their regular education programming. Students can register for full courses or they can complete a smaller subset of the course that pertains to a specific competency. Each module in each VLACS course aligns with specific state or national competencies, standards, and frameworks, depending on the course. Students move at their own pace through academic work. VLACS teachers, many of whom also work in traditional schools, are assigned a cohort of students to follow through their course or courses. Since online modules deliver direct instruction, the role of a VLACS teacher is very different than in a traditional school. VLACS teachers spend much of their time monitoring student progress and providing students with the reteaching, intervention, and enrichment needed to personalize their academic experience. For the VLACS student, the experience is self-paced. Students are able to move on when ready. When they start a new course, they are assigned a teacher who monitors their progress, provides ongoing feedback and assessment of their work, and conducts regular virtual meetings with them and, in some cases, their parents, throughout the learning experience.

Southern New Hampshire University (SNHU; http://degrees.snhu.edu) in Manchester, New Hampshire, has a similar model for its College for America (http://collegeforamerica.org) program. Through its redesigned model, SNHU has managed to change the role of its teachers from classroom-based lecturers or instructors to professionals who are part instructor, part learning coach, and part curriculum and content developer. The notion of a *learning coach*—an individual who can help students set academic goals for themselves and put all of the pieces together when they are learning a new concept or skill—is a new idea for colleges or universities, much like it is for traditional K–12 schools.

Most traditional schools don't have the luxury or the desire to use an online model to deliver all direct instruction. For these schools, developing a move-when-ready model includes the use of blended learning. Michael B. Horn and Heather

Staker (2015) explain their (and the most widely used) definition for *blended learning* in education:

> Blended learning is any formal education program in which a student learns at least part through online learning, with some element of student control over time, place, path, and/or pace. (p. 34)

Blended learning takes place at least in part in a supervised physical school location, often the student's neighborhood school. It is an integrated experience that brings together in a seamless balance both face-to-face instruction and online coursework for individual students based on their learning needs.

Horn and Staker (2015) propose several blended learning strategies that schools can use to develop move-when-ready systems. There are *rotational models* in which students rotate on a fixed schedule between face-to-face and online learning modalities. There are *flex models* that rely on online modules as the foundation and then bring in face-to-face instruction when it is relevant or appropriate to do so. There are *à la carte models* that provide students with the option to take full courses either traditionally or online during the school day. Finally, there are *enriched virtual models* that require students to engage in a set number of face-to-face learning sessions but then allow students to customize the rest of their learning experience with online work. These blended learning strategies are the key to helping schools develop structures for students to advance upon demonstrated mastery, the first characteristic of a competency-based learning system.

Competencies Include Explicit, Measurable, and Transferable Learning Objectives That Empower Students

Typical competency-based learning schools organize their courses into a series of measureable learning objectives that provide the foundation for the courses and ultimately for the grades that a student receives. A common practice in competency-based learning schools is to require that students demonstrate mastery on each learning objective in order to receive credit for the course as a whole. This practice, many argue, encourages students to take responsibility for their learning, increasing both student engagement and motivation. To understand this organizational structure, it helps to examine some real-life examples.

In the Henry County Schools (n.d.a) in McDonough, Georgia, students in high school language arts classes work toward several graduation competencies. For example, "Read closely to analyze and evaluate all forms of *(i.e. complex literary and informational)* texts" (Henry County Schools, n.d.a, p. 10). From this overarching statement, each language arts course then has the following explicit, measurable, transferable learning objectives (called *performance indicators* in Henry County's competency system):

> Cite strong and thorough textual evidence to support an analysis of the text, including any applicable primary or High School sources, and determine both explicit and implicit meanings, such as inferences that can be drawn from the text and where the text leaves matters uncertain.

> Determine the central ideas of the text and provide an objective summary.

> Analyze a complex set of ideas or sequence of events and explain how specific individuals, ideas, or events interact and develop over the course of the text.

> Determine the meaning of words and phrases as they are used in the text, including figurative, connotative, and technical meanings; analyze the impact of specific word choices on meaning and tone of a text or texts, including words with multiple meanings or language that is particularly effective for a desired purpose.

> Analyze how an author chose to structure a text and how that structure contributes to the text's meaning and its aesthetic and rhetorical impact.

> Determine an author's point of view, purpose, or rhetorical strategies in a text, analyzing how style and content contribute to the power, persuasiveness, or beauty of the text.

> Evaluate information from multiple sources presented in diverse media and formats (e.g., print, digital, visual, quantitative) to address a question or solve a problem.

> Delineate and evaluate the argument and specific claims in a text, assessing whether the reasoning is valid and the evidence is relevant and sufficient; identify false statements and fallacious reasoning.

> Integrate information from diverse sources into a coherent understanding of an idea or event, evaluating discrepancies among sources. (p. 10)

In the Rochester (New Hampshire) School Department (n.d.), the grade 3 mathematics curriculum is organized into the following learning objectives:

> Operations and Algebraic Thinking: Students will demonstrate the ability to compute accurately, make reasonable estimates, understand meanings of operations and use algebraic notation to represent and analyze patterns and relationships.

> › Number and Numeration in Base Ten/Fractions: Students will demonstrate the ability to understand the meanings, uses, and representations of numbers as well as equivalent names for numbers.
>
> › Measurement: Students will demonstrate the ability to understand the systems and processes of measurement, using appropriate techniques, tools, units, and formulas in making measurements.
>
> › Data: Students will demonstrate the ability to represent and analyze data.
>
> › Geometry: Students will demonstrate the ability to investigate characteristics and properties of two and three dimensional geometric shapes and apply transformations and symmetry in geometric situations.
>
> › Fact Fluency: Students will demonstrate the ability to quickly and accurately verbalize and compute fact fluency. (p. 1)

There is nothing inherently unique about the learning objectives in the Henry County and Rochester schools. Many will recognize them as being based on English language arts and mathematics CCSS (National Governors Association Center for Best Practices [NGA] & Council of Chief State School Officers [CCSSO], 2010a, 2010b). What sets both of these school systems apart is not that they have developed these learning objectives, but rather that the objectives have been integrated into courses and are used to promote both student engagement and motivation at a level that most schools have not yet reached.

What sets both of these school systems apart is not that they have developed these learning objectives, but rather that the objectives have been integrated into courses and are used to promote both student engagement and motivation at a level that most schools have not yet reached.

Henry County and Rochester teachers, for example, do not organize the assessment systems for their courses around grading categories such as tests, quizzes, homework, classwork, and participation. The learning objectives themselves are the grading categories. It follows, then, that when a teacher gives a formative or summative assessment, he or she is able to link the assessment directly to the learning objective. Students follow their progression through the various learning objectives for each of their courses. At the high school level, when students reach the end of the course, they earn credit only if they have mastered each of the learning outcomes. If they have not, a plan is put in place to help them recover those outcomes. At Rochester's Spaulding High School, competency recovery can take a variety of forms depending on what the student needs. Plans could include the completion of online courses or modules within courses that address specific competencies, the completion of a specific teacher-assigned performance task for a specific competency, or other similar demonstrations of learning. Once the student has demonstrated mastery of the course outcomes, he or she is awarded credit for the overall course.

The Henry County and Rochester models place student learning and mastery of learning objectives as the ultimate goal for all students. Both schools increase student engagement and motivation because at all times in the learning process, students know exactly what it is they need to know and be able to do to be successful. They take away the guessing games that many students play in traditional school models. In these traditional models, grades are simply a game of earning points. If a passing grade is a numerical score of 70, students simply have to complete enough work to earn the points necessary to reach the passing threshold. Oftentimes when students struggle in a traditional model, the feedback they receive is connected more to their behavior toward learning than to the actual learning itself. Teachers tell students to try harder, stay after school for help, raise their hands more during class, and do more homework. In contrast, if a student is struggling at a Henry County or Rochester school, he or she can tell the teacher exactly what skills or learning outcomes he or she needs help with, and teachers see when students are struggling with certain skills or learning outcomes, rather than finding out when a student doesn't do well on a summative assessment. The teacher works with the student to develop academic plans to improve his or her learning in those areas.

Assessment Is Meaningful and a Positive Learning Experience for Students

Not all assessments are created equally. If you talk to any student at any grade level in a traditional school, he or she is likely to tell you that his or her teacher approaches assessment in a way that is very different from other teachers. To effectively implement a competency-based learning model, you have to change this mindset and standardize the assessment process. The Center for Collaborative Education (CCE; http://cce.org) in Boston laid much of the foundation for this in its Quality Performance Assessment (QPA) framework (see figure 1.1). CCE (2012) defines a *performance assessment* as "multistep assignments with clear criteria, expectations, and processes that measure how well a student transfers knowledge and applies complex skills to create or refine an original product" (p. vi). Performance assessments can be formative or summative.

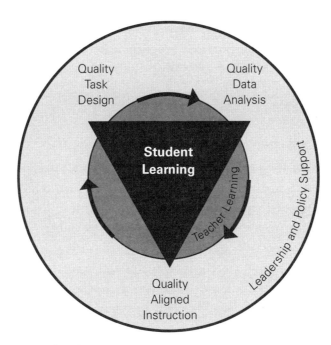

Quality
Task
Design

Quality
Data
Analysis

**Student
Learning**

Teacher Learning

Leadership and Policy Support

Quality
Aligned
Instruction

Source: CCE, 2012. Used with permission.

Figure 1.1: Center for Collaborative Education QPA framework.

The QPA framework places student learning at the center of the cycle. Teachers focus on standards-aligned quality instruction and assessment practices, providing students with multiple opportunities to demonstrate mastery. Working collaboratively, teachers use quality task design strategies to develop an appropriate set of prompts and a common understanding of content and cognitive complexity for each grade level. Finally, using quality data analysis, teacher teams examine both teacher and student assessment data to ensure that assessments are reliable, valid, free of bias, and provide sufficient evidence of learning.

CCE Executive Director Dan French (CCE, 2012) writes, "Embedding high-quality performance assessments throughout the core academic curriculum will result in an increased use of curriculum aligned to the CCSS, robust assessment data, and enhanced student learning" (p. iv). The QPA framework focuses teachers on developing formative and summative performance assessments and using those assessment results to inform instruction and greater revisions of curriculum, which ultimately lead to high-stakes decisions related to graduation and promotion. In this book, we explore several effective strategies collaborative teams can use to implement a quality performance assessment system in their school. The work often starts, however, with schools and districts developing a vision for assessment and a common understanding of how assessment will inform instruction and ultimately impact student learning.

Educators cannot think about assessment without also looking at grading and how grading practices support or don't support a school's vision for assessment. In the following sections, we outline some key considerations for effective competency-based learning grading practices in the following sections. We expand on this topic in chapter 4 (page 69).

Grade to Communicate Student Learning

The purpose of grading should be to communicate student achievement. Grades should not be about what students *earn*; rather, grades should be about what students *learn*. Unfortunately, this is not the case in most traditional classrooms. Traditional grading practices are flawed, at best. One of the hardest hurdles to overcome for any school or community that wants to adopt a competency-based learning model is reaching consensus on the grading practices that each teacher must practice in each course. Students must see consistent practices from classroom to classroom and teacher to teacher, and those practices must support the competency-based learning model.

Use Both Formative and Summative Assessment

The grading system must separate and acknowledge the role of both formative and summative assessment. A *formative assessment* is an assessment *for* learning—a snapshot that captures or a dipstick that measures student progress through the learning process (Stiggins, 2005). It explains to what extent a student is learning a concept, skill, or knowledge set. Teachers use formative assessments to monitor the learning process and obtain feedback on their instruction. Formative assessments also provide students with feedback to help them improve their learning. A *summative assessment* is a comprehensive measure of a student's ability to demonstrate the concepts, skills, and knowledge embedded within a course competency (Stiggins, 2005). An assessment *of* learning occurs at the end of an instructional unit with a teacher who evaluates the level and degree of a student's learning by comparing his or her work to a rubric-defined standard or benchmark.

Stop Averaging Grades

The grading system must no longer include the practice of averaging averages to get more averages. Mathematics teachers know that you can never get reliable data when using averages to produce more averages; yet traditional schools average grades all the time. Teachers average category grades (tests, quizzes, homework, and so on) to get a quarter average. They average quarter averages to get a course-grade average. This makes no sense. A better approach would be to compute a final course grade as a single term over the entire length of a course (a grade that opens on the first day of class and closes on the last). The best grading systems have mechanisms in place to allow the most recent assignments to carry more weight than earlier ones. This practice promotes the idea that the most recent student work offers a more accurate representation of what a student has learned and is able to do at that particular moment in time. Not fully understanding content at the beginning of a unit should not negatively impact a student's grade later on.

Separate Academics From Behaviors

The grading system must separate academics from behaviors. If educators are to trust grades and use them as a measure of learning, the grades must simply measure what a student knows and is able to do, and nothing more. The challenge for most school leaders is to find ways to maintain the academic purity of grades without losing the ability to motivate students to practice good behaviors.

Allow for Reassessment

If students are not proficient on a particular assignment, they must have the opportunity to be reassessed for a new grade. Doing this ensures that their final grade is a more accurate representation of what they know and are able to do. The trick to reassessment is developing a system that is manageable for teachers and the school. Reassessment should be an expectation, and the student must play an active part. Students must first complete a reassessment plan with their teacher. This plan may include an opportunity for the student to go back and redo formative tasks related to the assessment, the scheduling of specific intervention or reteaching time with the teacher, and a timeline to complete the plan. For younger students, teachers may need to take the lead in creating the plan in the beginning by scaffolding the conversation for students or providing them with a template of the action items in the plan that they must complete. Schools must not allow students to fail; so it should be understood that a student will continue to be assessed and retaught until he or she demonstrates proficiency.

Use Rubrics and Scales, Not Percentage Scores

The grading system must use rubrics and rubric scales, not percentage scores. Most U.S. high schools still use the same flawed one hundred–point scale they have for generations. With a traditional one hundred–point scale, all grades typically start at 100 percent and the teacher deducts for missing or incorrect components to arrive at a final percentage score. These deductions can vary from assignment to assignment and teacher to teacher, and they depend on the expectations the teacher sets for each assignment. Many students think they must accumulate a certain number of points over time to reach a passing grade in this system. With a rubric scale, a teacher determines a grade by first looking at the student work and then determining which rubric level is the most appropriate match for that work. Teachers generally develop rubrics specific to the course, competency, or skill they are assessing. Students receive the rubric along with the assignment or task so they have a clear expectation of what they need to do to complete the work at a proficient level or higher.

Students Receive Timely, Differentiated Support Based on Their Individual Learning Needs

As a school administrator, take a moment to consider how you respond when parents ask you what supports are in place to help their child be successful. If, when responding to the question, you have to hesitate—even for just a minute—to think about *which teacher* the student is assigned to before you can answer, then your school has a problem. If there is no consistency in how teachers approach differentiated support, your school is not going to be effective at responding to the individual learning needs of each student. In effective schools, it doesn't matter which teacher a student is assigned to; all students receive differentiated support. Effective schools not only have consistent practices at the classroom level but also schoolwide. This is important for any school, but for schools that embrace competency-based learning, it is essential. Here are some examples of ways such schools ensure all students receive timely, differentiated support based on their individual learning needs.

Create Flexible Time for Differentiated Support

Effective schools build time into the school day for all students to access differentiated support, which often takes the form of intervention, extension, or enrichment.

▸ **Intervention:** Small groups of students work with the teacher on content support, remediation, or other kinds of proactive support in the area of study skills and other work-study practices.

▸ **Extension:** Whole-class groups work with the teacher, who extends the current curriculum beyond the learning objectives that students have already mastered.

▸ **Enrichment:** Students do activities beyond the work outlined in the curriculum to expand their experiences and also receive differentiated first instruction, particularly those students the teacher or education team has identified as benefiting from such support.

This time is as flexible as possible, meaning that students can attend different support sessions on different days based on their learning needs. Many schools that offer differentiated supports do so for thirty to sixty minutes at least two to three times per week and often daily. At the elementary and middle school levels, grade-level teacher teams often handle the scheduling for this flexible time. At the high school level, scheduling can be a mixture of teacher team input and student input. There are several software systems available that allow schools to schedule students efficiently for intervention, extension, and enrichment. In chapter 6 (page 129), we explore in more detail how schools can structure and maximize this time for student learning.

Group Teachers and Students in Collaborative Teams

DuFour et al. (2016) write extensively about the power of a PLC as a "group of people working together *interdependently* to achieve a *common goal* for which members are held *mutually accountable*" (p. 36). When teachers share students, they are mutually accountable to each other for meeting all of the learning needs of those students. In schools focused on competency-based learning, students often organize into smaller groups that share the same set of teachers who work collaboratively with those students. In these teams, teachers are able to become laser focused on the four essential questions that every team must answer (DuFour et al., 2016).

1. **What knowledge, skills, and dispositions should every student acquire as a result of this unit, this course, or this grade level?** The answer to this question becomes the course competencies and performance indicators that guide the team's instructional planning. Teams work together to align their curriculum and instructional practices with these learning objectives.

2. **How will we know when each student has acquired the essential knowledge and skills?** Teams work together to develop quality performance assessments as the ultimate measure of student mastery. Since team members share students, they have a mutual interest in making sure all students demonstrate competency.

3. **How will we respond when some students do not learn?** The answer to this question defines how the team will approach intervention, both at the classroom level and beyond. Effective teams work together to use flexible time to support the needs of all learners. Some teachers on the team may offer reteaching sessions to students, while others may offer targeted intervention. Students recognize that it will be not just their own classroom teacher, but any teacher on the team who will work with them when they have not demonstrated mastery.

4. **How will we extend the learning for students who are already proficient?** Teams work together to develop opportunities for extensions and enrichment for students who have already mastered a skill or concept. Perhaps some will need a blended learning approach to allow them to extend their thinking in a new way or even move ahead. The team can also use flexible learning time to provide additional instruction and resources for students who already demonstrate mastery.

At many high schools, the concept of a *freshman academy* (or ninth-grade small learning community) is an example of an effective way a school focused on competency-based learning can use collaborative teacher teams to group students. Souhegan High School (n.d.) in Amherst, New Hampshire, uses such a concept. In its model, teams in one area of the building (part of an organizational structure it calls *Division I*) schedule students in grades 9 and 10. The teams are called 9A, 9B, 10Y, and 10Z and share common teaching areas separated by an accordion wall, which allows for flexible collaboration space. The team structure promotes a strong sense of community and encourages the development of meaningful relationships between adults and students, and between peers. Each team consists of a teacher from English, social studies, science, and mathematics, and a reading specialist. Teachers collaborate on all aspects of planning and preparation, curriculum and instruction, and assessment and grading. Each collaborative teacher team also has access to guidance counselors and special educators to assist in their efforts to differentiate instruction to meet the needs of each student on the team. There is also a support period known as *saber support* that allows teachers to provide personalized preteaching, reteaching, intervention, or enrichment options for students as needed.

Offer Recovery Options for Students Who Aren't Successful the First Time

Schools that focus on competency-based learning believe that failure is not an option. *All* students can learn, and *all* students must reach competency. It is simply not good enough to allow a student to fail a course or an individual course competency and not provide him or her with recovery options. Failures represent gaps in student understanding, and if not addressed, these gaps will get wider and wider. In a perfect world, no student would ever reach the point of failure in a course. Helping a student recover a course after he or she has already failed is as effective as using an autopsy to determine what is wrong with someone in an effort to keep him or her alive. Once a student has failed, it is too late. It is far better to work with students who are failing while there is still time to recover the credit, much like it is easier for a medical professional to discover a potential life-threatening medical condition through preventative screening.

In a competency-based learning system there is always time because time is not the constant that dictates when learning can occur. This does not mean that schools need to move away from time-bound organizational structures such as school years, terms, or semesters. It is acceptable to assign students to a grade level or course for a set period of time. The question becomes, What will a school do for a student who has not reached competency by the end of the course? Schools must have recovery options for these students.

Elementary schools focused on competency-based learning can achieve recovery with additional targeted instruction during the summer or during the next school year. At middle and high schools, courses are tied to credit, so students receive credit for a course only when they have demonstrated mastery in each of the course competencies. If that doesn't happen, students are placed in an appropriate competency-recovery program, which could take many forms—from summer work to online learning or a blended model that includes both. Oftentimes, students must reach mastery before they are allowed to continue to the next course of study.

Learning Outcomes Emphasize Competencies That Include Application and Creation of Knowledge, Along With the Development of Important Skills and Dispositions

All educators have had students who did well not because they mastered the material, but rather because they learned how to play "the game of school." They may not be the best test-takers, but they come to class each day with the right attitude and their homework complete, and they make sure to raise their hands every day to ask important questions or contribute to a class discussion or activity. Subconsciously, teachers look out for these students. They exhibit the behaviors and dispositions that teachers want all students to exhibit. Teachers find ways to weave these behaviors into these students' grades, sometimes without even realizing it. By doing this, teachers create grades that are no longer a pure representation of what it is the students know and are able to do.

In schools focused on competency-based learning, the fundamental purpose of grading is to communicate student achievement toward mastery of learning targets and standards. Grades represent what students *learn*, not what they *earn*. Academic grades must be separate from academic behaviors. These behaviors are critical to academic achievement, but commingling them with academic grades does not provide an accurate picture of the students' achievement levels with their academic course competencies. For much of this chapter, we focused on the importance of learning outcomes that emphasize competencies, including the application and creation of knowledge.

« ————————————

In schools focused on competency-based learning, the fundamental purpose of grading is to communicate student achievement toward mastery of learning targets and standards. Grades represent what students *learn*, not what they *earn*.

———————————— »

Competencies That Address Important Skills and Dispositions

Now, we turn our attention to the importance of competencies that address the development of important skills and dispositions. The New Hampshire Department of Education (2014) provides a foundation for this work:

> New Hampshire's system of educator support should promote the capacity of educators to deeply engage students in learning rigorous and meaningful knowledge, skills, and Work-Study Practices for success in college, career, and citizenship. . . . Work-Study Practices [are] those behaviors that enhance learning achievement and promote a positive work ethic such as, but not limited to, listening and following directions, accepting responsibility, staying on task, completing work accurately, managing time wisely, showing initiative, and being cooperative. (p. 1)

From there, the department identifies four overarching work-study practices that could be embedded in any school, at any grade level, in any course of study (New Hampshire Department of Education, 2014):

1. **Communication:** I can use various media to interpret, question, and express knowledge, information, ideas, feelings, and reasoning to create mutual understanding.

2. **Creativity:** I can use original and flexible thinking to communicate my ideas or construct a unique product or solution.

3. **Collaboration:** I can work in diverse groups to achieve a common goal.

4. **Self-Direction:** I can initiate and manage my learning, and demonstrate a "growth" mindset, through self-awareness, self-motivation, self-control, self-advocacy and adaptability as a reflective learner. (p. 2)

Effective competency-based learning schools adapt these skills and dispositions into their competencies. They create rubrics for different grade levels and courses and develop assessment strategies so the competencies are regularly assessed, with progress reported to students and parents. Even more powerful, teachers are focusing instruction on how each student can individually develop further within specific work-study practices, and students are well aware of their own needs related to these important skills and dispositions. By embedding these work-study practices and dispositions into different aspects of a competency-based learning program, they take on more relevance for students. This ultimately helps students on the road to becoming college and career ready.

Reflection Questions

According to Sturgis (2015), competency-based learning models have five components. To start thinking about how to apply this model to your school's current situation, consider the following five reflection questions with your team.

1. In schools focused on competency-based learning, students advance upon demonstrated mastery. Are there instances in your school where this happens? If so, what are they?

2. Competencies include explicit, measurable, transferable learning objectives that empower students. How will your school develop competencies? Will educators be required to develop them for each grade level or course or will the school provide them?

3. Assessment is meaningful and a positive learning experience for students. If you surveyed students, to what extent would they see assessment in this way? What about parents? What about teachers?

4. Students receive timely, differentiated support based on their individual learning needs. To what extent does this happen for students in your school? Are there barriers that limit this support?

5. Learning outcomes emphasize competencies that include application and creation of knowledge, along with the development of important skills and dispositions. In your school, do teachers always consider depth of knowledge when developing learning outcomes? How do you assess skills and dispositions?

CHAPTER 2

Building the Foundation of a Competency-Based Learning System Through PLCs

Teacher collaboration is one of the best supports a school leader can provide to his or her school staff (DuFour et al., 2016). In this chapter, we explore how that ongoing process, one in which educators work collaboratively in recurring cycles of collective inquiry and action research to achieve better results for the students they serve, best supports a competency-based learning model. We identify the PLC framework as the single best support network that schools need in order to successfully implement competency-based learning. When implemented correctly, the PLC framework cultivates teachers who become collectively responsible and mutually accountable for the learning of students in their school. Teachers become supports for each other, and teacher teams become integral parts of both the decision-making process and instructional leadership for competency-based learning. And, the work of collaborative teams and work done throughout the school is transparent. Student learning, a collaborative culture, and constant reflection become the norm, and these are the levers that will effect change through the work of the PLC.

Any systems change requires hard work, dedication of the entire staff, and the understanding of why the change is necessary. It is imperative to have the foundational structures in place to allow collaboration to occur within a school. The PLC framework is the vehicle for this change.

It is important to recognize, however, that transforming into a PLC does not happen overnight. Many administrators and educators have sought a silver bullet that not only allows them to build and implement high-functioning PLCs but also simultaneously implement standards-based grading and competency-based learning. If high levels of learning for all learners is the *why*, we maintain that PLCs are the *how*, and competency-based learning is the *what* (see figure 2.1).

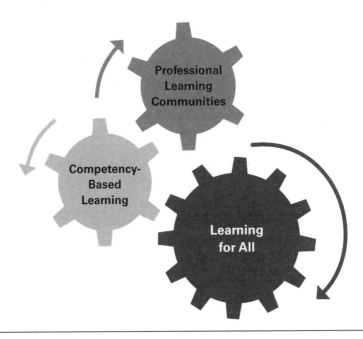

Figure 2.1: Competency-based learning and PLCs.

> To attempt to embark down the road to a competency-based learning system without working as a highly functioning PLC will lead to failure.

Competency-based learning and PLCs are a true fit if implemented correctly and with fidelity. To attempt to embark down the road to a competency-based learning system without working as a highly functioning PLC will lead to failure. We've seen it happen, and it undercuts this learning model before it even has a chance to get off the ground. The implementation of PLCs provides the initial steps that must develop in a competency-based learning model.

The Foundation of a PLC

The architects of the PLC model, Richard DuFour, Rebecca DuFour, and Robert Eaker, along with Thomas W. Many and Mike Mattos (2016), describe the four pillars of a PLC—the mission, vision, values (collective commitments), and goals—as the foundation of a PLC. Questions guide each of the four pillars, providing opportunities for staff members to engage in dialogue to build consensus. Utilizing the four pillars of a PLC can help a district or school build a road map for competency-based learning. Educators and other staff must understand and commit to the reasons for transforming their educational system. Outlining the mission, vision, values, and goals of the organization together helps build a common understanding and commitment to the work. From there, teams in PLCs will work collaboratively to define the specifics at each grade level.

Mission: Why Do We Exist?

The first pillar of a PLC is the *mission*. The mission answers the question, Why do we exist (DuFour et al., 2016)? Staff must explore this question together. There are many successful ways to do this; the common thread is that conversations occur in an honest and safe environment at both the district level, within the collaborative leadership team at schools, and within teacher teams. Those within a school must be clear on their fundamental purpose, and those within a community should be clear about student expectations within that community. This common understanding at all levels promotes a sense of "we are all in this together," leading to a collective effort to achieve a mutually desired outcome.

Schools transitioning to a competency-based learning model should frame their work around this question: "Do we accept high levels of learning for all students as the fundamental purpose of our school and therefore are willing to examine all practices in light of their impact on learning" (DuFour et al., 2016, p. 14)? This one question will not only frame short-term conversations as teams work together to develop the mission and vision, determine collective commitments (values), and build goals together but also the many follow-up conversations for years to come.

This question should be the beacon for a school implementing such transformative change. Staff members can go back to this question to determine if a strategy truly supports the belief that *all* students in the school are learning at high levels, and staff won't make excuses when multiple data points suggest things should be done differently.

Successful competency-based learning schools typically use data to identify groups of students who are not demonstrating the expected growth over the course of many years. When this happens, it makes sense that a school will need to take a hard look at its practices. This is a difficult and time-consuming process, and even after several years of implementation, it is important to continue to analyze multiple data points to ensure growth is occurring for all students.

Competency-based learning meets learners where they are and allows them to progress at their own speed along a developmental continuum.

Competency-based learning meets learners where they are and allows them to progress at their own speed along a developmental continuum.

Asking the question of why an educational institution exists will lead to learning for all. Remember, a competency-based learning model is based on what students learn, not what they earn. It wholly supports the mission and vision of becoming a system that focuses on learning and provides students every opportunity to demonstrate that learning at a high level.

Vision: What Must We Become to Accomplish Our Fundamental Purpose?

The *vision* question (DuFour et al., 2016) specifically asks teachers to focus on what needs to change. The school can determine the answer only through honest and open dialogue. The outcome of that dialogue provides inspiration not only to educators within the school but also the greater community.

In many schools going through this reflective process, adults in the school identify their focus on adult issues instead of what they should be expending their energy on—the student-centered issues that truly matter within their school. Once staff make that distinction, it becomes much easier to focus collective energy. Teachers will start to look at how the school can truly commit to learning for all.

In many successful U.S. competency-based learning districts, educators have made a concerted effort to deeply involve their communities in the systems change process. The Lindsay Unified School District in California asked the following five questions of its entire community to frame its shared purpose (or vision):

1. Why do we exist?
2. What are the values that will govern how we interact with each other?
3. What are the principles by which we will make decisions?
4. What is our vision for the future?
5. What is the description of our graduates? (Sturgis, 2015, p. 22)

Chugach School District is small, but spread out over twenty-two thousand miles in Prince William Sound, Alaska. Chugach began its journey to a competency-based education system in the mid-1990s and has made impressive growth since. Director and founder of MetisNet (www.metisnet.net) Chris Sturgis (2015) describes Chugach Superintendent Bob Crumley's effort:

> Chugach solidified the school board and district leadership commitment to a long-term strategy and created an intentional communication strategy that reinforced the idea that the system transformation will take several years. They also used data to intensify the sense of urgency by reminding people of the poor results in the traditional system as well as

> celebrating small steps of progress. Most importantly, they kept their
> community engaged so members could continue to deepen their under-
> standing and celebrate alongside the students who were beginning to
> thrive and enjoy coming to school. (p. 64)

Superintendent Crumley was honest when communicating to the local school board and community; he made it very clear that the change process would take years, and that the traditional system resulted in poor outcomes, further amplifying the need for change. Sharing this upfront is incredibly important.

Similarly, John Freeman, superintendent for Pittsfield School District School Administrative Unit (SAU) 51 in Pittsfield, New Hampshire, describes his district's move to competency-based learning as a process developed with the entire community, literally during a pig roast.

Practitioner Perspective

Virgel Hammonds, Chief Learning Officer, KnowledgeWorks; Former Principal, Lindsay Unified High School; and Former Superintendent, Regional School Unit 2

Though thousands of miles apart and culturally very different, Lindsay Unified School District (LUSD) in California and Regional School Unit 2 (RSU2) in Maine share a common vision for learning. Both aspire to empower students to be drivers of their education in a highly personalized, competency-based system. Each learning community's journey is unique, but the vision is the same: to ensure every child's dreams become reality.

In 2005, LUSD was at a crossroads. The city of Lindsay and the school district had made concerted efforts to improve and had seen some gains; however, the school and community both believed growth could be accelerated. School district and city leaders agreed to hold a series of community forums to discuss how LUSD could become a world-class district. Neighbors, businesses, civic and school employees (LUSD is the city's largest employer), community organizations, clergy members, nonprofits, and students were invited to collaborate on how to make this vision a reality. Over the course of a year, the LUSD community established guiding principles for how they would serve and support one another. They established a commitment to lifting each stakeholder while holding all accountable to the vision of Empowering and Motivating for Today and Tomorrow.

Purposely, the community left out the words *child, learner, student*, and so on as they believed this vision was an opportunity to collectively support the evolution of everyone in or serving the community. At that point, the school district and city had come together to form a strong, collaborative union—a learning community.

Like any great school district, LUSD provided its instructional teams with strong professional development. With a large migrant population, the district placed heavy emphasis on literacy and instructional pedagogy. The staff focused on grading practices and had hard conversations about averaging and scoring work. Educators and support staff established collaborative teams to discuss strategies, data, and lessons learned in the classroom.

continued →

Despite LUSD's efforts, student gains were not as strong as the district desired. Staff believed the district, their learners, and the community could do more; however, the next step toward making the vision a reality was unclear.

In the summer of 2007, LUSD was finalizing its plans for a new high school—an opportunity to rethink learning strategies in the high school. The secondary team took an instructional audit and realized they had a passion for ensuring each learner's success. The team always strived to support its learners both within the classroom and throughout the community. However, academic success did not reflect their efforts. As a team, members dug deeper. They asked one another, "How are you holding students accountable and to what expectations?" Realizing their expectations for teaching and learning varied greatly, the team members made a commitment to establishing common expectations for learning (designed competencies for all courses) and agreed to advance students solely based on mastery, not seat time. And, if that wasn't a large enough lift, they created a new learning ecosystem where students were empowered and motivated to prove their mastery in highly personalized ways. These action steps were bold, but the team believed it (and its learners) was up to the challenge.

After daily process checks with staff, learners, and parents, teams made adjustments and refinements—such as grouping and regrouping kids, strategic direct instruction, design thinking, refinement of personal goals, assessment, and so on—and implemented them immediately.

Process checks were so frequent, the teams became masterfully collaborative. Discuss, confirm (data), design, implement, observe, and repeat became the Lindsay High School routine. At times the team did the twist, but often it was poetry in motion.

At the conclusion of the 2007–2008 school year, LHS had far surpassed its previous academic gains. Adequate yearly progress (AYP) target scores quadrupled. More important, stakeholders were excited. With support from the superintendent's office, LHS shared its momentum with other district schools that then replicated (in unique ways) its successes. In 2017, LUSD is known as an exemplar in personalized and competency-based learning. And LHS ranks in the top 1 percent of schools on the California Healthy Kids Survey, which focuses on school climate and learner success.

When the Maine school consolidation law passed, many communities expressed Dorothy's sentiments—"We're not in Kansas anymore." In 2007, the Maine legislature passed LD 2323, An Act to Remove Barriers to the Reorganization of School Administrative Units (Maine Department of Education, 2008). The law was established to ensure learning opportunities, rigorous academic programs, uniformity in delivering programs, a greater uniformity in tax rates, more efficient and effective use of limited resources, preservation of school choice and maximum opportunity to deliver services in an efficient manner.

With this passage, the State of Maine saved $66 million annually, but it also forced highly independent school districts into a loss of local control to consolidation and thus their culture and community identity. This loss of local tradition and processes was a concern.

A tornado of anxiety tore through the state.

Regional School Unit 2, which serves the towns of Dresden, Farmingdale, Hallowell, Monmouth, and Richmond, saw this law as an opportunity to think differently about how they could collectively support the unique needs of the 2,400 students living within this new, extended family within five towns. The region held countless meetings in schools, homes, churches, town halls, farms, theaters, and any other location where people congregated within each community. Everyone—from students to the senior town spokesperson—was invited to discuss how all RSU2 community members could support each student in meeting learners' desired personal and professional goals.

RSU2 educators discussed the following four questions with the community.

1. What is our ultimate commitment to each student?

2. What are we preparing our students for?

3. How may each community member be a part of the solution?

4. How will the support of our community accelerate the growth of our students and our five towns?

Throughout 2009, the RSU2 towns evolved from five independent communities into one community of learners focused on putting students at the center of all learning decisions. The RSU2 learning community wanted to establish an ecosystem that embraced learner voice and choice through varied year-round learning opportunities occurring both inside and outside the schools.

The RSU2 learning community would work collaboratively to support highly personalized, competency-based learning opportunities via community projects that needed new solutions; internships with community and state partners; experiential learning engagements nurtured by educators and community members alike; and the students themselves. RSU2 parents and business leaders wanted their high school graduates to analyze and think critically, write and speak effectively, and collaboratively solve complex problems today and in the future. Equally important, the learning community requested students also be given the opportunity to learn at different paces based on their individual learning needs.

RSU2's engagement of the entire community allows for the exponential growth of learning supports available to students, educators, and families. Though the consolidation law forced RSU2 communities to collaborate, it also allowed them to think differently about their schools, students, and commitment to regional prosperity.

LUSD and RSU2 are two unique stories separated by thousands of miles, but unified by one common vision: "A Community of Student Centered Learning." To establish a highly personalized learning ecosystem, schools cannot continue to solely depend on the miraculous measures of our educators. (V. Hammonds, personal communication, October 2016)

Values: How Must We Behave to Achieve Our Vision?

As education visionary Thomas J. Sergiovanni (2007) writes:

> When people are gathered together to share ideas and to commit to these ideas, their relationships change. They make promises to each

other—implicitly perhaps, but promises nonetheless. And thus they are likely to feel morally obliged to keep their promises. (p. 3)

The *values* pillar is crucial. As Richard DuFour (2015) writes in *In Praise of American Educators*, the shift in thinking changes from the future of the vision to today. Shifting to competencies is a result of educators identifying the need for change today to prepare students for tomorrow.

As districts and schools move forward in their learning together, they must adhere to three specific collective commitments that will guide them. These commitments align precisely with the three big ideas that drive the work of a PLC (DuFour et al., 2016).

1. We accept learning as the fundamental purpose of our school and therefore are willing to examine all practices in light of their impact on learning.

2. We are committed to working together to achieve our collective purpose.

3. We will assess our effectiveness on the basis of results.

Schools must then delineate what each of these ideas will look like. This is a very important part of the process because these commitments state the conditions for what everyone will expect of each other. A safe, orderly, and respectful environment for all learners within a school, for example, is inclusive of both students and adults. The moral authority and collegial pressure of such an expectation is far more effective than any edict from an administrator deeming certain behaviors inappropriate.

Schools and teams need to revisit these three collective commitments and, using multiple data points, determine their growth within each area. They can then refine their practices based on this data.

Goals: How Will We Mark Our Progress?

The fourth pillar involves developing shared *goals* (DuFour et al., 2016). The process of developing school, team, and individual goals is an indicator of progress toward attaining a shared purpose. This process allows educators to confront their current reality together, and then make informed decisions about how they can move forward both as a system and as individuals to effect positive change.

SMART (strategic and specific, measurable, attainable, results oriented, and time bound) goals are a very productive way to track progress on a short-term or long-term basis (Conzemius & O'Neill, 2014). Schools that develop building-level goals based on their current reality provide common goals for teams to build their own goals based on their own data. Teams should formally assess their SMART goals at least midyear and again at the end of the year, although ongoing data collection and analysis are imperative throughout the year. During the midyear check, teams can report on which goals they are on track to meet or not meet, and how they are going to address any areas of deficiency. This provides teams with a road map to make any needed changes. During the end-of-year reporting, teachers should identify what helped them achieve each goal and what instruction may have been missing that didn't allow students to effectively progress. This helps teachers become cognizant of each student's individual needs so they can adjust instruction appropriately to provide the support and intervention necessary for continued growth.

Teams that develop SMART goals have a clear understanding of why the goals are important, how they relate to daily instruction, and how they support and, in many ways, define the work of their PLC. Teams can report progress on these goals to parents, the community, and a district's school board throughout the year.

SMART goals allow schools to become even more focused as they transition to a competency-based learning model. Teams look very closely at growth data across all cohorts and even down to each individual student in the school. When teachers are aware of this information, it causes them to change instructional practices to become crystal clear about how to help each student attain growth in demonstrating the competencies.

Transparency is crucial in any system, and schools and districts that successfully navigate this change process openly acknowledge areas of progress and areas in which progress has proven difficult. There will be times of celebration, but there will also be times when the trajectory may need to change. Leaders must recognize and act during these times. If leaders believe strongly that what they are doing is best for students and their school, then they must be willing to communicate in an honest and forthright manner. This makes parents aware of the progress (or lack of progress) being made as a school and begins to develop the trust necessary for the community to work hand in hand with the school.

The Four Critical Questions of a PLC and Competency-Based Learning

One of the greatest indicators as to how well a PLC will support competency-based learning is by examining the four critical questions of a PLC (DuFour et al., 2016). As DuFour (2015) states:

> [The] curriculum needed to provide all students with the knowledge, skills, and dispositions required for the 21st century will be far more rigorous and challenging than either teachers or students are accustomed. . . . Educators

must now ensure that *every* student who graduates from high school is ready for college or a career. (p. 138)

This quote speaks directly to competency and the need for a system to ensure that all students have opportunities to engage in experiences that provide chances to practice and learn these abilities:

> Critical-thinking skills and problem-solving skills
> Creativity and innovation
> Effective communication through clear and convincing written and oral expression
> Collaboration skills
> Inferential reasoning
> Analytical-thinking skills
> Self-directed learning (in other words, having learned how to learn)
> Transference of learning to new situations
> Evaluation of sources for importance and credibility
> Openness to and utilization of critical feedback (DuFour, 2015, p. 138)

Competency, by definition, is the "ability to transfer content and skill in and/or across content areas" (Bramante & Colby, 2012, p. 65). So the four critical questions of a PLC help determine precisely what students must be able to demonstrate to successfully show their competency, assist teachers in building assessments that allow students to demonstrate competency, and provide integrated opportunities for support or extension, depending on each student's needs.

We will examine each question to further support this assertion.

What Do We Expect Students to Know and Be Able to Do?

Teachers should be crystal clear about what students are expected to know and demonstrate in their learning. Grant Wiggins and Jay McTighe (2005) outline a backward design process for answering this question:

We cannot say how to teach for understanding, or which material and activities to use, until we are quite clear about which specific understandings we are after and what such understandings look like in practice." (pp. 14–15)

Utilizing a backward design planning system, teams make the outcomes for any unit clear to learners.

Many educators have difficulty determining the difference between a standard and a competency. In their book *Off the Clock*, Bramante and Colby (2012) describe *standards* as the *what* of learning and *competencies* as the *why* of learning. Another way to look at it is to think of competencies as the umbrella, with the leverage and enduring standards beneath the umbrella of competency.

Larry Ainsworth (as cited in DuFour et al., 2016) provides clarity on *priority standards* (those that provide leverage and those deemed to be enduring) by explaining that students will be able to apply *leverage standards* across subject areas, while with *enduring standards*, students will need to know and be able to demonstrate competency beyond the specific course or grade level.

It is impossible for any teacher to cover the sheer number of existing standards. Competency-based learning focuses on depth over breadth. As Robert J. Marzano and Mark W. Haystead (2008) note, "Schooling, as currently configured, would have to be extended from kindergarten to grade 21 or 22 to accommodate all the standards" (p. 7). The important skills involve transfer at a depth of knowledge (DOK) level 3 or 4. Norman Webb's (2005) *depth of knowledge* refers to the complexity of thinking required to successfully and appropriately complete a task or assignment (Aungst, 2014):

Level 1: Recall and Reproduction

Tasks at this level require recall of facts or rote application of simple procedures. The task does not require any cognitive effort beyond remembering the right response or formula. Copying, computing, defining, and recognizing are typical Level 1 tasks.

Level 2: Skills and Concepts

At this level, a student must make some decisions about his or her approach. Tasks with more than one mental step such as comparing, organizing, summarizing, predicting, and estimating are usually Level 2.

Level 3: Strategic Thinking

At this level of complexity, students must use planning and evidence, and thinking is more abstract. A task with multiple valid responses where students must justify their choices would be Level 3. Examples include solving non-routine problems, designing an experiment, or analyzing characteristics of a genre.

Level 4: Extended Thinking

Level 4 tasks require the most complex cognitive effort. Students synthesize information from multiple sources, often over an extended period of time, or transfer knowledge from one domain to solve problems in another. Designing a survey and interpreting the results, analyzing multiple texts by [sic] to extract themes, or writing an original myth in an ancient style would all be examples of Level 4.

Table 2.1 provides examples of the types of activities students would be engaged in at the various DOK levels.

Table 2.1: Depth of Knowledge Chart

Describe, Explain, Interpret			
Level 1 (Recall)	**Level 2** (Skill and Concept)	**Level 3** (Strategic Thinking)	**Level 4** (Extended Thinking)
Arrange	Infer	Revise	Design
Calculate	Categorize	Assess	Connect
Define	Collect and display	Develop a logical argument	Synthesize
Draw	Identify patterns	Apprise	Apply concepts
Identify	Organize	Construct	Critique
List	Construct	Use concepts to solve nonroutine problems	Analyze
Label	Modify		Create
Illustrate	Predict	Critique	Prove
Measure	Interpret	Compare	
Memorize	Distinguish	Explain phenomena in terms of concepts	
Who, what, when, where, why	Use context cues	Formulate	
	Make observations	Draw conclusions	
Repeat	Summarize	Investigate	
State	Show	Hypothesize	
Recall	Graph	Differentiate	
Tell	Classify	Cite evidence	
Recite	Separate		
Tabulate	Cause and effect		
Recognize	Estimate		
Name	Compare		
Report	Relate		
Use			
Quote			
Match			

Source: Webb, 2005.

Better understanding competencies allows teachers to delve deeply into the import-ant critical-thinking aspects for students in a course or unit of study. It is crucial for teacher teams to identify the enduring understandings (Wiggins & McTighe, 2005) and *power standards* and then build backward from there. Power standards are those standards that are critical to students' success (Ainsworth, 2003). Teacher teams working through this process together develop not only a greater understanding of their grade-level competencies and standards but also a greater focus on what is imperative for all students to learn in each grade level or course. As this is articulated across a school (K–5, 6–8, and 9–12) or district, the work of each teacher aligns not only horizontally but also vertically. Students clearly benefit from this scaffolding of learning.

Teachers' increased understanding of competencies in relation to standards ensures a guaranteed and viable curriculum, a curriculum that (1) gives students access to the same essential learning regardless of who is teaching the class and (2) can be taught in the time allotted (Marzano, 2003). Many districts and states are developing high-leverage competencies to guide students' learning. Underneath the umbrella of the competencies and within the design of the assessments (both formative and summative) themselves, teachers must identify the leverage standards to assess.

Assessing the many other standards (not identified as leverage standards) throughout a unit of study may be formative or as a check to ensure understanding (see the following section on critical question two). The important thing to remember is that every single standard to assess does not need to be a leverage standard. These are all important skills to understand, but competency is the assimilation of the entirety of the skills and the subsequent transfer into a real-world situation.

Competency is the assimilation of the entirety of the skills and the subsequent transfer into a real-world situation.

How Will We Know Students Have Learned It?

"Competency-based learning asks students to learn important content information and skills . . . [and] demonstrate that learning by applying the content and skills in unique ways" (Bramante & Colby, 2012, p. 63). Team-designed rubrics outline precisely what students are expected to know. Competency is the ability of students to transfer their learning in and across content areas; therefore, teachers should provide real-world problems and cross-curricular assessment opportunities for students to demonstrate this transfer of knowledge into other situations.

Team-created common assessments are the driving force behind gathering data specific to each student's learning progression. Teams then collaboratively analyze these data to inform the next instructional steps and learning pathways for each student.

Understanding whether a student has learned must be a fluid process. In a competency-based learning model, this means ingraining the learning in a student's knowledge base. It doesn't mean that students can recite memorized facts, only to lose these facts two weeks later when asked to recite them again. In a competency-based learning model, *learning* means transferring knowledge repeatedly and to different tasks, truly reflecting a deeper level of understanding. As Linda Darling-Hammond and Frank Adamson (2014) proffer:

> A successful education can no longer be organized by dividing a set of static facts into the twelve years of schooling, to be doled out to students bit by bit each year. . . . Schools must teach disciplinary knowledge in ways that also help students learn how to learn. (p. 4)

In a competency-based learning model, *learning* means transferring knowledge repeatedly and to different tasks, truly reflecting a deeper level of understanding.

Understanding whether a student has learned also requires assessment structures that incorporate both formative and summative measures. Creating a balanced assessment system that honors and values assessment *for* learning (formative) and assessment *of* learning (summative) is critical as both are integral for accuracy (Stiggins, 2005). Assessment for learning is the formative form that teachers utilize to assist them in determining where a student is along his or her individual pathway to demonstrating competency. Teachers can and should make changes in instruction. Students should self-assess as well, and this can formatively indicate to the learner what areas he or she may need to further explore to solidify understanding.

A rigorous common summative performance assessment truly requires a higher DOK for students to demonstrate competency or proficiency. These types of assessments are superior in that they "allow the development and assessment of more complex skills that cannot be measured in a two-hour test on a single day" (Darling-Hammond & Adamson, 2014, p. 5). Additionally, in the preface of *Quality Performance Assessment: A Guide for Schools and Districts*, Dan French (as cited in CCE, 2012) explains that "performance assessments add a fuller, more in-depth picture of student learning, lead to more rigorous and relevant learning experiences, and result in greater equity of access to postsecondary skills, knowledge, and credentials for all students" (p. v).

Developing a high-quality, rigorous performance assessment requires teachers to have a high level of assessment literacy. A deep understanding of building essential questions that are truly at a higher DOK and that will elicit student responses that allow them to demonstrate competency is not an easy task. McTighe and Wiggins (2013) outline characteristics that make questions *essential* and can be great guides for teachers as they learn to develop rigorous questions to guide students' learning experiences. When developing essential questions, teachers should ask themselves the following.

- ▸ "Is the question open-ended?"

- ▸ "Is it thought provoking and engaging?"

- ▸ "Does it require higher-order thinking (analysis, inference, evaluation, or prediction)?"

- ▸ "Does it allow for transfer of learning, both in and across content areas (competency)?"

- ▸ "Does it raise more questions or require further research to develop deeper understanding?"

- ▸ "Is the question meaningful over time? Can you revisit the question again and again?"

Developing questions that reflect these characteristics takes time, and teachers must work and learn together in both horizontal and vertical teams (grade-level and cross-grade teams).

Once teachers become more comfortable and familiar with these processes, they naturally incorporate them into everyday planning. Teachers better understand the standards and competencies they are assessing, they are working diligently to enhance differentiation within their everyday instruction, and most important, they are collaborating together to home in on students' areas of strength and areas needing support. By teachers collaboratively providing the focused support needed (differentiation) within their instruction with their students, each student will be able to move along his or her own learning progression.

We believe that these rigorous performance assessments are the best way to truly assess a student's competency. They require students to transfer their learning at a higher DOK. Because teams within a PLC develop, refine, administer, and review assessments, students receive the timely support they need to progress along their continuum.

How Will We Respond When Some Students Don't Learn It?

A structured time to provide support for students who have not demonstrated competency is imperative within any education system committed to learning for all. Schools and districts must have a multitiered K–12 support system for all learners. Not learning foundational knowledge is not an option. Because students will inevitably walk into classrooms every year lacking skills they need to be successful with essential grade-level standards, schools need multiple tiers of support.

Austin Buffum, Mike Mattos, and Chris Weber (2012) describe response to intervention (RTI) as a way to provide "every child with the additional time and support needed to learn at high levels" and that this model should "provide timely, targeted, systematic interventions to all students who demonstrate the need" (p. xiii). The authors represent the three tiers of the RTI model through an inverted pyramid, where all students receive core instruction, some students receive supplemental interventions, and intensive interventions are reserved for individual students (Buffum et al., 2012).

Schools must develop a schedule that allows every student within the school to receive additional instruction or support, depending on each student's particular needs. This should occur at each grade level, in each school, ideally every day. One of the most effective ways to maximize support is to build this schedule collaboratively with teachers, maximizing the resources available within the school and across grade levels to allow for smaller-group instruction for those students who benefit from it.

This schedule may look different across schools, but one constant will emerge: dedicated time within the school day for teachers to work with students to provide support and preventative maintenance within their learning progression. One school's schedule may outline Tier 2 for each grade level at a different time so that each grade level can be flooded with support resources. Or, like in Pittsfield, New Hampshire, a somewhat traditional high school schedule was developed for four days per week:

> Wednesdays [have] a late start and shorter classes to create time for teachers to meet and pursue professional development, to have a block of time to support students academically and in leadership development, and to offer the high interest, project-based learning. (Sturgis, 2015, p. 62)

It is important to remember that this support is above and beyond what all students are exposed to during Tier 1 core classroom instruction, and students who may require additional support after Tier 2 (a much smaller percentage) receive Tier 3 instruction as well. The Tier 3 intervention is for students who have still not mastered the prioritized grade-level standards.

In a competency-based learning model, students may not be working on grade-level standards yet, but the K–12 competencies may be the same. This allows each student to still work on the same competencies, but possibly at different standard levels. It is imperative to identify precisely which skills each student needs to work on and provide the appropriate resources (human and time). Looking at data together in collaborative teams is the best way to accomplish this, as all teachers can determine together the appropriate learning progression and support necessary.

How Will We Extend the Learning for Students Who Have Demonstrated Proficiency?

A competency-based learning system lends itself very well to students who need to be challenged. The same tiered system that provides support also provides various opportunities for extension. Students receive opportunities to demonstrate a deeper DOK (level 4) on their assignments, and to extend through personalized experiences.

Extension can also occur during Tier 2, but it is important to note that competency-based learning, by design, allows for a more personalized approach to learning. This means that this more personalized approach does not need to be limited to the defined Tier 2 time within the day. Students in a competency-based learning system have a much better understanding of their own learning needs than students in a traditional system, and therefore must have more ownership of their learning. Opportunities for these students to extend their learning must be present not only throughout the school day but also outside of the school day.

In a competency-based learning system, teachers access many resources to assist in developing a more personalized and blended approach. Technology enhances competency-based learning, but educators must utilize it effectively. Computers, for example, provide the opportunity for students to engage in activities that may be geared for their learning style and needs, and also provide remediation in specific areas of need. Teachers must harness all of this and still guide the learning. However, as Horn and Staker (2015) note in *Blended*, an "important part of student-centered learning is that students develop a sense of agency and ownership" (p. 10)—whether it be choice of time or location, thus fulfilling the five design principles of competency-based learning.

The Three Big Ideas of a PLC

Earlier in this chapter, we referenced various questions for leaders related to developing a vision for learning within their school. That question is based on the first of the three big ideas of a PLC (DuFour et al., 2016) related to the fundamental purpose of the school. The three big ideas of a PLC are as follows (DuFour et al., 2016).

1. We accept learning as the fundamental purpose of our school and therefore are willing to examine all practices in light of their impact on learning.

2. We are committed to working together to achieve our collective purpose. We cultivate a collaborative culture through the development of high-performing teams.

3. We assess our effectiveness on the basis of results rather than intentions. Individuals, teams, and schools seek relevant data and information and use that information to promote continuous improvement.

Big Idea 1

We accept learning as the fundamental purpose of our school and therefore are willing to examine all practices in light of their impact on learning. Reviewing this statement allows you to successfully navigate your journey to a competency-based learning system. When everyone agrees on a fundamental purpose, a shift to competency-based learning will provide educators with even more data to support the benefits of this move (despite its many struggles), and that a traditional model of education will not make sense as it relates to individualized, personalized learning.

Making this transition, and examining all practices, allows for innovation in the classroom. Teacher autonomy is a hallmark of a competency-based learning environment because teachers rely on their own and each other's expertise. Teachers make instructional decisions based on experience and what teams feel will work best to support students' growth, but the reality is you don't know what will work until you try it.

The second big idea of a PLC is related to a team-based collaborative culture.

Big Idea 2

We are committed to working together to achieve our collective purpose. We cultivate a collaborative culture through the development of high-performing teams. We argue that there is no more successful way to support a competency-based learning model than by doing so collaboratively. It truly tests the resolve of all, but the overarching calling to provide a better way for our students to prosper in their learning is too powerful to resist.

A true test of the strength of PLCs lies in a school's ability to work vertically (across grade levels). This is incredibly important in a competency-based learning system that still recognizes grade levels for social, emotional, and developmental reasons. By engaging in vertical work, teachers' awareness and understanding of the scaffolding standards and competencies increases significantly, which translates to their classrooms.

In a competency-based learning system, it is imperative to understand what comes next in a learning progression. PLC structures allow these conversations and experiences to occur organically, as part of the natural process. For example, Lucy Calkins's (2017) Units of Study follow a developmental progression. *Developmental learning progressions* are "descriptive continuums of how students develop and demonstrate more sophisticated understanding over time" (Hess, 2010, p. 57).

Therefore, you may have a second-grade student writing at the same level as a fourth-grade student. It is very important for the fourth-grade teacher to understand how to help his or her fourth-grade student writing at a second-grade level improve. Conversely, it is important for the second-grade teacher who has a second-grade student writing at a fourth-grade level to understand how to push his or her student to progress to the next level.

The third big idea of a PLC relates to measuring effectiveness based on results.

Big Idea 3

We assess our effectiveness on the basis of results rather than intentions. Individuals, teams, and schools seek relevant data and information and use that information to promote continuous improvement. In a competency-based learning system, teachers have more focused data and information about their students than ever before. Each assessment, whether formative or summative, provides a wealth of information about a student's progress. The goal is for *every* student to be college and career ready, think critically, solve problems, and understand what learning looks like, feels like, and consists of, so he or she can apply those skills to any problem. Because a competency-based learning system is geared to the individual learner, this all happens naturally.

Information is everywhere, but teams have to know what to do with the data they have in front of them. They must share with each other what they are learning. As Sturgis (2015) notes:

> The emphasis on sharing denotes that these approaches differ from those commonly used in traditional systems. These are collaborative approaches that generate respect and trust. They contribute to the formation of a different type of school culture—one that is student-centered rather than system-centered, empowering rather than compliance-oriented, cooperative rather than dependent on individual leadership, and motivated by learning rather than by carrots or sticks. (p. 11)

The collaborative processes inherent in a PLC provide the structure to analyze these data and put the information to good use. What may have once been a pile of numbers is now a piece of the puzzle that can help teachers dissect what is keeping a student from demonstrating growth and success. Staff members need to be encouraged to try various approaches when considering student learning needs. Teachers will develop their sense of autonomy based on the success of their action plans. At other times, these action plans may not work as predicted, but this is part of the learning process as well. In fact, teachers will often learn more from experiences that don't go as planned because they will carry the experiences forward, making changes based on their professional expertise.

A majority of the behind-the-scenes work in a competency-based learning system is accomplished during collaborative team time. All stakeholders must support a widely dispersed mission and vision for learning. Goals must be set by individuals, teams, schools, and the district to support this vision. Teams must identify the competencies and anchor standards to assess in their units of study; build performance assessments that truly measure those competencies; run the performance assessments through a vetting process for quality assurance; review and assess student work together; and then revise and refine the assessment accordingly. In addition, teacher teams must provide reteaching and opportunities for extension based on assessment results. This must be coordinated within the teams to ensure that every student is receiving what he or she needs. Highly functioning PLCs are imperative for this work to occur at high levels. The result is high levels of student growth and learning.

> **A majority of the behind-the-scenes work in a competency-based learning system is accomplished during collaborative team time.**

Reflection Questions

Consider the following four reflection questions with your team.

1. Developing a clear vision of where you want to go as a school community sets the stage for learning. Have you defined your school's mission, vision, values, and goals? Is everyone clear on what these are, why they are important, and how they can guide your efforts?

2. Collaborative teams are integral to a competency-based learning model. Do you function as a PLC? Is time set aside within the school day for collaborative teaming? Is this time focused on student learning?

3. Providing tiered supports for students at all levels of learning is imperative in a competency-based learning system. Do you currently maximize your resources to meet the needs of all learners? How might you do that more effectively?

4. Data inform decisions. Do you utilize the available data to inform your decisions regarding next steps? Do you seek additional data to assist you in promoting a culture of continuous improvement?

CHAPTER 3

Developing Competencies and Progressions to Guide Learning

S chools that have made the transition to competency-based learning systems have undoubtedly run into the issue of how to determine what competencies to use within a grade or course. The education system has been so intent on breadth versus depth that it is not uncommon to hear a teacher respond, "Oh, I covered that" when asked about a specific standard. This is by no means any fault of the teacher; the mindset of breadth versus depth has been hammered into generations of educators, and punitive accountability reinforces this thinking. Our response to the teacher's statement would be, "OK, you have *taught* it, but have the students *learned* it?" Competency-based learning reframes the mindset about the purpose of educators.

This chapter focuses on the first critical question of a PLC in the context of a competency-based learning model: What is it we want students to learn (DuFour et al., 2016)? This requires developing effective competency statements. Readers will learn how to develop schoolwide and course-specific competencies that include explicit, measurable, and transferable learning objectives that empower all students.

We have long understood that true learning is the result of making meaning of experiences, connecting them to things already understood or known, and then applying the knowledge to similar situations the learner encounters. In *The Process of Education*, Jerome S. Bruner (1960) explains the importance of ensuring that true understanding happens when topics are placed into a larger context, but learners must also have the ability (and opportunity) to apply that learning to future similar situations. In 1897, John Dewey underscored the importance of making meaning of learning by considering its relationship to other things, making connections, and eventually making meaning of the gathered information. Wiggins and McTighe (1998) describe the concept of these understandings being "linchpin" ideas, that is, an idea that is "essential to understanding" (p. 4). Although recognition of these important components of learning isn't new, we believe that competency-based learning ties these understandings together in a way that allows for a personalized, rigorous approach to prepare learners for success in their careers, college, and life.

Developing meaningful K–12 competencies that align with district and state standards to ensure students are career and college ready is only part of the equation. In a competency-based learning system, the stepping stones to achieving competency are an integral component for development and refinement. Each student, regardless of where he or she is on the learning path, is able to clearly understand how to move forward.

A competency-based learning system is built on whether students have learned *it*. But, what is *it*? In this chapter, we explore the development of competencies, and further define what constitutes competency. This is challenging, rigorous work that will expand teachers' knowledge not only of the curriculum but also of the instructional and assessment practices that will allow students to truly reach mastery.

The following pages examine the relationship between competencies, standards, and learning progressions; multiple pathways; grain size; the development of competencies; learning progressions and grading; embedded professional development; vertical teaming; and project-based learning and competencies.

The Relationship Among Competencies, Standards, and Learning Progressions

Understanding the relationship among competencies, standards, and learning progressions is a crucial component of teachers' assessment literacy and will allow educators to fluidly provide support and guidance in a focused and meaningful way. The overlap among the three can be somewhat confusing, however. To simplify, we borrow from Bramante and Colby (2012), who note that competencies are the *why* of learning, while standards are the *what* of learning. *Learning progressions* represent the *how to get there*.

The following sections discuss competencies, standards, and learning progressions in more detail.

What Are Competencies?

A competency is specific to the higher-order skill or transfer of knowledge required within a specific content area or within skills and dispositions. At the secondary level, a course may be made up of several course-specific or grade-level-specific competencies, or a subject area may contain multiple competencies; they are the bigger ideas that students must be proficient in within that course or subject. See figures 3.1 and 3.2 for examples of academic and nonacademic competencies.

Mathematics

State of New Hampshire, grades 9–12: Students will reason abstractly and manipulate symbolic expressions and models to represent relationships and interpret expressions, equations, and inequalities in terms of a given context (including real-world phenomena) for determining unknown values.

English Language Arts

Rochester, New Hampshire, English language arts grade 3, competency 2: Informational texts—Students will demonstrate the ability to comprehend, analyze, and evaluate increasingly complex informational texts.

Social Studies

Rochester, New Hampshire, social studies grade 7, competency 2: Foundations of geography—Students will understand that within a region the physical geography impacts how the people and their environments interact and affect each other.

Science

Henry County Schools, Georgia, elementary science graduation competency 2: Earth and space sciences, hydrology and meteorology—Students will understand and analyze the role of water in Earth processes, the dynamics and composition of the atmosphere, and global processes influencing water and climate.

Source: Henry County Schools, n.d.c; New Hampshire Department of Education, n.d.; Rochester School District, n.d.

Figure 3.1: Examples of academic competencies.

Communication

State of New Hampshire work-study practices: Communication—I can use various media to interpret, question, and express knowledge, information, ideas, feelings, and reasoning to create mutual understanding.

Collaboration

Henry County Schools, Georgia: Collaboration focus—Collaborate with diverse teams to accomplish a common goal (accompanying performance indicators).

Source: Henry County Schools, n.d.b; New Hampshire Department of Education, 2014.

Figure 3.2: Examples of nonacademic competencies.

As you can see from the examples in figures 3.1 and 3.2, teams have written the competencies in various ways. The use of "I can" statements (State of New Hampshire) provides student-friendly language. A broad competency (Henry County Schools) may then be broken down even further, by grade level, through performance indicators (accessible through the website). The competencies related to skills and dispositions, or success skills, appear as high school graduation competencies in figures 3.1 and 3.2. Teacher teams can break these competencies down even further into their respective grade bands to build a learning progression.

What Are Standards?

The CCSS provide a basis and structure for exploring standard-level learning goals in greater detail. In 2009, state education leaders from forty-eight states, two territories, and the District of Columbia began the process of developing rigorous, aligned learning goals to prepare America's youth for college, careers, and life (NGA & CCSSO, 2010a, 2010b). These learning goals outline what a student should know and be able to do at the end of each grade level. The standards ensure all students graduate from high school with the skills and knowledge necessary to succeed, regardless of where they live. According to the Common Core State Standards Initiative (n.d.a), learning goals should be:

1. Research- and evidence-based

2. Clear, understandable, and consistent

3. Aligned with college and career expectations

4. Based on rigorous content and application of knowledge through higher-order thinking skills

5. Built upon the strengths and lessons of current state standards

6. Informed by other top performing countries in order to prepare all students for success in our global economy and society

Although a majority of states have adopted the CCSS, there are those who have not. Texas, for example, developed the Texas Essential Knowledge and Skills (TEKS), which outline the grade-level expectations for learning for students. There is some alignment within many of these individually developed state standards and the Common Core. For example, in grade 5, the TEKS outline that students in grade 5 will be able to:

> (a) compare and contrast the themes or moral lessons of several works
> of fiction from various cultures (Texas Education Agency, 2010)

The CCSS outline that a fifth grader will be able to:

compare and contrast two or more characters, settings, or events in a story or drama, drawing on specific details in the text (e.g., how characters interact) (RL.5.3; NGA & CCSSO, 2010a)

Learning goals are single standards, an intermediate goal on the way to a standard or competency, or a combination of standards. Wiggins and McTighe (2005) differentiate learning goals even further by comparing various types of learning goals in relation to three characteristics: (1) acquisition, (2) meaning making, and (3) transfer. All three are important, but each represents a different DOK. *Application* and meaning making would typically fall into DOK 1 or 2, while anytime students are asked to *transfer*, they have moved into DOK 3. What are the differences? *Acquisition* requires learners to acquire basic information and skills. *Meaning making* requires learners to construct the meaning of important ideas and processes. *Transfer* (which we say is the competency level) requires learners to transfer their learning autonomously and effectively in new situations, representing their proficiency within this specific arena. Just acquiring the knowledge doesn't mean a student is going to be able to apply the knowledge. In a competency-based system, we are concerned with students making meaning of information they have acquired, then being able to transfer it in and across subject areas.

But how do students take these incremental steps to ensure they attain the building blocks needed to further their competency? This is done when students master the necessary skills and build on that mastery to move along to the next critical component or learning within that competency. These are *learning progressions*.

What Are Learning Progressions?

Learning progressions are the linchpins to understanding and implementing a competency-based learning system. We all want to get our students to competency, but how to get there is the million-dollar question. Learning progressions provide the pathways to learning that are crucial in a successful competency-based learning system.

Karin K. Hess (2012) describes *learning progressions* as "research-based, descriptive continuums of how students develop and demonstrate deeper, broader, and more sophisticated understanding over time" (pp. 2–3). Similarly, W. James Popham (2007) describes *learning progressions* as the "carefully sequenced set of building blocks that students must master en route to mastering a more distant curricular aim. These building blocks consist of subskills and bodies of enabling knowledge" (p. 83). These progressions provide a basis for how understanding will progress, or how students will *deepen* their understanding over time.

Achieve's (2015) publication, *The Role of Learning Progressions in Competency-Based Pathways*, provides helpful definitions of terminology specific to learning progressions, as an accepted, common understanding does not yet exist within the education community. *Learning progressions* map out commonly travelled paths students take to achieve a competency. Teachers can (and should) use learning progressions to design or modify instruction. *Student learning path* describes the unique, personalized approach each student may take to achieve the intended learning goal. "In a competency-based system, teachers can apply what is known about common learning progressions to track and move students along their individual paths" (Achieve, 2015, p. 2).

Learning progressions are crucially important because they allow both teacher and student to understand precisely where the learner is in relation to the bigger picture of learning development. Margaret Heritage (2008) expands:

> With clear connections between what comes before and after a particular point in the progression teachers can calibrate their teaching to any missing precursor understanding or skills revealed by assessment, and determine what the next steps are to move the student forward from that point. (p. 4)

Teachers and students who utilize these competency building blocks internalize that learning is interconnected and not only a result of previous understandings but also provides the necessary glimpse into what students will learn in the future.

Figure 3.3 outlines a visual diagram of the relationship between standards and competencies. It outlines all of the CCSS that flow into the competency. For the purposes of this diagram, we have used the State of New Hampshire's Language Arts Model Competencies for Reading Foundational Skills, K–8. This example is specific to grades 5 and 6.

In this example, each of the major standards are in either black or dark gray. In the instances that a standard is addressed in both grades 5 and 6, the grade 6 standard is closer to the level of competency (L.6.3, L.6.4, L.6.5, and L.6.6, for example). Leading to these standards are substandards (A, B, C, and so on) that flow into the larger standards. Under L.5.3, for example, there are the two standards, smaller in grain size, that flow into it. The term *grain size* is often associated with competencies, standards, and learning progressions. Grain size directly reflects how big the standard or competency might be.

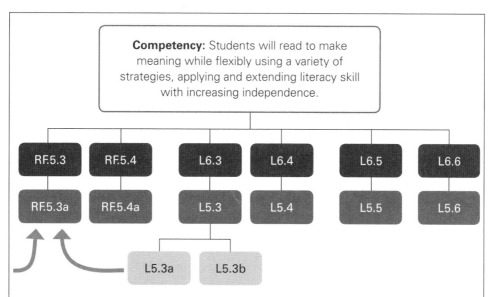

RF.5.3: Know and apply grade-level phonics and word analysis skills in decoding words.

RF.5.3a: Use combined knowledge of all letter-sound correspondences, syllabication patterns, and morphology (e.g., roots and affixes) to read accurately unfamiliar multisyllabic words in context and out of context.

RF.5.4: Read with sufficient accuracy and fluency to support comprehension.

RF.5.4a: Read grade-level text with purpose and understanding.

RF.5.4b: Read grade-level prose and poetry orally with accuracy, appropriate rate, and expression on successive readings.

RF.5.4c: Use context to confirm or self-correct word recognition and understanding, rereading as necessary.

L.6.3: Use knowledge of language and its conventions when writing, speaking, reading, or listening.

L.6.3a: Vary sentence patterns for meaning, reader/listener interest, and style.

L.6.3b: Maintain consistency in style and tone.

L.5.3: Use knowledge of language and its conventions when writing, speaking, reading, or listening.

L.5.3a: Expand, combine, and reduce sentences for meaning, reader/listener interest, and style.

L.5.3b: Compare and contrast the varieties of English (e.g., dialects, registers) used in stories, dramas, or poems.

L.6.4: Determine or clarify the meaning of unknown and multiple-meaning words and phrases based on grade 6 reading and content, choosing flexibly from a range of strategies.

L.6.4a: Use context (e.g., the overall meaning of a sentence or paragraph; a word's position or function in a sentence) as a clue to the meaning of a word or phrase.

Figure 3.3: The relationship among competencies, standards, and learning progressions.   continued ➜

L.6.4b: Use common, grade-appropriate Greek or Latin affixes and roots as clues to the meaning of a word (e.g., *audience, auditory, audible*).

L.6.4c: Consult reference materials (e.g., dictionaries, glossaries, thesauruses), both print and digital, to find the pronunciation of a word or determine or clarify its precise meaning or its part of speech.

L.6.4d: Verify the preliminary determination of the meaning of a word or phrase (e.g., by checking the inferred meaning in context or in a dictionary).

L.6.5: Demonstrate understanding of figurative language, word relationships, and nuances in word meanings.

L.6.5a: Interpret figures of speech (e.g., personification) in context.

L.6.5b: Use the relationship between particular words (e.g., cause/effect, part/whole, item/category) to better understand each of the words.

L.6.5c: Distinguish among the connotations (associations) of words with similar denotations (definitions) (e.g., *stingy, scrimping, economical, unwasteful, thrifty*).

L.6.6: Acquire and use accurately grade-appropriate general academic and domain-specific words and phrases; gather vocabulary knowledge when considering a word or phrase important to comprehension or expression.

L.5.6: Acquire and use accurately grade-appropriate general academic and domain-specific words and phrases, including those that signal contrast, addition, and other logical relationships (e.g., *however, although, nevertheless, similarly, moreover, in addition*).

Source for standards: NGA & CCSSO, 2010a.

Grain Size

Competencies, naturally, are quite large in grain size, while standards and learning progressions may vary in size. The grain size of any standard or learning progression can be best associated with the leverage and endurance of that particular standard.

> ➡
> **The grain size of any standard or learning progression can be best associated with the leverage and endurance of that particular standard.**
> ⬅

Again, the *leverage* refers to the standard's ability to be applied across curriculum and its *endurance* refers to applicability beyond the grade level or course. In some instances, a specific learning goal within a standard may take a week to learn and demonstrate, whereas another learning goal within a standard may take a month's worth of learning and demonstration. But these are both important learning goals that will provide the building blocks for a student to attain the competency.

It is important to rely on both experience and research of developmental progressions when designing the learning path and progressions that will lead to successful attainment of a learning goal for each student.

We recognize that progression development is a process. Teachers, through their increased understanding and experience with competencies, will refine and iterate their progressions over time. It is important to remember that educators cannot include every subskill within a learning progression. Educators should only include the skills and knowledge that will provide the leverage to get to proficiency. The other subskills will be captured within these building blocks.

It is important to understand the relationship among competencies, standards, and learning progressions. As mentioned earlier, competencies are the *why* of learning. The College and Career Readiness standards outline the knowledge and skills within academic disciplines that students should demonstrate at the end of high school, giving teachers at each grade level responsibility for moving students toward that ultimate goal (NGA & CCSSO, 2010a, 2010b). The study and development of learning progressions can help teachers understand the learning that must take place—*what* learning will look like for students during the school year as they work toward a competency. Teachers and students together then determine the best pathway to take in pursuit of annual academic goals (Achieve, 2015). Figure 3.3 provides a simple visual for understanding how one flows into the other, and the among between competencies, standards, and progressions of learning.

Multiple Pathways

Students in traditional classroom settings typically have one way to learn content or a new skill. Those students who did not learn content and skills in the way the teacher teaches them are often left behind. One of the greatest strengths of a competency-based learning system is there are multiple pathways for students to achieve success within a given competency.

The whole concept of developing research- and experience-based learning progressions is to provide teachers and students with a logical pathway based on known information. If we know that to get from point A to point B a student must demonstrate understanding of specific key skills, the teacher is able to provide support and the student is able to clearly understand his or her next steps. Research demonstrates that students often learn specific skills through a similar process. Teachers, through trial and error, begin to understand the steps necessary, both within their instruction and within students' learning, for development and growth within a particular learning goal. Frederic Mosher (2011) describes this as "a sequence of distinguishable levels or constellations of understanding and skill that are stable for a student for at least some period of time, and represent steps advancing along a path" (p. 6).

However, learning paths will look different for every student, and that is OK. For classroom teachers, this may seem like a daunting consideration. How is it possible for teachers to support twenty-five students, all at different points within a learning progression? It is not easy to do. But teachers, through increased understanding of the learning building blocks and experience and professional development opportunities that provide research-based theory, will begin to intrinsically understand how to support and group their students accordingly to maximize their time.

This doesn't mean that students will be tracked in any way. Skill by skill, competency by competency, students will have the opportunity to work independently, in small groups, and with direct support from their teacher to clearly understand how to move forward on their own learning continuum. Student ownership of learning is a critical component of a competency-based learning system and allows teachers to effectively support students. It is not all up to that one person in the classroom—the teacher—to ensure a student's success. The student, given the opportunity to be in control of his or her own learning, will be more engaged and committed to the learning process.

Technology can play a major role in providing personalized pathways. Teachers must know how to effectively integrate technological tools to support personalized learning. Technology itself is not personalized learning, but rather a resource to provide opportunities for personalized learning experiences. Managing all of these resources can be tricky, so it is imperative to access a learning management system (LMS) that can support teachers in this work. An LMS "manages" the various components related to instruction, grading, curriculum, assessment, student reporting, and state reporting. Developing tasks, warehousing and sharing tasks, uploading student work, and integrating systems are integral parts of an LMS. In a competency-based system, an LMS can significantly streamline these various components for students, teachers, and administrators, so that teachers are able to collaborate effectively together and with students and parents in supporting student learning goals. Ideally, students are able to provide evidence of learning directly within this system, and teachers are able to work collaboratively to develop, refine, and assign assessments, as well as provide ongoing feedback to students.

Competency Development

There are a number of ways schools and districts can go about developing their competencies, but there is a common, important theme in all successful implementation scenarios: teachers are involved from the beginning.

In many schools and districts, the difference between competencies and standards (especially leverage standards) is not wholly different. In fact, many standards are considered to be *competency level*—that is, they are at a much higher DOK level and require a greater level of critical thinking from students.

The process for developing competencies is very similar to one utilized in many schools and districts that have gone through the process of identifying leverage standards. DuFour et al. (2016) outline the importance of teachers working collaboratively to build shared knowledge and come to a collective understanding. Educators should utilize this process when developing competencies, as well as when identifying learning pathways that will lead to successful demonstration of proficiency within these competencies.

Teachers do not have to begin from scratch. In some states, the departments of education have identified model competencies that can be starting points for schools. For example, New Hampshire's Department of Education staff worked closely with experts in the field, as well as teachers and curriculum coordinators, to develop model competencies available for educators to use and access.

This approach is ideal because it combines a research base and the ever-important experience of teachers. Heritage (2008) outlines examples of a *top-down approach* in which experts create the progressions based on their knowledge within a specific field. In a *bottom-up approach*, teachers develop the progressions based on their experience and work "collaboratively to identify the sub skills or sub concepts that would lead to understanding of the concept or acquisition of the skill" (Heritage, 2008, p. 17).

We posit that this bottom-up approach with top-down *support* is the most conducive to developing rigorous, developmentally appropriate competencies and learning progressions that teachers base on other teachers' and their own input and recognized expertise. This also provides teachers with the leeway to refine the competencies and progressions as necessary, truly allowing them to evolve organically.

In New Hampshire, districts and schools also develop their own competencies by utilizing a competency validation rubric to guide them and to assess the quality of their own competencies (New Hampshire Department of Education, 2010). This rubric outlines the four major areas to consider while developing competencies— (1) relevance to content area, (2) enduring concepts, (3) cognitive demand, and (4) relative to assessment—as well as determines what is necessary to develop stronger competency statements. This is particularly helpful at the secondary level, where teachers must develop competencies for elective courses that don't necessarily have national or state standards. Visit the New Hampshire Department of Education website to view the complete rubric (goo.gl/TfaFqB). Figure 3.4 (pages 56–57) shows another example—a design criteria chart from the Maine Department of Education (2013).

Criteria	Weaker Statements . . .	Stronger Statements . . .
Alignment With Reporting Standard *To what extent does the statement align with the relevant reporting standard? Is the statement central to understanding the standard as described?*	• Are either too abstract (and cannot be measured) or too specific (and fail to address broadly applicable content-area skills and knowledge) • Are so detailed that they obscure their connection to the graduation standard	• Describe and define what students need to know and be able to do to demonstrate proficiency in and achievement of the content-area reporting standard • Use precise, descriptive language that clearly communicates what is essential to achieving the graduation standard
Enduring Knowledge *To what extent does this statement provide students with knowledge and skills that will be of value beyond a particular point in time, such as when students take a test or complete the unit?*	• Are limited to the scope and sequence of a specific textbook, resource, or program • Describe only knowledge and skills that are relevant or unique to a specific unit • Are nice to know but not essential for students to learn if they are going to succeed in next unit, course, or grade level	• Require students to develop and demonstrate skills and knowledge that will endure throughout their education, professional careers, and civic lives. • Answers the question, "What do we want students to remember, understand, and be able to do several years from now, perhaps long after they have forgotten the details?"
Cognitive Demand *What level of conceptual comprehension, knowledge acquisition, and skill development does the statement encourage? What DOK does this statement promote? Is the level of cognitive demand that is expected measurable?*	• Require only basic recall and lower-level cognitive skills, such as identifying, defining, summarizing, or listing • Do not encourage the application of knowledge to diverse or novel problems and situations	• Require students to demonstrate higher-order cognitive skills • Promote deeper comprehension of content and the acquisition of transferable skills such as reasoning, planning, interpreting, hypothesizing, investigating, or explaining • Are measurable

Assessment Facilitation		
To what extent does the statement allow for a broad range of formative and summative assessments?	• Suggest only limited options for assessing and demonstrating learning • Fail to describe in precise and understandable language what will be measured • Focus narrowly on factual recall and rote skills • Suggest that a single task or activity can be considered a valid demonstration of proficiency	• Help define the specific knowledge and skills that will be assessed and measured • Promote the assessment of deeper content comprehension and the acquisition of transferable skills • Promote multiple and varied options for students to demonstrate evidence of learning, particularly through performance assessments and body-of-evidence strategies such as portfolios

Source: Adapted from Maine Department of Education, 2013.

Figure 3.4: Maine Department of Education design criteria chart.

Some schools have the opportunity to work closely with an expert, allowing the implementation and learning process to occur over a period of time. This embedded support and access provides teachers and administrators with a point person who not only provides relevant, timely professional development but also can be available to answer the inevitable questions that come up in the day-to-day implementation of competencies within a curriculum area.

Regardless of how your district or school chooses to move forward, teachers should play an integral role. Developing the initial competency statements is only the beginning of this process. More important, developing the learning progressions, instructional approaches, and assessment processes that determine student growth will result in a comprehensive, balanced approach to a personalized model that supports students where they are.

Competency-based learning specialist Rose Colby, who assists schools and districts in transitioning to a competency-based system, describes the process involved in beginning this transition and the types of questions to consider as educators begin this process in their own schools and districts.

Practitioner Perspective
Rose Colby, Competency-Based Learning Specialist

When accepting an invitation to a school or district that is considering taking its first steps into designing personalized, competency-based teaching and learning systems, I find that it is important to identify the assets and liabilities as well as the reasons for moving in this direction.

My first question always is, "Why change?" If teachers and educators are going to do the hard work of systemic shifts in teaching and learning, there must be compelling reasons to move forward. Again, what is the vision of the community for the education of their students?

In one district, educational leaders felt this question deserved time and effort. They asked community members exactly what their vision for their children's future looked like. With this information, they could then design teaching and learning in the community, relying on that community vision for long-term planning of finances, instructional resources, and technology supports. This vision setting also created a laser-like focus for sustainability, as leaders and teaching staffs would inevitably change.

The vision work in this community took a year to complete. Every principal in the district invited parents to simply answer, "Who is our graduate?" or "What does it take to get the handshake at graduation?" Central office staff asked the same questions of school board members, municipal employees, and members of community organizations. Most parents and community members want only the best for their children, and often, they identify important values that go well beyond an academic report card showing credits earned.

It is also important to determine the assets of a school or district when considering what practices and policies are in place in the teaching and learning programs in the school. This needs assessment can identify what strengths a school has in different areas. Schools can then use these areas as the design levers for the transformational practices in competency-based learning.

Figure 3.5 can help with a simple determination of a team's level of readiness to begin planning for a long-range transformation to competency-based learning. Teams use the questions to assess their progress relating to competencies, performance assessment, learning pathways, and grading.

Competencies	Have you identified your graduation competencies and personal success skills?
	Are competencies in place for all curriculum areas, including electives and the arts?
	Do you use local and national standards as benchmarks for teaching and learning in all K–12 disciplines?
	Do students move on in a curriculum when they demonstrate proficiency?
	How do you currently support students who need more time to meet proficiency?
	How do you support students who already know the curriculum learning targets?
Performance Assessment	Give examples of how students at various grade levels demonstrate proficiency.
	What types of performance tasks and projects do you use throughout all curriculum areas?
	How do you create performance tasks and assessments within units of instruction?
	Do students take a summative assessment when formative assessments indicate they are ready, or are all students given the summative assessment at the same time?
	How do you use DOK in performance task design and assessment?
	Do you validate performance tasks in team meetings?
	Do you calibrate rubrics for tasks against student work?

Figure 3.5: Level of readiness assessment questions. continued →

Learning Pathways	Is a learning management system in place to support student learning?
	Do teachers collaborate in the design of instruction units?
	What learning environments are available for learners: online learning courses? Blended learning strategies? Adaptive online curriculum?
	Do high school students have the opportunity to follow their passions and interests through extended learning opportunities in the community?
	To what degree do students have voice, choice, and agency in their everyday learning opportunities?
	How do students engage with their personal learning plans (a student-created journey map for learning that students use for academic short-term and long-term planning and continual reflection along the K–12 continuum?
Grading	Does your school or district have research-based best grading practices in place? Are they identified in a grading philosophy statement?
	Is standards-based grading in place within your school or district?
	Is a standards-based report card used throughout the district?
	How do you assess and report nonacademic (personal success skills) areas on report cards? Are these areas consistent for K–12?

Asking these questions can begin the discernment process for what might be the best steps forward for a school or district. For example, a school district that has developed standards-based approaches for its curriculum may wish to develop its K–12 competencies as a first step, then move into developing professional development supports in assessment literacy. For districts that have weak K–12 articulated curriculum, this may the most important area to develop.

This work often isn't sequential. While a district works on developing a competency-based curriculum (units of instruction), it may wish to explore blended learning. The assessment questions in figure 3.5 can present an opportunity for districts to identify where they want to plan comprehensive, collaborative, deep work. The shifts in the time-based model of traditional education are significant, as shown in figure 3.6.

Taking the time to set a vision for the future of learning in a community, identifying starting points for the work, and moving from teacher-centric instruction to student-centered learning is at the heart of moving toward personalized, rigorous, competency-based learning. (R. Colby, personal communication, September 2016)

Learning Progressions and Grading

In our experience, many schools at the forefront of implementing competency-based learning practices have struggled greatly with how to actually grade the

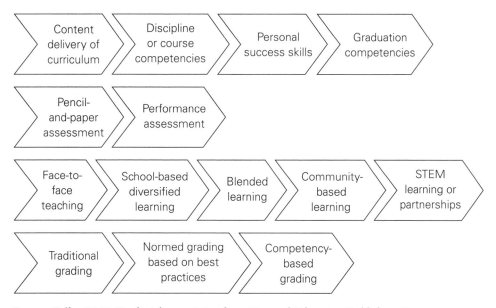

Source: Colby, 2017. Used with permission from Harvard Education Publishing Group.

Figure 3.6: The shift from a traditional to a competency-based learning system.

competencies they are supposed to assess. This is especially true in public schools that are still grade based (first grade, second grade, and so on). Once the school develops the competencies, teachers must then do the significant work of determining precisely where students should be at various times in the year to reach them. In many schools implementing competency-based learning, teachers were, without realizing it, developing the learning progressions for each competency they were assessing.

This work inspired more questions. For example, if teachers are grading students at the end of the first trimester on a specific standard or competency, and a student has not mastered the competency yet, but is exactly where the teacher expects him or her to be at that point in the year, what should his or her grade be? Many schools solve this problem by grading students as *emerging* (a 2 on a four-point scale) or *proficient* (a 3 on a four-point scale).

In a competency-based learning system, teachers describe precisely where a student is in relation to the competency; some argue it is OK that a student is at the emerging level because this is where the teacher would expect him or her to be. However, some teachers might assess the same level of evidence as proficient because they are utilizing benchmarks to assess, meaning the student has met the standard set forth and therefore is proficient. These teachers would say the student is where they would expect him or her to be.

We argue that the latter argument is the best way to report a student's progress because it is about the progression of learning; the student has demonstrated that he or she is proficient specific to where he or she is expected to be at that moment in time. Regardless of which way your district chooses to report competency, teachers within the same school or district must be clear about how they are going to grade, and they must be consistent in this approach. As a student or a parent of a student, it would get very confusing if teachers were using different indicators to report the same level of progress.

Embedded Professional Development to Support Understanding of Learning Progressions

Embedded professional development is a crucial component when transitioning to a competency-based learning environment. The learning curve is steep, so the professional development available for teachers must align with the work happening in the school. Some of the greatest learning happens while teachers are deeply involved in the work within their collaborative teams. Let's take a deep look through an example specific to writing.

Writing progressions are a tremendous example of developmental learning progressions. When utilized correctly, the grade level of the student is not the indicator of success or growth. Each student is following his or her own progression in writing.

A very valuable professional development experience some schools use to better understand progressions is to look at writing across grade levels to determine learning gaps in various stages of the writing process. This is also invaluable in developing inter-rater reliability across the entire school, as well as developing a deep understanding of learning progressions and competencies.

In our experience, the PLC framework supports this activity by providing the structure in which both horizontal and vertical teacher teams work together to dig deeply into writing progressions. Identifying writing as the focus area for digging deeply into curriculum, instruction, and assessment practices has tremendous positive impacts. Structure this activity with the following five steps.

1. Teams should agree on which research-based writing method they will use to assess writing samples at each grade level or grade band. This can be somewhat difficult because students may be engaged in different units of writing in different grades.

2. Teachers must then decide on a time when all initial writing will be complete. If this is an activity that teachers will engage in at various times during the year, then it could be divided up by trimester. It is always beneficial to assess growth over time, so three times a year for an activity like this is reasonable.

3. Teachers must ensure they analyze and assess all writing samples, ideally in teams, and through the use of a protocol. Teams assessing writing together will develop assessment literacy to a greater degree, as all team members learn from each other.

4. Teams must identify exemplar writing samples to share with their vertical colleagues for *each level of writing* that students achieve within the grade level. This is important because it allows for comparison across grade levels.

5. Teams should place exemplars (without names) visually so that groups of teachers have the opportunity to read the writing across the grade levels.

Figure 3.7 shows teachers how to visually compare writing at various levels across different grades. At each grade level, a shaded box indicates student work assessed at that level (one exemplar per writing level per grade).

Grade Level	Writing Level							
	1	2	3	4	5	6	7	8
K	■	■	■					
1	■	■	■					
2	■	■	■	■				
3		■	■	■	■	■	■	
4			■	■	■	■	■	■
5			■	■	■	■	■	■

Figure 3.7: Example of a chart comparing writing vertically on a developmental continuum.

When digging more deeply into the writing, you will notice that each paper should be assessed using the same common rubric, regardless of the grade level. The conversations teachers have will be specific to the content of the writing, not what the writing might actually look like.

Shared Understanding Through Vertical Teams

Learning through vertical teams is incredibly valuable and productive, especially in a competency-based learning model. We find that teachers tend to know their own grade's standards and competencies very well. But, in a system that allows students to move on when ready, it is imperative for all teachers to have a deeper understanding of more than just their grade-level competencies. This helps teachers begin to develop an awareness of not only the building blocks to get to a certain level but also to extend learning well beyond previous knowledge.

> ⟫
> **It is imperative for all teachers to have a deeper understanding of more than just their grade-level competencies.**
> ⟪

Vertical teams should work together to look at the displayed student work exemplars for each grade level. These vertical teams should include a teacher from each grade level (if possible), as well as specialists and special educators. As a leader, you can provide guiding questions, but the intent is to allow teachers the opportunity to look carefully at the work. From this, teachers invariably ask questions of each other about how to get a student from a 4 to a 5 (for example) or why a certain piece of work was assessed at a certain level.

Additionally, conversations generally evolve into deeper dialogue focused on specific activities that can help students get to the next level. When teachers engage in this process, they truly begin to tap into the expertise of those around them. We have also found that teachers are then more likely to approach their colleagues at other grade levels for specifics on how to support learners who may not be making the progress they would expect or desire.

Project-Based Learning and Competencies

Competencies ensure that learners are acquiring the requisite skills as well as a deep understanding of content they can then transfer within learning experiences. Project-based learning (PBL) is a model within competency-based learning schools that fits incredibly well with competency-based learning. PBL is an instructional method that allows learners the opportunity to develop their knowledge and skills through an extended project (Buck Institute for Education, n.d.a). These projects are authentic, engaging, and typically challenge students to solve issues and problems directly connected to their world. Students develop the knowledge and then build the habits and skills through PBL that are necessary for success in today's world.

A number of factors integrate PBL with competency-based, personalized pathways for student learning. The Buck Institute for Education (n.d.b) identifies a number of ways that PBL supports personalized student learning:

> **PBL makes school more engaging for students.** Today's students, more than ever, often find school to be boring and meaningless. In PBL, students are active, not passive; a project engages their hearts and minds, and it provides real-world relevance for learning.

> **PBL improves learning.** After completing a project, students understand content more deeply, remember what they learn and retain it longer than is often the case with traditional instruction. Because of this, students who gain content knowledge with PBL are better able to apply what they know and can do to new situations.

> **PBL builds success skills for college, career, and life.** In the 21st century workplace and in college, success requires more than basic knowledge and skills. In a project, students learn how to take initiative and responsibility, build their confidence, solve problems, work in teams, communicate ideas, and manage themselves more effectively.

> **PBL helps address standards**. The Common Core and other present-day standards emphasize real-world application of knowledge and skills, and the development of success skills such as critical thinking/problem solving, collaboration, communication in a variety of media, and speaking and presentation skills. PBL is an effective way to meet these goals.

> **PBL provides opportunities for students to use technology.** Students are familiar with and enjoy using a variety of tech tools that are a perfect fit with PBL. With technology, teachers and students can not only find resources and information and create products, but also collaborate more effectively, and connect with experts, partners, and audiences around the world.

> **PBL makes teaching more enjoyable and rewarding.** Projects allow teachers to work more closely with active, engaged students doing high-quality, meaningful work, and in many cases to rediscover the joy of learning alongside their students.

> **PBL connects students and schools with communities and the real world.** Projects provide students with empowering opportunities to make a difference, by solving real problems and addressing real issues. Students learn how to interact with adults and organizations, are exposed to workplaces and adult jobs, and can develop career interests. Parents and community members can be involved in projects.

These are crucial components of a successful competency-based learning system.

Practitioner Perspective
Jeff Heyck-Williams, Director of Curriculum and Instruction, Two Rivers Public Charter Schools

As we think about the competencies that students need to be successful in college and careers, we realize that each individual competency in isolation is relatively useless unless it can be transferred from the original learning setting and applied in the context of solving complex problems. As David N. Perkins (2009) suggests in his book, *Making Learning Whole*, when learning particular competencies, students need opportunities to see how concepts and skills interrelate, to experience drawing on a developing bank of competencies in solving problems, and to evaluate the effective use of those competencies in context. When a child learns a sport through practice that includes drills of techniques and scrimmaging, the true test of learning the sport is when the child applies his or her learning from practice in the context of the game. We need to give students opportunities *to play the game* with the competencies they learn in school.

At Two Rivers Public Charter School (a preschool through grade 8 English language education network of schools in Washington, DC), project-based learning is our approach to giving students the opportunity to play the game. We believe that students deepen their skills and knowledge when given real-world contexts in which to apply their competencies. The projects, which we call *learning expeditions*, are ten to twelve weeks in which students develop new competencies and explore solutions to authentic problems.

A grade 8 learning expedition on public spaces is an excellent example. The students in this learning expedition were tasked with developing competencies in understanding the history of the ancient civilizations of Greece and Rome utilizing the mathematics concepts of scale and transformations of shapes; formulating well-reasoned written arguments in English; and collaborating and communicating. Drawing on an understanding of each of these competencies and an understanding of our local context of a city in the midst of urban renewal, teachers crafted the following problem for students to tackle.

> DC is a divided city, and not everyone feels their participation as citizens is valued. Robert F. Kennedy Memorial Stadium sits on a symbolic dividing line in the city (the Anacostia River). In the future, this space will be redeveloped. How could this space be used to address some of these divisions and engage more residents as citizens? Draw on ideas from ancient Athens and Rome to design and defend a public space that enables citizenship and strengthens our community.

This problem was given to students with the understanding that the strongest proposals for redesigning the space would be pitched to our local Advisory Neighborhood Commission, a community-based governing body that advises the DC government on community affairs.

Through the course of the learning expedition, the students developed their competencies in history, mathematics, and English because they knew that their knowledge and skills would be put to the test in front of adults who had a stake in how the land could be redeveloped. They began by gaining an understanding of public space in history and how it has been used to promote civic engagement in ancient Greece and Rome. Simultaneously, in mathematics, they developed an understanding of scale and transformations of shapes that included dilations of a shape. Then building on this study of history and mathematics, they created scale drawings of the parcel of land near the stadium under consideration for redevelopment. In their drawing, they incorporated design elements that would promote civic engagement. Through multiple drafts, critiques, and revisions, teams of two students settled on some essential elements for the public space redesign and began working on pitches. These pitches had to incorporate the effective reasoning skills that they had been learning in their English classes. Each team formulated claims and supported them with a combination of understanding the uses of ancient spaces in antiquity and the modern context of Washington, DC's, neighborhoods. After giving all of the pitches to panels of guest experts including local architects, school administrators, and city planners, three designs were chosen to be presented before the Advisory Neighborhood Commission, which took the recommendations seriously in its work in taking public comment on the development in the neighborhood.

Situating the learning of competencies within a real-world context like the public space learning expedition was more than an engaging context for students to learn competencies. Students understand why the concepts that they were learning in history and mathematics class mattered. In addition, they transferred the skills they learned in class into a product that had relevance beyond the school. In other words, they *played the game*. (J. Heyck-Williams, personal communication, October 2016)

Developing competencies that challenge, inspire, and engage students and teachers is not an easy process. In fact, this process takes years. But the result of this hard work is an aligned system of learning that provides students with the opportunities for engagement, ownership, development of mindset, and growth necessary to solve the complex issues our world will face in the very near future.

Reflection Questions

Consider the following four reflection questions with your team.

1. Teacher teams must be clear on what students should be demonstrating a deep understanding of. Has your school developed competencies (the *why* of learning) that reflect a deep understanding of your school's or district's standards? Are these competencies written in student-friendly terms?

2. The relationship among competencies, standards, and learning progressions is important to understand. Do teachers in your school have a shared understanding of competencies, the standards that feed into these competencies, and the role of learning progressions in the overall learning process?

3. Developing shared knowledge through focused horizontal and vertical professional development opportunities increases the knowledge and overall literacy of collaborative teams. Does your staff participate in professional development together as a school, sharing student work in and across grade levels to enhance their understanding of developmental learning progressions?

4. PBL provides meaningful, real-world opportunities for students to learn through a project. Do teachers in your school plan instruction units in which a project provides the learning opportunity, not just as a summative way to demonstrate learning?

CHAPTER 4

Changing to Competency-Friendly Grading Practices

One of the most difficult, yet necessary, tasks to transform a school from a traditional to a competency-based learning model is to develop a schoolwide approach to grading with competency-friendly practices. This chapter focuses on changing traditional grading practices. Readers will learn how collaborative teams support competency-friendly grading practices for both academic skills and academic behaviors. To introduce this topic, consider the day Brian's outlook on grading (and assessment) changed forever.

Have you ever had a moment in your life when you had the stark realization that everything you have ever known to be true about a particular topic is completely wrong? Sometimes this moment develops gradually, over a period of months or even years. Sometimes, it hits you like a ton of bricks. Brian experienced that brick-crashing moment on November 22, 2005.

It was the last period of the day, and Brian was busy finishing up a precalculus lecture on rational functions before his students in the affluent town of Andover, Massachusetts, left for Thanksgiving break. Waiting outside his classroom door was Jeff, one of his former students who was coming back to visit after his first few months in college. Brian thought very highly of Jeff, as he was one of those students every high school mathematics teacher longs for. Mathematics did not come easy for Jeff, but Brian marveled at the way Jeff would keep plugging away at it. He was an extremely hard worker, perhaps one of the most memorable of Brian's career. Jeff was often the first one to enter the classroom with a question from the previous night's homework assignment, and he always chose to sit right in the front row during class so that he could capture everything Brian wrote on the board. During lectures, Jeff always asked great questions. His homework was always complete, neat, and organized. The same could be said of his notebook too.

Brian got to know Jeff on a personal level because he would spend at least one to two afternoons a week with him for extra help after school. It was during this time that the pair prepared for taking tests, a skill that Jeff believed he was very weak in. Brian was known back then for giving very difficult mathematics tests. For Brian, these tests were an opportunity to separate the A-students from the rest of the class. It was not uncommon for very few students to get As on tests. Generally, a student's test score average was about a grade lower than his or her overall course average. At the time, this made sense to Brian. He would soon discover, however, that this logic was very flawed.

Despite Jeff's low test scores, he managed to earn a B+ in class. This academic accomplishment, however, was a disappointment for a young man who was used to earning straight As. Brian recalled a deep conversation with Jeff who was nervous that the B+ was going to stick out as his only poor grade from his junior year transcript and make it difficult for him to get into the college of his choice. Brian offered to write his college recommendation letter, explaining that he would write about how hard Jeff worked for that B+ and how, if Brian were grading on effort alone, Jeff's grade would have been higher. Jeff agreed, and the letter became part of his college application packet that fall. Throughout his senior year, Jeff and Brian stayed close, with Brian tutoring the student once a week in calculus. When Jeff graduated that spring, he enrolled in a computer engineering program at Boston University, Brian's alma mater. Brian couldn't have been prouder as Jeff was well on his way to having a successful college career. Brian hoped that in some small way he had helped Jeff finally overcome his mathematics weaknesses and set him up to be successful in college.

As soon as the bell rang and the students cleared the room, Jeff entered. It was clear he was on a serious mission. "Mr. Stack, we need to talk," he said.

"Absolutely, Jeff, and how is your semester going?" Brian asked.

"It's going really well, Mr. Stack, but I have some advice for you that I believe is going to make you a better teacher. I don't want you to be offended by what I am about to tell you, but I respect you so much for the passion and the enthusiasm you display each day in your class. There are some places where you are falling short, and you can do better," Jeff replied.

Never in Brian's professional life had a student been so direct with him. Brian was half intrigued and half scared about what he was about to hear. With great hesitation, Brian took a deep breath and asked Jeff to continue.

For the next fifteen minutes, Jeff explained in detail how he wasn't prepared for mathematics in college. Although he had developed the work-study habits to be successful in high school, his mathematics skills were extremely weak, which wasn't surprising based on Jeff's low test scores in Brian's class; however, Jeff shared that this wasn't the issue.

"Mr. Stack," he explained, "I earned a B+ in your class because I knew how to play the game of school. As hard as your tests were, I knew that they only counted for 30 percent of my grade. To compensate, I aimed to have perfect homework, classwork, notebook, and participation grades. I assumed that I could do OK on the smaller quizzes because they were focused on smaller amounts of the material. Then, when it came to your tests, I knew that as long as I could get at least a 65 percent on the test, I would still be in the ballpark to get a B or a B+ in the class. I never considered myself to be a good test-taker, and your tests always asked us to connect too many mathematics concepts than I could handle. I could only do small amounts at any one time. The problem was I didn't learn the mathematics by doing this. Over the last few months in college, I have spent hours and hours trying to learn the skills that I should have gotten from high school. Now that I am in college, I see that my professors are still giving me really difficult tests that ask me to apply and extend my thinking, but I am still having trouble with the basics!"

Brian's jaw dropped. One of his favorite students just told him that he had failed him as a teacher.

Jeff could sense his former teacher's heightened anxiety. "Don't take this the wrong way, Mr. Stack," he went on to explain. "Your class was engaging and there is no doubt in my mind that you love mathematics, you love your job, and you are committed to helping your students be successful. What I am trying to tell you is that as a high school student, I didn't take advantage of the opportunities you presented to

← —————

Brian's jaw dropped. One of his favorite students just told him that he had failed him as a teacher.

————— ⇒

me to really dig deep into the mathematics and learn it to the extent that I should have. I took the easy way out, and I only cheated myself. I am paying for it now."

After a brief hesitation, Brian asked, "Jeff, what could I have done differently to prevent this?"

Jeff put his hand up to his mouth and let out a sigh. He began shaking his head as he mumbled, "I'm not sure, Mr. Stack. I knew you were going to ask me that question, too. I'm not sure what you could have done differently. Maybe you could have weighted tests more in your grade? I know it would have made my grade even lower, but maybe it would have motivated me to try harder? That is just a guess. I don't know what the solution is, but I just wanted you to know how things played out for me in hopes that you could figure out a better solution for future students, like my younger sister, Katie, who is in your class right now."

At that moment, Brian realized he would never look at grading and assessment the same way again.

That day, Jeff taught Brian a valuable lesson. As a teacher, Brian had become so focused on providing opportunities for "nice" students to earn points toward their grade that he was missing the fundamental purpose of grades: representing what students *learn*, not what they *earn*.

The Flaws of the Traditional Grading System

Cathy Vatterott (2015) makes a strong case for the need to rethink grading practices in competency-based learning schools, suggesting that such a philosophical shift in a school is a "complete overhaul of the teaching-learning process" which leads to a grading shift from one of a compliance culture to a "performance culture driven by student empowerment and mastery of learning" (p. 26). In a competency-based school, this philosophy needs to permeate every teacher, every student, every assignment, and every grade, every day. To understand why such a philosophy must be present in a competency-based school, you must start by recognizing the following flaws in the traditional point-based system.

Lack of Consistency in Grading Structures

For the majority of schools, grading practices differ greatly between teachers, and this results in teachers using a variety of sources to determine student grades. University of Kentucky Professor Thomas R. Guskey (2009) refers to this issue as *hodgepodge grading.* If you are in the mood for a lengthy faculty discussion, simply ask people to weigh in on how much homework should count toward a course grade. Inevitably, after two hours, the group members will be no closer to consensus on that question than they were when they started. Imagine being a student in a school where this is the norm. When grades are driven by teachers through a compliance culture, students come to see grading as a game, and the best students are the ones who learn how to play that game successfully with each of their teachers. Besides being an unjust way of assessing learning, this lack of consistency creates a host of other issues.

School administrators dread no conversation more than when a parent calls to question his or her child's grade. Without a consistent set of grading practices, the leader is forced into a debate with the parent over whether the teacher's grading practices are fair and consistent. The leader will have no immediate answer or explanation to provide the parent. In an effort to defend the teacher and his or her professional judgment, the leader would have to look into each complaint on a case-by-case basis. It is difficult for the leader to defend the teacher without consulting a collaboratively created team rubric in a PLC.

In some schools, teams and departments band together to reach consensus on how to approach grading. While this is certainly a step in the right direction, nothing can be more frustrating than explaining to a parent why the mathematics department believes that homework should count for 40 percent of a grade when it only counts for 20 percent in social studies. To eliminate this flaw, schools need one consistent set of grading practices that every teacher in the building uses. We discuss this topic in more detail later in this chapter.

Blending of Academic Behavior With Academic Evidence

This second flaw is apparent in Brian's story about Jeff. When Brian spoke about Jeff as a good student, he was defining Jeff as a hard worker who did his homework, raised his hand in class, and stayed after school for extra help. For Jeff, this good academic behavior didn't necessarily translate into learning, yet Brian continued to reward him by letting those behaviors influence his grade. This issue gets to the heart of Vatterott's (2015) claim that the traditional grading system is built on a compliance culture where grades reward compliance and punish noncompliance.

As an example of this, let's look at how Brian assigned homework grades. Back then, Brian believed that a student couldn't learn everything in the classroom and, therefore, homework was an essential part of the learning process. Homework was 40 percent of the course grade, which was actually more than test scores. Each night, Brian would assign a problem set consisting of twenty to twenty-five problems of varying degrees of difficulty. The next day at the beginning of class, he would walk around the room and check in with each student to review his or her effort on the homework. The grading scale is shown in figure 4.1.

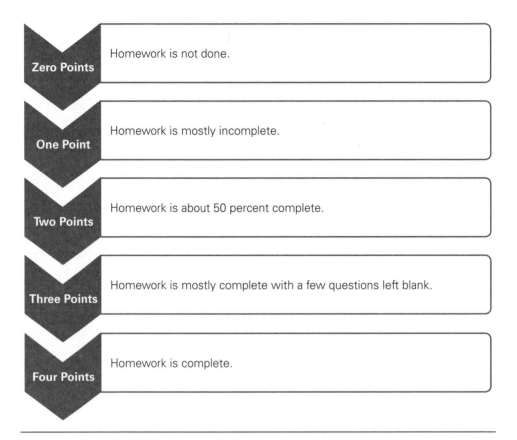

Figure 4.1: Brian's traditional homework grading scale.

This scale only addresses a grade for effort—the number of homework problems that the student attempted as a percentage of how many Brian assigned. To grade the content of students' homework, Brian would collect it at the end of class and review it for accuracy. Since he often did not have time to grade each homework answer for each student, he would randomly select two to three problems to grade for accuracy. Students then received an accuracy grade and an effort grade, and these were combined to produce their overall homework grade for the day.

Brian's homework example demonstrates two important points. First, if homework is such an important part of the learning process, what good is a homework grade when 50 percent of it comes from effort alone with no evidence of whether learning has occurred? The act of blending academic evidence with academic behavior results in a watered-down homework grade that is not indicative of what the student knows and is able to do. Second, and perhaps most important, why is homework graded at all? The very act of grading formative work is flawed. Homework is a time to practice. It is a time to make mistakes and learn from them. By grading those mistakes, students are given the message that the entire learning process, from development to exhibition, is under review. It tells them that part of their grade will depend on how quickly they learn something and how many mistakes they make practicing a new skill. This is not the message we want to send to students.

Schools focused on competency-based learning must take steps to separate academic evidence from academic behaviors. While it is necessary to help students develop positive academic behaviors, schools need to find ways to do so without taking away from the integrity of the academic grade. If a school cannot find a way to meaningfully hold students accountable for academic behaviors, this could become a major stumbling block to a successful implementation of a competency-based learning system. Later in this chapter, we revisit this idea and outline a list of strategies to help schools be successful.

Accumulation of Points With No Direct Correlation to Learning

Jeff raised an interesting point when he described his education as *a game of school*. Jeff quickly figured out how he could earn as many points as possible. If 40 percent of his grade was based on homework, he just had to do his homework. If 10 percent came from keeping an organized notebook, he could do that. If another 10 percent came from an obscure category called *participation*, he would make sure he raised his hand once in every class to earn those points. From those three categories alone, Jeff already had sixty of one hundred possible points, and he hadn't actually started demonstrating his learning yet. From there, his quiz and test scores became a shell game where he tried to earn as many points as he could to bring him to the threshold of the minimum grade he was trying to earn.

Brian experienced something similar. In his first year as a high school principal, he was confounded by an issue a student brought to his attention. Three months into the school year, the student learned from her teacher that she had performed so poorly on her assessments that it would be mathematically impossible for her to pass the class. The teacher advised the student to drop the class and take something else. Think about that. With seven months left in the school year, a student was told to give up. How could we do such a disservice to a student?

From the teacher's perspective, the one hundred–point scale is also a game. Consider participation for a minute. What criteria do teachers use to assess something like participation? Most teachers do not assess skills and dispositions until the end of a grading term, and many move a student's grade slightly up (or down) to the grade that they believe the student earned for the quarter. This grade may be loosely based on how often the teacher believes the student contributes to class discussions and, as many teachers admit, their most recent experience with the student. This certainly does not take into account a body of evidence.

Another common teacher malpractice in the grading game is extra credit—or points a teacher makes available to students to help them boost their grade to a higher level. Rick Wormeli (2006) argues that there is no connection to the practice of giving extra credit and learning. He writes, "If a student falters in his or her demonstration of mastery with the regular test items, but overcomes those scoring losses with points from a bonus section, then we have to reconsider whether the new, bonus-inflated grade really represents what the student knows and is able to do" (p. 125). Teachers, like students, have come to recognize the flaws of a points-based system and develop strategies to make the system work to meet their needs and their students'.

As a school leader, changing grading practices can be one of the most difficult things to do. Assistant superintendent Kyle Repucci shares how he approached this work as a middle and high school principal.

Practitioner Perspective
Kyle Repucci, Assistant Superintendent, Rochester School District, New Hampshire

Moving to a competency-based grading and reporting system is an opportunity to focus your school on what matters—academic performance. Grades in a traditional system have so many independent variables (assignment categories, category weighting, assessment frequency, reassessment, extra credit, effort, and so on) that assessing academic performance is nearly impossible. When I was the principal of Epping Middle and High School in Epping, New Hampshire, in 2011, our school worked to understand how what we were doing in a traditional grading system actually masked academic performance instead of supporting it.

Over the course of an entire school year, our faculty constructed a model based on a simple maxim we created after many spirited conversations: grades should reflect a student's academic performance. As principal during our journey to competency-based learning, I worked to build consensus and shape many traditional practices into a competency-based learning model. It was important for me to be considerate of those more traditional staff members, but I also needed to be the instigator of philosophic change.

The goal of our new system was to more accurately report academic achievement, to provide meaningful feedback, and to be fair and transparent. Like any good coach, I worked with my staff to create systems that made our maxim more tangible. Our first task was to better understand our grading scale. In our case, we kept a traditional scale, but we drafted language to describe each performance level. This new language became more important than the number associated with a grade. For example, staff determined that advanced students understand and apply key concepts and skills with consistency and independence instead of earning ninety-three points. Performance-level descriptors help teachers craft richer and more authentic tasks that allow students to demonstrate their understanding of course content and competencies.

Much of our work focused on creating common grading practices and common definitions for all things pertaining to our grading and reporting system. For example, we analyzed the topic of homework, and we discovered that it was much easier to see how we were different than similar in our practices pertaining to homework. In our case, we decided that homework was important for students, but wanted it to serve a much more significant and consistent purpose in our grading and reporting system, so homework became formative assessment. As a faculty, we defined formative assessment and calibrated our implementation of this new schoolwide definition. It became the first of many that we documented in our school's grading and reporting guidelines. The entire faculty worked together to craft, revise, and approve this document.

In creating clear and consistent grading practices, our faculty decided on a democratic process where consensus ruled; not everyone agreed all the time. In addition, our grading and reporting guidelines were not perfect or written in stone. During our first year of implementation, we realized that a few philosophic tenets, like a rolling grade and late work, were problematic in the reality of our brick-and-mortar school and traditional school calendar, so we revised these practices the following summer.

We wanted students to take ownership of their learning, so we tried to remove the guesswork and mystery associated with grades. Our grading and reporting guidelines helped create a system with total transparency that provided a foundational understanding of what comprised the measurement of a student's academic performance or grade. We sought to remove outside factors like effort, extra credit, and aesthetic performance unrelated to course content and competencies from the grading practices. Our schoolwide grading and reporting system allowed students and parents to be more reflective and proactive when evaluating a student's performance. In addition, the normed grades and grading practices yielded student performance data that help teachers better modify and plan instruction, as well as determine additional supports and opportunities. As a school, we are also better able to evaluate the effectiveness of our instructional programs.

Our school now has consistency among teachers and students in discussing, applying, and understanding grading guidelines. In our system, the only independent variable in grading is what each student brings to the table. (K. Repucci, personal communication, October 2016)

Essential Grading Practices of a Competency-Based Learning System

One of the first tasks a school should undertake in its efforts to make the shift to a competency-based learning system is to identify a common set of grading expectations for all teachers. Although schools will need some autonomy to develop practices for their unique situations, these are the considerations for any common grading practices in competency-based learning schools.

- ▸ Grades must reflect what students learn, not what they earn.

- ▸ Grading must consider the use and purpose of diagnostic testing, formative assessment, and summative assessment.

- ▸ Rubrics must replace the traditional one hundred–point scale with a smaller rubric scale based on three, four, or five points.

- ▸ Grades must separate academics from academic behaviors.

- ▸ Students must have the opportunity to reassess their work without penalty.

Grades Must Reflect What Students Learn

At the secondary level, a final course grade (if required) should reflect the student's actual degree and level of learning. When possible, divide the grade into separate grades for each course competency or skill. At the elementary level, because the emphasis is more on the reporting of individual skills, an overall grade for credit is not necessary. All emphasis should be on making sure that each competency grade is an accurate reflection of what the student knows and is able to do.

Author and grading consultant Ken O'Connor (2009) describes this approach: "Grades should be effective communication vehicles, and the methods used to determine them need to provide optimum opportunities for student success and to encourage learning" (p. 47). O'Connor (2009) goes on to state:

> Grades must be directly related to the learning goals for each grading period in each classroom. Teachers must understand clearly what learning results are expected and then base their assessment and grading plans on these learning goals. Students must also understand clearly what the learning goals are so that they know what is expected of them. (p. 47)

Implementing a competency-based grading model that focuses on student learning follows naturally from the standards-based learning process. Collaborative teams start this process by adopting a common set of standards such as the CCSS (www .corestandards.org); Next Generation Science Standards (www.nextgenscience.org); or College, Career, and Civic Life (C3) Framework for Social Studies Standards (www.socialstudies.org/c3). Using backward design, teams create *learning targets* that Connie M. Moss and Susan M. Brookhart (2012) define as follows: "A learning target describes, in language that students understand, the lesson-sized chunk of information, skills, and reasoning processes that students will come to know deeply and thoroughly" (p. 164). Teams organize learning tasks in a way that makes sense to teachers, allowing them to develop performance assessments, a topic that we focus on in greater depth in chapter 5.

Standards-based learning positively impacts student agency, giving students power and autonomy over their learning that would never happen in a system where students have to accumulate points to earn a particular grade. To maximize this potential for student agency, teachers must know when and how to provide feedback to students through grades and other means. There are differences between diagnostic testing and formative and summative assessment. Knowing when to use these methods is the next must-have.

Grades Must Consider the Purpose of Diagnostic Testing and Formative and Summative Assessment

The learning process often starts with diagnostic or pretesting to determine where students are, and gives teachers important data on the prerequisite skills and knowledge that students will need to meet the upcoming learning target. While diagnostic testing is an important part of the learning process for which teachers must provide students with feedback, it should never carry weight as a grade in a competency-based learning system.

Formative assessment refers to feedback given to students during the learning process and explains to what extent a student is learning a concept or skill. More commonly, formative assessment occurs when teachers provide students with feedback while they are practicing a new concept or skill. As mentioned earlier in this chapter, there is a fundamental flaw in the logic of heavily weighting formative work, such as homework, because teachers don't want to penalize students or detract from their opportunity to freely practice, make mistakes, and learn from them. For these reasons, grading formative assessment should be done only for the purpose of providing a student with feedback on his or her understanding during the learning process. Vatterott (2015) stresses the importance of this point, stating:

> Most teachers view informal feedback and formative assessment as two different things. They don't consider the actions of checking for understanding or helping students correct mistakes as formative assessment—it's just good teaching. It's easier to think of *formative assessment* as structured tasks designed by the teacher, the results of which may be marked or documented in some fashion, so students and parents can have a record of the student's progress toward the learning targets. (p. 57)

When possible, formative work should carry little, if any, weight in a student's final course grade. In grading systems where teachers assign weights to certain grading categories, formative work should never count for more than 10 percent of an overall grade.

If formative assessment is no more than 10 percent of an overall grade (or not counted at all), this leaves at least 90 percent (if not 100 percent) of the grade for *summative* assessments, a term that O'Connor (2009) defines as "an assessment designed to provide information about a student's achievement at the end of a period of instruction" (p. 246). The reason for such a high weight is that summative assessments are the true measure of what students have learned, whereas formative assessments are the opportunity for students to practice and prepare for their demonstration. Summative assessments should be organized by learning targets, and should be given to students when they are ready to demonstrate what they know and are able to do. Ideally, students should not take a summative assessment until there is mutual agreement between student and teacher that the student is ready to demonstrate his or her evidence of learning. When students have multiple opportunities to demonstrate their learning of a particular target, more recent summative assessment grades should be weighted more heavily as these are the best indicators of how well a student has learned the knowledge or skill. According to Marzano and Haystead (2008), this concept is often referred to as a *learning trend model*.

Marzano and Haystead (2008) point out that some grading software systems have the capability to compute a grade based on a learning trend that weights more recent work using a mathematical process known as a learning power law. Teachers can apply this process when at least four distinct data points exist. Figure 4.2 illustrates the difference between averaging and a trend line.

In figure 4.2, a student has received grades of 2.0, 3.0, 3.0, and 4.0, in that order. The average of these grades is a 3.0. Although the student had a strong finish with a high grade, the first score of 2.0 brought down the average score. Looking at all four grades collectively, the trend tells us that this student has gained considerable knowledge from the first assessment to the last assessment; that attainment isn't apparent in the average calculation. Using a learning trend calculation (marked by the solid black line in the diagram), it's clear that the student is not penalized for the fact that he or she was still learning the concept on the first assessment. In the learning trend calculation, the final result is a score of 3.5, and this best represents the student's learning and positive upward trend over the duration of the learning process.

This diagram also highlights another consideration for a competency-based grading system: the need for smaller scales that align closely with rubrics that have clear descriptors. These result in a much more accurate representation of what a student knows and is able to do at the end of the learning process. This also becomes the rationale for our next consideration.

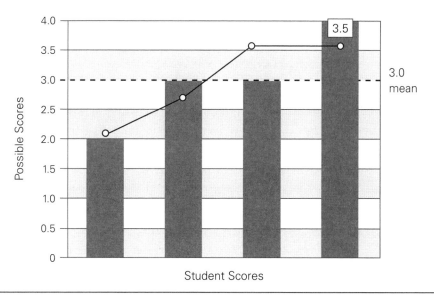

Figure 4.2: Averaging versus a trend line.

Rubric Scales Must Replace the Traditional One Hundred– Point Scale

Brookhart (2013) defines a *rubric* as "a coherent set of criteria for students' work that includes descriptions of levels of performance quality on the criteria" (p. 4). Designed correctly, rubrics allow teachers to objectively match student performance to clearly defined descriptions rather than forcing them to make judgment calls on performance. This eliminates the subjectivity of grading. Rubrics are the tools collaborative teams use to determine how they will know when a student has learned something, the second of the four critical questions of a PLC (DuFour et al., 2016). Brookhart (2013) makes a case for why rubrics play such an important role for teachers and teams: "Really good rubrics help teachers avoid confusing the task or activity with the learning goal, and therefore confusing completion of the task with learning. Rubrics help keep teachers focused on criteria, not tasks" (p. 11).

In addition to helping teachers align their instruction and assessment, rubrics also assist students in the learning process by helping them understand what the desired performance level looks like. When crafted in student-friendly language, rubrics play an important role in increasing student agency by providing them with a tool to self-assess their own learning and a road map for improvement toward the learning target.

For these and many other reasons, the use of rubrics is essential to developing quality assessments in a competency-based learning system. It follows, then, that teachers should report final grades using the same rubric-based scale they use at the assessment level. Every effort should be made to shift people's thinking from a percentage-based points system to a criterion-referenced system. Scales need to be built from clear, concise rubrics that clearly articulate the level and degree of learning that students must demonstrate.

There are many inequities and flaws in using the one hundred–point-scale system. First and foremost, teachers should not use a grade if they cannot create a clear descriptor of student performance for that particular grade. If a teacher has defined what it looks like to get a grade of 90 percent versus a grade of 80 percent, the teacher cannot award a grade between 80 and 90 unless he or she can clearly define that grade as well. It is too subjective and not specific enough to justify a grade of 85 as one for which a student demonstrates his or her learning at a level halfway between the 80 and the 90 descriptors. If we extend this logic, the teacher would need clearly defined descriptors for each of the one hundred percentages in the one hundred–point scale. This expectation would be unwieldy, impractical, and ultimately too subjective for any teacher to accomplish. For that reason, a smaller rubric-based scale is the only grading scale teachers should use in a competency-based learning school.

> **Although they sound very mathematical, one hundred–point-scale systems promote subjectivity and a lack of consistency. In competency-based learning schools, the one hundred–point system is generally replaced by a smaller, more appropriate grading scale such as a three-, four-, or five-point system.**

Although they sound very mathematical, one hundred–point-scale systems promote subjectivity and a lack of consistency. In competency-based learning schools, the one hundred–point system is generally replaced by a smaller, more appropriate grading scale such as a three-, four-, or five-point system. For example, in a four-point system, a student would receive a rating of 0, 1.0, 2.0, 3.0, or 4.0.

Rick Wormeli (2006) writes at length about the higher level of inter-rater reliability of such smaller-scale systems. *Inter-rater reliability* is when a team of teachers come to consensus on the parameters a student needs for a particular grade on an assignment. Done correctly through a collaborative team process, a student who receives a grade of 3.0 in one class would likely receive that same grade regardless of his or her teacher. This is because the collaborative team vets a calibrated rubric for what level and degree of learning the 3.0 represents. In a one hundred–point system, does a teacher really have a way to distinguish a grade of 93 percent from that of 94 percent? Teachers do if they are simply asking students one hundred right or wrong answers and looking for a percentage that the student answers correctly. In competency-based learning schools, teachers frequently don't do that. Instead, they make use of assessment opportunities like essays, short-answer questions, and other performance tasks. In competency-based learning schools, assessment goes so much further than lower-level assessments. We will get into the topic of quality assessments in chapter 5.

Grades Must Separate Academics From Academic Behaviors

In the very first chapter of this book we pointed out that a flawed logic exists in a grading system that assigns value to academic behaviors, which can include such things as neatness, organization, participation, effort, and meeting deadlines. This is because doing so makes a dangerous assumption that students who practice these good behaviors have ultimately met the learning target. These academic behaviors are sometimes also referred to as *dispositions* or *work-study habits*. While it makes sense that good academic behaviors often lead to increased learning, grading systems that blend these grades miss the point—grades are about what students learn, not what they earn.

According to Wormeli (2006), teachers and schools often include academic behaviors in an academic grade to motivate, punish, or sort students. He writes, "When we grade to motivate, punish, or sort students, we do three things: we dilute the grade's accuracy; we dilute its usefulness; and we use grading to manipulate students, which may or may not be healthy" (Wormeli, 2006, p. 103). It is a common misconception that grades will motivate students to improve, especially students who receive low grades. Rather, this practice has the opposite effect (Wormeli, 2006). Low grades further separate and disenfranchise students from the learning process, sending them the message that they have dug themselves into a hole that they cannot get out of, leaving them hopeless and in despair.

It is common practice in many schools to include a student's level of participation or effort in an overall grade. This practice is especially apparent in many nonacademic courses such as fine and performing arts, physical education, and public speaking. In these instances, teachers must ask themselves whether participation and effort are necessary to *reach* the standard or whether they *are* the standard. A typical example of this is a middle or high school physical-education class that requires students to change for class and includes that behavior as part of an overall course grade. Changing into appropriate attire for class is not a standard; it is simply a way to arrive at a standard. A student's ability to run a mile may indeed be a standard for the class, and the student must participate in that activity in order to demonstrate his or her mastery of that skill. In this instance, it is appropriate to grade participation as an academic grade.

Another common practice in schools is to grade students on whether they complete a summative assessment according to a specific time line or by a certain date.

Oftentimes, a student will receive a deduction in his or her grade for lateness. This is another example of a flawed grading practice. Students learn at different paces. Teachers cannot penalize students for not completing the learning target according to the pace that adults predetermine. If and when a student demonstrates evidence that he or she has reached the target, that student should receive the same grade as a student who demonstrates the same learning earlier in the learning process. What is important in a competency-based learning system is that the student *has* learned it, not how long it took *to* learn it. It can become especially difficult to uphold this practice at the secondary level. Teachers are often concerned that if they do not enforce deadlines, they will create unrealistic situations where they cannot manage how and when they receive students' work. This can be avoided. In effective competency-based learning environments, teachers treat avoiding doing work like any other classroom misbehavior. If a student breaks a classroom rule, the teacher points that out to the student and works with him or her to correct the behavior by any means necessary. A refusal to do work is a behavior treatable in exactly this manner.

Related to the topic of allowing students to learn at their own pace is the practice of encouraging students to reflect, learn from their mistakes, and reassess their work. This becomes the fifth and final necessary grading consideration in a competency-based grading system.

Students Must Have the Opportunity to Reassess Their Work

Schools that do not permit reassessment lose out on the great potential for learning that such a practice encourages. Teachers can harness the power of reassessment as a learning tool by doing the following.

- ▸ **Reserve the right to reassessment:** Often, the first step in the reassessment process is for a student and a teacher to develop a mutually agreed-on reassessment plan. The plan outlines the scope and sequence of reassessment work with a time line for completion and requires a signature from a parent who agrees to support his or her child in the learning process at home.

- ▸ **Don't look at a reassessment as simply a redo or a retake of the exact same assessment:** Teachers should reserve the right to change the reassessment format. Ultimately, a student should only reassess the parts of the original assessment for which he or she fell short, not the whole assessment.

- ▸ **Have the student include his or her original work when submitting the reassessment:** This makes it easier for the teacher to determine student growth in the learning process over time.

A common question is whether the reassessment grade should supplant or combine with the original grade in some way. As mentioned in the learning trend discussion, it is a student's more recent work that is a better indicator of what he or she has learned, knows, and is able to do. For that reason, the reassessment grade should *always* supplant the original grade, even when the reassessment grade is lower than the original one. Teachers should resist the urge to water down this process by using techniques such as averaging the two grades or worse, counting the higher of the two grades. Doing this only promotes grades and the grading process as a points-accumulation exercise, and that is what teachers in schools that practice competency-based learning cannot do.

Another caution for teachers and school leaders with a reassessment policy is to remember that this process should be reserved for students who submit work and are looking for an opportunity to better their performance and their learning. A student who simply refuses to submit work or evidence of learning by an agreed-on deadline should not have the opportunity for reassessment. This student has failed to submit evidence for the first time, and the teacher should treat this as academic misbehavior.

School leaders need to find creative and nonthreatening ways to bring the community together to talk about deep topics such as a philosophical shift to a competency-based model. Superintendent John Freeman shares how he found a creative way to do this in his small community.

Practitioner Perspective
John Freeman, Superintendent, Pittsfield Schools, Pittsfield, New Hampshire

After devoting two years to the transition from our traditional system to a competency-based learning system at Pittsfield Middle High School, we provided families with opportunities to learn about the forthcoming shift for students, teachers, and families. We connected families with information through several typical channels: written updates in our newsletters and websites; one-to-one conversations during our student-led conferences; and open forums during which we discussed the rationale for the change, the practices that would shift for students, and changes to our grading and reporting systems.

These opportunities proved to be very positive, with parent engagement, understanding, and support characterizing these events. However, the events didn't attract the large numbers of parents we had hoped to reach. We wondered how we could help parents (who had chosen not to join us or were unable to join us at our school-based events) to be ready for the shift, especially when it came to grading and reporting.

Our brainstorming led us to a method of bringing people together that we'd not tested in the past: a free pig roast held in a small park located in our downtown area (within walking distance for many of our families) in the early evening during the opening weeks of school. Yes, a pig roast! Our plan was to hook folks with the pig, and then engage parents in using

continued →

the computers to learn about the shift—in a hands-on way—that would happen with grading and reporting in our new competency-based system.

On the day of the roast, we temporarily installed a bank of computers in the park (with power provided by a close-by youth services program office). Teachers donned school shirts and stationed themselves at computers to help guide students and parents though the process of accessing individual student progress records while explaining the competency systems.

The result was an excellent turnout of parents, importantly including many parents who we don't usually see at typical school events. Our teachers made informal connections with students and parents, both throughout the park as well as at the computers. Parents learned about the competency-based system and how to keep track of their children's progress as they shifted to the new system. Students and parents came to the table for both a fine meal and to gain new knowledge about competency-based education. (J. Freeman, personal communication, September 25, 2012)

The Need to Change Grading Practices Over Time

Most schools looking to make the transition from a traditional to a competency-based learning model do not have the luxury of starting with a blank slate. In many cases, there are existing procedures, policies, beliefs, and traditions within the school culture and school community that you must carefully acknowledge and consider when developing a plan to change grading practices over time. These existing practices and beliefs should not influence or impact what grading changes you ultimately implement in your school. However, school leaders should recognize and work to change the mindset of teachers, students, and parents who may be accustomed to these practices and beliefs, and how they manifest themselves in the school's grading system. In chapter 7 (page 149), we'll discuss many change-management strategies that will come into play during this transition. There are a few other considerations that school leaders should reflect on.

Make a Plan

First, school leaders should implement the change according to a predeveloped plan over several years. For example, a school may choose to focus on developing rubrics and using a rubric scale at the assignment level only for the first few years to allow teachers, students, and parents an opportunity to get accustomed to the idea of receiving grading feedback on assignments from a rubric. Although it is not ideal to then convert the assignment rubric score into a one hundred–point-scale score, it may be a concession worth making for a year or two if it helps stakeholders develop an appreciation for the rubric-based feedback system. They will ultimately become more receptive to a final grade reported on a rubric scale. As another example, a school may choose to limit reassessment in the first year or two to only students who receive below a certain score. Although not ideal, doing this will give stakeholders time to adjust to the process and philosophy behind reassessment. It is often easier to accept the need for reassessment for students who receive low grades rather than for those who receive moderately high grades (like a B) and are looking to improve beyond that proficient level. It is quite likely, however, that any conversation about providing only intervention will segue into a discussion about how to provide those students who are already proficient opportunities to extend their learning. It is a logical next step.

Effectively Communicate the Plan

Second, school leaders must effectively communicate the plan to change grades over time to all stakeholders. Failure to do this will result in a school community that sees every new school year as an opportunity for the school and teachers to change another aspect of the grading system without notice, and that produces an environment where students believe they are forever working toward a moving target. To the extent possible, a multiyear plan should clearly identify annual benchmarks, and at the onset, school leaders should communicate these benchmarks to the entire school community. This will give all stakeholders an understanding of how the plan will work.

Maintain Some Grading Traditions

Lastly, school leaders should not be afraid to continue to uphold some grading traditions as long as they do not detract from the overall purpose of grading—communicating evidence of learning. The best example of this point comes from the debate over whether to continue to calculate class rank. Schools can fall into a trap of losing stakeholder trust and buy-in by eliminating this tradition entirely from a school community. As much as the practice of sorting and comparing students to each other instead of to a standard goes against the competency-based learning philosophy, class rank is still a data point that many colleges, universities, and scholarship organizations look for when reviewing a student application. Rather than eliminate class rank altogether, a school can minimize the extent to which this data point and tradition contributes to the learning process. One way to do this is to minimize the role that class rank plays at the graduation ceremony. Does the valedictorian have to be the chosen graduation speaker, or could the school invite interested students to submit a graduation speech in advance for consideration by a jury of faculty and students to review? Does the school have to use class rank as the criteria for academic honor recognition (such as honor roll or a graduation title) or could the school grant that recognition to any student who demonstrates his or her learning at a certain level? Colleges award the cum laude, magna cum laude, and summa cum laude distinctions to any student who achieves above a set grade point average. Why can't this same logic apply in secondary schools? For many of these traditions, there are ways to modify or minimize their impact on a school community without completely eliminating them. The willingness of a school to do this as it develops its grade transition plan will help the school gain traction, buy-in, and ultimately support for the grade changes from stakeholders. And that will help embed the competency-based learning philosophy in the school's culture in the long term.

Reflection Questions

Consider the following five reflection questions with your team.

1. Grades are about what students learn, not what they earn. Think about how this philosophy and mindset will need to change for different stakeholders such as teachers, parents, and students. Which group will have the easiest time changing its mindset and why? Which group will have the hardest time and why?

2. Grading practices must clearly articulate the use and purpose for diagnostic testing, formative assessment, and summative assessment. In your current situation, do teachers have a clear understanding of when to use diagnostic, formative, and summative assessment? If not, what can you do as a school leader to help change that?

3. Grading systems must replace the one hundred–point scale with a smaller rubric scale based in three, four, or five points. In your school, what will be the most straightforward part of converting from a one hundred–point to a rubric-based scale? What will be the biggest challenge?

4. Grades must separate academics from academic behaviors. How does your school currently recognize and assess academic behaviors? How will this change in a competency-based learning model, or will it?

5. Grading practices must allow all students the opportunity to reassess their work without penalty. As a school leader, what will you do to guarantee the reassessment practice is consistent classroom to classroom and grade level to grade level in your school?

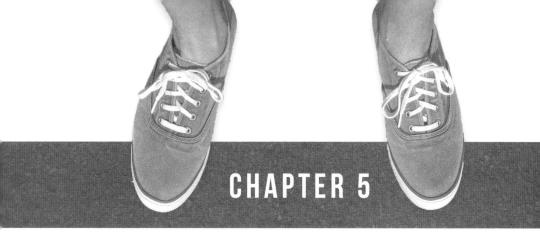

Creating and Implementing Competency-Friendly Performance Assessments

Developing and using performance assessments is not only a necessary component of competency-based learning but also a transformative component. This chapter focuses on the critical components of performance assessments and how teacher teams develop them in a competency-based learning environment, specifically addressing the second critical question of a PLC: How will we know when students have learned it (DuFour et al., 2016)? Readers will then learn how teams develop comprehensive assessment systems to formatively and summatively assess students' competency and growth.

In *Quality Performance Assessment*: *A Guide for Schools and Districts*, the CCE (2012) defines *performance assessments* as "multistep assignments with clear criteria, expectations, and processes that measure how well a student transfers knowledge and applies complex skills to create or refine an original product" (p. vi). In this chapter, we explore how educators within a PLC can support performance assessment development and implementation. These assessments help students apply their knowledge in the context of new settings or problems, and provide students with the opportunity to demonstrate transfer in an authentic task, a hallmark of an effective competency-based learning system.

To begin, consider the following example. The U.S. military has been utilizing performance assessments since its founding. Jonathan discovered this firsthand in 1993 when, as a twenty-one-year-old entering basic training, he was thrust into an environment in which he had to master and demonstrate every task successfully to move forward. All recruits saw their instructors demonstrate tasks the recruits needed to learn, had time to practice, and then ultimately had the opportunity to demonstrate. Tasks ranged from the fairly simple (for example, understanding military time and recognizing rank) to the more difficult (for example, taking apart, cleaning, and putting together an M16 thoroughly, quickly, and correctly, or successfully navigating in the forest using a compass, map, and pace count). Every task truly required the demonstration of not only understanding but also being able to apply and transfer that learning across various situations and settings. This was not Jonathan's first experience demonstrating his learning through transfer, but it was one that left an indelible impression for the simple fact that everything he learned was for a reason, serving a greater purpose.

With each step recruits take, drill sergeants provide feedback and encouragement, pointing out when something is not done up to the expected standard. Granted, this encouragement and feedback looks and sounds very different than it would in a school. However, teachers and drill sergeants have in common that they are truly expert at the tasks they are teaching and make it their mission to ensure that every single student or recruit under their watch is competent. For the drill sergeant, for a recruit to be incompetent could be devastating to the efficacy of a fighting unit. For a teacher, a lack of student competency could have dire consequences as the learning gap grows wider.

Jonathan recalls that reassessment was also part of his training. During his time in the military, Jonathan began to learn that growth and learning were not stagnant; he was always engaged in a learning process and had the opportunity to demonstrate this learning and grow from his mistakes.

For example, later in his military career, Jonathan attended the U.S. Army Air Assault School, where soldiers are taught how to correctly tie the rigging for various vehicles so helicopters can lift and transport them. Part of the training required trainees to carefully examine a Humvee rigged for lifting. Trainees must find a certain number of mistakes, and if they do not, they have not completed that task and are in danger of failing. Jonathan missed one of the major faults in the rigging for the Humvee and was sent to another area to retrain. This provided the opportunity for Jonathan to learn from his mistake, and when he was ready to be retested, he went back to the Humvee and found all possible errors in the rigging, successfully demonstrating his competence and completing this portion of the course successfully.

The preceding example is important because it shows that the military recognizes that there are a number of important factors in assessment (see figure 5.1).

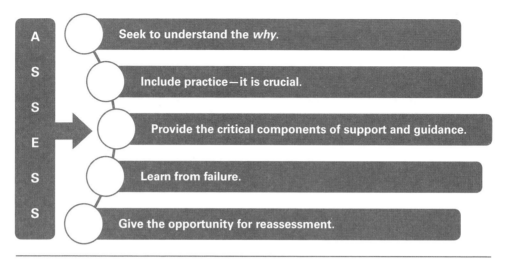

Figure 5.1: Factors in performance assessment.

In this chapter, we examine the creation and implementation of performance assessments by first examining the difference between competencies and standards in assessment building. We then look at the components of competency-based performance assessment and how teams must take collaborative action to transition away from traditional assessment systems and use a validation process before implementing assessments. Next, we discuss the student's role in assessment, instructional alignment, how to build common summative performance assessments, and assessment of skills and dispositions. The chapter ends with a section on student self-reflection in regard to assessment.

The Need for Change in Performance Assessment Practices

Evolving assessment practices in our schools are the lever to the significant transformation of all practices in competency-based learning environments. Once teachers' assessment literacy evolves to a point at which it is impacting instructional practices, the various pieces of quality assessment no longer seem like separate initiatives but rather pieces of the larger puzzle of informing successful learning.

The difference between what is happening in some schools compared to the mid-2000s is staggering. It has become very apparent that traditional teaching and learning methods are not going to prepare students for the world today and tomorrow. Through evolving instructional and assessment techniques, many schools and districts integrate practices that will better assist students in being even more engaged and successful in their learning. But this takes time, and educators have to let that process take hold in our schools to let true changes in practice occur.

> Evolving assessment practices in our schools are the lever to the significant transformation of all practices in competency-based learning environments.

Assessment changes drastically in successful competency-based learning schools. Teachers traditionally gave students a test, typically most of it at a very simplistic depth of knowledge level, and asked students to show what they knew (or really, could remember and regurgitate) to determine their grades. Admittedly, this paints teachers' traditional assessment practices with a very broad stroke, but it illustrates typical assessment practice for many teachers. Most, but certainly not all, teachers then took that information and provided some sort of remediation for any students who demonstrated difficulty. But this step was left up to the individual teacher. This step *cannot* be at the discretion of the individual teacher. All students should have the opportunity to continually demonstrate their learning with adult support to guide them. In the traditional model, once teachers provided additional support, they moved on to the next unit. This left (and continues to leave in traditional schools) major gaps in learning for students at all levels who may be at a very peripheral level of competency or not competent at all. In her many presentations on this topic, Rose Colby, a competency-based specialist, describes this as *Swiss cheese learning*.

Students who truly master the content will demonstrate their understanding anytime and in any setting. Their transfer is not dependent on how long ago they studied the content or when it was taught. Deep understanding of skills and knowledge is ingrained in the learner, and he or she can apply it across any subject matter, problem, or situation.

The Difference Between Competencies and Standards in Assessment Building

Part of the learning process of transitioning to a competency-based learning model is developing an understanding regarding the difference between competencies and standards. Specifically, if you are developing an end-of-unit summative performance assessment, what do you start with? When beginning with the end in mind, we recommend starting with the *why*. As we explain in chapter 3, competencies are the *why* of learning, so this is where to start when developing an assessment.

It is impossible to focus on every single standard. Obviously, this is not a feasible way to assess growth and learning, nor is it fair for either teachers or students. Competencies allow teachers to focus on depth, not necessarily breadth, with the underlying leverage standards falling beneath each respective competency.

In our experience, and the experience of those we have worked with, schools that successfully implement a competency-based learning system typically start with a core group of teachers who begin to investigate a better way to assess competency, often through training on how to build common summative performance assessments. This is a crucial component in a competency-based learning model. Teacher leaders who participate in the direction and focus of the school's work are able to help the school move forward through a combined understanding and collective commitment to the vision. A collaborative leadership team should work together to implement the process of developing performance assessments. A trained, smaller teacher leader and administrator group should formulate a plan to introduce the performance assessment model to teacher teams during common staff time together, but before beginning to build summative assessments together that teachers can administer in their own classrooms. It is imperative to consistently gauge where the staff is in this process and make changes based on what the teacher leader and administrator group is noticing specific to the school's needs.

Teacher leaders who participate in the direction and focus of the school's work are able to help the school move forward through a combined understanding and collective commitment to the vision.

School teams and the school as a whole face many potential hurdles as they begin the journey to transform assessment practices. For example, as a school introduces the concept of implementing performance assessments and begins the necessary professional development that will allow teachers to begin to engage in this process, the school may find that there is the need to explore DOK or assessment essential questions to a greater degree. It may become very clear that teachers are at tremendously varied levels of understanding within both areas. At this point, we advise that the school undergo the very important process of building a common understanding and literacy in these particular areas. It is sometimes necessary to take a step back to move forward.

Schools may need to completely reorganize their professional development calendar to allow teams to engage in the process of learning together while building performance assessments. Each team might set a goal to complete one performance assessment (developed, validated, administered, and validated again with student work) over the course of the school year. This may make it seem like the process is not moving quickly enough, but if teachers dig deeply into this process (and do it well), it will have a significant impact on all aspects of the school's teaching and learning moving forward. Teachers will begin to alter all their assessments to reflect their increased understanding of quality assessment because they want to, not because they have to.

Components of Competency-Based Performance Assessment

A well-designed competency-based assessment model has many components. We begin by talking about what a competency-based assessment model includes, and then provide examples of what this might look like in action.

Kim Bailey and Chris Jakicic (2012) describe the necessary components of a balanced assessment system. A balanced system includes classroom assessments, common formative assessments, interim benchmark assessments, and external summative assessments—both summative and formative assessments. Common summative assessments are within the category of benchmark assessments.

Summative Assessment

The difference in a competency-based learning system is that collaborative teacher teams design these end-of-unit common summative assessments, not the district, and teachers do not create them in isolation. There is a level of ownership inherent in a product that you help develop. And when reflecting on the results of these assessments, it will help teams to not only plan for how to better instruct students but also to inform future assessment practices and areas for further development.

Formative Assessment

As we mentioned previously, it's critical to identify the standards necessary for a student to master to be successful in a summative assessment. Teachers, utilizing the three stages of the backward design model (Wiggins & McTighe, 2005), should develop a time line to assess the various skills and standards throughout the unit that lead to a specific competency. In the three stages of backward design, teachers ensure that they have (1) identified desirable results (what students should know and be able to do is clear); (2) determined what successful evidence they will accept from students that demonstrates their competency; and finally, (3) planned learning experiences and instruction by considering the most appropriate instructional strategies. These time lines may look very different, depending on the skill or standard teachers assess. For example, if the competency being assessed is a fifth-grade argumentative essay, teachers need to assess a number of different items prior to administering the performance assessment. Students should not take a performance assessment if there is any question whether they will be successful on it or not. The point of a performance assessment is to allow students to demonstrate their learning; therefore, the importance of formative assessment as an integral component of a balanced system of assessment cannot be overstated.

> **The point of a performance assessment is to allow students to demonstrate their learning; therefore, the importance of formative assessment as an integral component of a balanced system of assessment cannot be overstated.**

We argue that every assessment is truly formative in nature; that is, teachers use the results to advance and not merely monitor each student's learning (DuFour et al., 2016). When teachers administer a summative performance assessment and students do not demonstrate competency, teachers and teams use this information to inform next steps. Perhaps a student demonstrates mastery on a portion of the competency or standard. Does the student have to take the entire assessment over? Absolutely not. The student has already demonstrated mastery of this other content, so it is unnecessary for the teacher to assess the student for the same material again.

Reassessment is a crucial component of an effective assessment system in a competency-based learning model; it must happen. Assessment can't be a one-and-done system. It must be ongoing and differentiate based on what teachers need to assess. Popham (2008) notes that "assessments play a role in the process—they are not the process itself" (p. 7). The learning process is ongoing, so assessment measures where a student is at one point in time. Results determine next steps. Bailey and Jakicic (2012) describe assessment feedback as "intended to help students reflect on their own learning and adjust their strategies as needed in order to meet or exceed the expectation and achieve deeper understanding of the important concepts" (p. 21).

Historically, schools have not used summative assessments to improve student understanding (Ainsworth & Viegut, 2006, as cited in Burke, 2010). In a competency-based learning model, it is imperative that all assessment data inform changes in individual students' instruction. At no point is a competency and the underlying standard "done" if students have not mastered it. This is an important distinction in competency-based learning.

So, learning occurs on a progression, and the key for teachers is to provide both feedback and guidance. O'Connor (2009) describes how traditional schools approach learning backward—specifically, teachers provide guidance first, rather than feedback first. This is an important factor in competency-based learning: teachers should first provide ongoing feedback from information they glean formatively, and then provide guidance to students as to how to best move forward.

Depth of Knowledge

Hess's (2013) rigor matrices assist teachers in developing the essential questions within their performance assessments. A well-developed essential question should be a DOK 3 or 4, and engage and connect to the students' world in some way. There should be no bias in a strong essential question (a difficult concept, but one teachers can become more adept at with practice and consistent feedback). Teachers find these matrices helpful as they write assessments because they ensure a task is written at a higher level of rigor. Hess's (2013) matrices combine both Bloom's (1956) taxonomy and Norman L. Webb's (2005) DOK. (See figures 5.2, 5.3, 5.4, and 5.5, pages 96–107.)

Revised Bloom's Taxonomy	Webb's DOK Level 1 Recall and Reproduction	Webb's DOK Level 2 Skills and Concepts	Webb's DOK Level 3 Strategic Thinking and Reasoning	Webb's DOK Level 4 Extended Thinking
Remember Retrieve knowledge from long-term memory, recognize, recall, locate, and identify.	• Recall, recognize, or locate basic facts, terms, details, events, or ideas explicit in texts. • Read words orally in connected text with fluency and accuracy.	Use these curricular examples with most close reading or listening assignments or assessments in any content area.		
Understand Construct meaning, clarify, paraphrase, represent, translate, illustrate, give examples, classify, categorize, summarize, generalize, infer a logical conclusion, predict, compare and contrast, match like ideas, explain, and construct models.	• Identify or describe literary elements (characters, setting, sequence, and so on). • Select appropriate words when intended meaning or definition is clearly evident. • Describe or explain who, what, where, when, or how. • Define or describe facts, details, terms, and principles. • Write simple sentences.	• Specify, show relationships, and explain why (such as with cause and effect). • Give nonexamples and examples. • Summarize results, concepts, and ideas. • Make basic inferences or logical predictions from data or texts. • Identify main ideas or accurate generalizations of texts. • Locate information to support explicit and implicit central ideas.	• Explain, generalize, or connect ideas using supporting evidence (such as quote, use examples, include text references). • Identify and make inferences about explicit or implicit themes. • Describe how word choice, point of view, or bias may affect the readers' interpretation of a text. • Write multiparagraph composition for specific purpose, focus, voice, tone, and audience.	• Explain how concepts or ideas specifically relate to other content domains (such as social, political, and historical) or concepts. • Develop generalizations of results or about strategies and apply them to new problem-based situations.

Apply Carry out (apply to a familiar task) or use (apply to an unfamiliar task) a procedure in a given situation	• Use language structure (pre and suffix) or word relationships (synonyms and antonyms) to determine meaning of words. • Apply rules or resources to edit spelling, grammar, punctuation, conventions, and word use. • Apply basic formats for documenting sources.	• Use context to identify the meaning of words and phrases. • Obtain and interpret information using text features. • Develop a text that may be limited to one paragraph. • Apply simple organizational structures (such as paragraphs and sentence types) in writing.	• Apply a concept in a new context. • Revise a final draft for meaning or progression of ideas. • Apply internal consistency of text organization and structure to composing a full composition. • Apply word choice, point of view, and style to impact readers' or viewers' interpretation of a text.	• Illustrate how multiple themes (historical, geographic, social, artistic, and literary) may be interrelated. • Select or devise an approach among many alternatives to research a novel problem.
Analyze Break into constituent parts, determine how parts relate, differentiate between relevant or irrelevant; distinguish; focus; select; organize; outline; find coherence; and deconstruct (for example, for bias or point of view).	• Identify whether specific information is contained in graphic representations (for example, in a map, chart, table, graph, T-chart, or diagram) or text features (such as headings, subheadings, and captions). • Decide which text structure is appropriate to audience and purpose.	• Categorize and compare literary elements, terms, facts and details, and events. • Identify use of literary devices. • Analyze format, organization, and internal text structure (signal words, transitions, and semantic cues) of different texts. • Distinguish between relevant and irrelevant information and fact and opinion. • Identify characteristic text features and distinguish between texts and genres.	• Analyze information within data sets or texts. • Analyze interrelationships among concepts, issues, and problems. • Analyze or interpret an author's craft (literary devices, viewpoint, or potential bias) to create or critique a text. • Use reasoning, planning, and evidence to support inferences.	• Analyze multiple sources of evidence, or multiple works by the same author, or across genres, time periods, and themes. • Analyze complex and abstract themes, perspectives, and concepts. • Gather, analyze, and organize multiple information sources. • Analyze discourse styles.

Figure 5.2: Tool 1 in Hess's rigor matrices.

continued →

Revised Bloom's Taxonomy	Webb's DOK Level 1 Recall and Reproduction	Webb's DOK Level 2 Skills and Concepts	Webb's DOK Level 3 Strategic Thinking and Reasoning	Webb's DOK Level 4 Extended Thinking
Evaluate Make judgments based on criteria, check, detect inconsistencies or fallacies, judge, and critique.	**Unsubstantiated generalizations (UGs) are stating an opinion without providing any support for it.**		• Cite evidence and develop a logical argument for conjectures. • Describe, compare, and contrast solution methods. • Verify reasonableness of results. • Justify or critique conclusions.	• Evaluate relevancy, accuracy, and completeness of information from multiple sources. • Apply understanding in a novel way and provide argument or justification for the application.
Create Reorganize elements into new patterns and structures, generate, hypothesize, design, plan, and produce.	• Brainstorm ideas, concepts, problems, or perspectives related to a topic, principle, or concept.	• Generate conjectures or hypotheses based on observations or prior knowledge and experience.	• Synthesize information within one source or text. • Develop a complex model for a given situation. • Develop an alternative solution.	• Synthesize information across multiple sources or texts. • Articulate a new voice, alternate theme, new knowledge, or new perspective.

Source: Reprinted from Hess, 2013. Adapted with permission.

Revised Bloom's Taxonomy	Webb's DOK Level 1 Recall and Reproduction	Webb's DOK Level 2 Skills and Concepts	Webb's DOK Level 3 Strategic Thinking and Reasoning	Webb's DOK Level 4 Extended Thinking
Remember Retrieve knowledge from long-term memory, recognize, recall, locate, and identify.	• Recall, observe, and recognize facts, principles, and properties. • Recall and identify conversions among representations or numbers (such as customary and metric measures).	Use these curricular examples with most mathematics or science assignments or assessments.		
Understand Construct meaning, clarify, paraphrase, represent, translate, illustrate, give examples, classify, categorize, summarize, generalize, infer a logical conclusion, predict, compare and contrast, match like ideas, explain, and construct models.	• Evaluate an expression. • Locate points on a grid or numbers on a number line. • Solve a one-step problem. • Represent mathematics relationships in words, pictures, or symbols. • Read, write, and compare decimals in scientific notation.	• Specify and explain relationships (such as examples and nonexamples and cause and effect). • Make and record observations. • Explain steps followed. • Summarize results or concepts. • Make basic inferences or logical predictions from data or observations. • Use models and diagrams to represent or explain mathematical concepts. • Make and explain estimates.	• Use concepts to solve nonroutine problems. • Explain, generalize, or connect ideas using supporting evidence. • Make and justify conjectures. • Explain thinking and reasoning when more than one solution or approach is possible. • Explain phenomena in terms of concepts.	• Relate mathematical or scientific concepts to other content areas, other domains, or other concepts. • Develop generalizations from results and strategies (from investigation or reading) and apply them to new problem situations.

continued →

Figure 5.3: Tool 2 in Hess's rigor matrices.

Revised Bloom's Taxonomy	Webb's DOK Level 1 Recall and Reproduction	Webb's DOK Level 2 Skills and Concepts	Webb's DOK Level 3 Strategic Thinking and Reasoning	Webb's DOK Level 4 Extended Thinking
Apply Carry out (apply to a familiar task) or use (apply to an unfamiliar task) a procedure in a given situation.	• Follow simple procedures (for example, recipe-type directions). • Calculate, measure, and apply a rule (such as rounding). • Apply an algorithm or formula (such as area or perimeter). • Solve linear equations. • Make conversions among representations or numbers, or within and between customary and metric measures.	• Select a procedure according to criteria and perform it. • Solve routine problems applying multiple concepts or decision points. • Retrieve information from a table, graph, or figure and use it to solve a problem requiring multiple steps. • Translate tables, graphs, words, and symbolic notations (such as graph data from a table). • Construct models with given criteria.	• Design investigation for a specific purpose or research question. • Conduct a designed investigation. • Use concepts to solve nonroutine problems. • Use and show reasoning, planning, and evidence. • Translate between problem and symbolic notation when not a direct translation.	• Select or devise an approach among many alternatives to solve a problem. • Conduct a project that specifies a problem, identifies solution paths, solves the problem, and reports results.
Analyze Break into constituent parts, determine how the parts relate, differentiate between what is relevant and irrelevant, distinguish, focus, select, organize, outline, find coherence, and deconstruct.	• Retrieve information from a table or graph to answer a question • Identify whether specific information is contained in graphic representations (such as in a table, graph, T-chart, or diagram). • Identify a pattern or trend.	• Categorize and classify materials, data, and figures based on characteristics. • Organize or order data. • Compare and contrast figures or data. • Select appropriate graphs and organize and display data. • Interpret data from a simple graph. • Extend a pattern.	• Compare information within or across data sets or texts. • Analyze and draw conclusions from data, citing evidence. • Generalize a pattern. • Interpret data from complex graph. • Analyze similarities and differences between procedures or solutions.	• Analyze multiple sources of evidence. • Analyze complex and abstract themes. • Gather, analyze, and evaluate information.

	DOK 1	DOK 2	DOK 3	DOK 4
Evaluate Make judgments based on criteria, check, detect inconsistencies or fallacies, judge, and critique.	**Unsubstantiated generalizations (UGs) state an opinion without providing any support for it.**		• Cite evidence and develop a logical argument for concepts or solutions. • Describe, compare, and contrast solution methods. • Verify reasonableness of results.	• Gather, analyze, and evaluate information to draw conclusions. • Apply understanding in a novel way and provide an argument or justification for the application.
Create Reorganize elements into new patterns or structures, generate, hypothesize, design, plan, and produce.	• Brainstorm ideas, concepts, or perspectives related to a topic.	• Generate conjectures or hypotheses based on observations or prior knowledge and experience.	• Synthesize information within one data set, source, or text. • Formulate an original problem to a given situation. • Develop a scientific or mathematical model for a complex situation.	• Synthesize information across multiple sources or texts. • Design a mathematical model to inform and solve a practical or abstract situation.

Source: Reprinted from Hess, 2013. Adapted with permission.

Revised Bloom's Taxonomy	Webb's DOK Level 1 Recall and Reproduction	Webb's DOK Level 2 Skills and Concepts	Webb's DOK Level 3 Strategic Thinking and Reasoning	Webb's DOK Level 4 Extended Thinking
Remember Retrieve knowledge from long-term memory, recognize, recall, locate, and identify.	• Complete short-answer questions with facts, details, terms, principles, and so on (such as label parts of a diagram).	**Use these curricular examples with most writing and oral communication assignments or assessments in any content area.**		
Understand Construct meaning, clarify, paraphrase, represent, translate, illustrate, give examples, classify, categorize, summarize, generalize, infer a logical conclusion, predict, compare and contrast, match like ideas, explain, and construct models.	• Describe or define facts, details, terms, principles, and so on. • Select the appropriate word or phrase to use when the intended meaning or definition is clearly evident. • Write simple complete sentences. • Add an appropriate caption to a photo or illustration. • Write fact statements on a topic (such as, "Spiders build webs").	• Specify, explain, and show relationships (explain why and cause and effect). • Provide and explain nonexamples and examples. • Take notes and organize ideas and data (for example, note relevance, trends, and perspectives). • Summarize results, key concepts, and ideas. • Explain central ideas or accurate generalizations of texts or topics. • Describe steps in a process (such as a science procedure).	• Write a multiparagraph composition for a specific purpose and audience (using specific focus, voice, and tone). • Develop and explain opposing perspectives or connect ideas, principles, or concepts using supporting evidence (such as a quote, example, text reference, and so on). • Develop arguments of fact (for example, "Are these criticisms supported by the historical facts?" and "Is this claim or equation true?").	• Use multiple sources to elaborate on how concepts or ideas specifically draw from other content domains or differing concepts (such as research papers and policy arguments). • Develop generalizations about results or strategies and apply them to a new problem or contextual scenario.

Apply Carry out (apply to a familiar task) or use (apply to an unfamiliar task) a procedure in a given situation.	• Apply rules or use resources to edit specific spelling, grammar, punctuation, conventions, or word use. • Apply basic formats for documenting sources.	• Use context to identify or infer the intended meaning of words and phrases. • Obtain, interpret, and explain information using text features (such as tables, diagrams, and so on). • Develop a brief text that may be limited to one paragraph. • Apply basic organizational structures (introduction, topic sentence, sentence types, paragraphs, and so on) in writing.	• Revise final draft for meaning, progression of ideas, or chain of logic. • Apply internal consistency of text organization and structure to a full composition or oral communication. • Apply a concept in a new context. • Apply word choice, point of view, style, and rhetorical devices to impact readers' interpretation of a text.	• Select or devise an approach among many alternatives to research and present a novel problem or issue. • Illustrate how multiple themes (historical, geographic, and social) may be interrelated within a text or topic.
Analyze Break into constituent parts, determine how the parts relate, differentiate between what is relevant and irrelevant, distinguish, focus, select, organize, outline, find coherence, and deconstruct (such as for bias or point of view).	• Decide which text structure is appropriate to audience and purpose (such as compare and contrast or proposition with support). • Determine appropriate, relevant key words for conducting an Internet search or researching a topic.	• Compare and contrast perspectives, events, characters, and so on. • Analyze and revise format, organization, and internal text structure (signal words, transitions, and semantic cues) of different print and nonprint texts. • Distinguish between relevant and irrelevant information and fact and opinion. • Locate evidence that supports a perspective and differing perspectives.	• Analyze interrelationships among concepts, issues, and problems in a text. • Analyze impact or use of author's craft (literary devices, viewpoint, and dialogue) in a single text. • Use reasoning and evidence to generate criteria for making and supporting an argument (for example, "Was FDR a great president?" or "Who was the greatest ball player?"). • Support conclusions with evidence.	• Analyze multiple sources of evidence, or multiple works by the same author, or work from across genres or time periods. • Analyze complex and abstract themes, perspectives, and concepts. • Gather, analyze, and organize multiple information sources. • Compare and contrast conflicting judgments or policies (such as Supreme Court decisions).

Figure 5.4: Tool 3 in Hess's rigor matrices.

continued →

Revised Bloom's Taxonomy	Webb's DOK Level 1 Recall and Reproduction	Webb's DOK Level 2 Skills and Concepts	Webb's DOK Level 3 Strategic Thinking and Reasoning	Webb's DOK Level 4 Extended Thinking
Evaluate Make judgments based on criteria; check and detect inconsistencies or fallacies; judge; and critique.	*Unsubstantiated generalizations (UGs) state an opinion without providing any support for it.*		• Evaluate validity and relevance of evidence used to develop an argument or support a perspective. • Describe and compare and contrast solution methods. • Verify or critique the accuracy, logic, and reasonableness of stated conclusions or assumptions.	• Evaluate relevancy, accuracy, and completeness of information across multiple sources. • Apply understanding in a novel way and provide an argument or justification for the application. • Critique the historical impact (policy, writings, discoveries, and so on).
Create Reorganize elements into new patterns and structures, generate, hypothesize, design, plan, and produce.	• Brainstorm facts, ideas, concepts, problems, or perspectives related to a topic, text, idea, issue, or concept.	• Generate conjectures, hypotheses, or predictions based on facts, observations, evidence and observations, or prior knowledge and experience. • Generate believable grounds (reasons) for an opinion or argument.	• Develop a complex model for a given situation or problem. • Develop an alternative solution or perspective (such as a debate).	• Synthesize information across multiple sources or texts in order to articulate a new voice, alternate theme, new knowledge, or nuanced perspective.

Source: Reprinted from Hess, 2013. Adapted with permission.

Revised Bloom's Taxonomy	Webb's DOK Level 1 Recall and Reproduction	Webb's DOK Level 2 Skills and Concepts	Webb's DOK Level 3 Strategic Thinking and Reasoning	Webb's DOK Level 4 Extended Thinking
Remember Retrieve knowledge from long-term memory, recognize, recall, locate, and identify.	• Recall or locate key facts, dates, terms, details, events, or ideas explicit in texts.	Use these curricular examples with most assignments, assessments, or inquiry activities in social studies, history, civics, geography, economics, or humanities.		
Understand Construct meaning, clarify, paraphrase, represent, translate, illustrate, give examples, classify, categorize, summarize, generalize, infer a logical conclusion, predict, observe, compare and contrast, match like ideas, explain, and construct models.	• Select appropriate words or terms when intended meaning is clearly evident. • Describe or explain who, what, where, when, or how. • Define facts, details, terms, and principles. • Locate and identify symbols and what they represent. • Raise related questions for possible investigation.	• Specify, explain, and illustrate relationships; explain why (cause and effect). • Provide and explain examples and nonexamples. • Summarize results, concepts, main ideas, and generalizations. • Make basic inferences or logical predictions (using data and text). • Locate relevant information to support explicit and implicit central ideas.	• Explain, generalize, or connect ideas using supporting evidence (quotes, examples, text references, and data). • Support inferences about explicit or implicit themes. • Describe how word choice, point of view, or bias may affect the reader's or viewer's interpretation. • Write a multiparagraph composition or essay for specific purpose, focus, voice, tone, and audience.	• Explain how concepts or ideas specifically relate to other content domains or concepts (social, political, historical, and cultural). • Apply generalizations to new problem-based situations. • Use multiple sources to elaborate on how concepts or ideas specifically draw from other content domains or differing concepts (such as research papers and policy arguments).

continued →

Figure 5.5: Tool 4 in Hess's rigor matrices.

Revised Bloom's Taxonomy	Webb's DOK Level 1 Recall and Reproduction	Webb's DOK Level 2 Skills and Concepts	Webb's DOK Level 3 Strategic Thinking and Reasoning	Webb's DOK Level 4 Extended Thinking
Apply Carry out (apply to a familiar task) or use a procedure in a given situation (transfer to an unfamiliar or nonroutine task).	• Apply basic formats for documenting sources. • Apply use of reference materials and tools for gathering information (do keyword searches).	• Use context to identify the meaning of words and phrases. • Interpret information using text features (diagrams, data tables, captions, and so on). • Apply simple organizational structures (such as paragraph outlines).	• Investigate to determine how a historical, cultural, or political context may be the source of an underlying theme, central idea, or unresolved issue or crisis.	• Integrate or juxtapose multiple (such as historical and cultural) contexts drawn from source materials (such as literature, music, historical events, and media) with intent to develop a complex or multimedia product and personal viewpoint.
Analyze Break into constituent parts, determine how parts relate, differentiate between what is relevant and irrelevant, distinguish, focus, select, organize, outline, find coherence, and deconstruct (such as for bias, point of view, and approach or strategy).	• Identify causes or effects. • Describe processes or tools used to research ideas, artifacts, or images reflecting history, culture, tradition, and so on. • Identify ways symbols and metaphors are used to represent universal ideas. • Identify specific information given in graphics (such as maps, T-charts, and diagrams) or text features (such as headings, subheadings, and captions).	• Compare similarities and differences in processes, methods, and styles due to influences of time period, politics, or culture. • Distinguish relevant from irrelevant information, fact from opinion, and primary from secondary sources. • Draw inferences about social, historical, and cultural contexts portrayed in literature, arts, film, political cartoons, or primary sources. • Explain and categorize events and ideas in the evolution of _____ across time periods.	• Analyze information within data sets or a text (such as the interrelationships among concepts, issues, and problems). • Analyze an author's viewpoint or potential bias (such as in a political cartoon). • Use reasoning, planning, and evidence to support or refute inferences in policy or speech. • Use reasoning and evidence to generate criteria for making and supporting an argument of judgment (for example, "Was FDR a great president?" or "Is this a fair law?").	• Analyze multiple sources of evidence across time periods, themes, and issues. • Analyze diverse, complex, and abstract perspectives. • Gather, analyze, and organize information from multiple sources. • Analyze discourse styles and bias in speeches, legal briefs, and so on, across time or authors. • Compare and contrast conflicting judgments or policies (such as Supreme Court decisions).

	DOK 1	DOK 2	DOK 3	DOK 4
Evaluate Make judgments based on criteria; check and detect inconsistencies or fallacies; judge, and critique.	**Unsubstantiated generalizations (UGs) state an opinion without providing any support for it.**		• Develop a logical argument for conjectures, citing evidence. • Verify reasonableness of others' results. • Critique conclusions, evidence, and credibility of sources.	• Evaluate relevancy, accuracy, and completeness of information using multiple sources. • Apply understanding in a novel way and provide an argument or justification for the application. • Critique the historical impact on policy, writings, and advances.
Create Reorganize elements into new patterns, structures, or schemas; generate; hypothesize; design; plan; and produce.	• Brainstorm ideas, concepts, problems, or perspectives related to a topic, principle, or concept.	• Generate testable conjectures or hypotheses based on observations, prior knowledge, and artifacts.	• Synthesize information within one source or text. • Develop a complex model or symbol for given issue. • Develop and support an alternative solution.	• Synthesize information across multiple sources or texts. • Articulate a new voice, alternate theme, new knowledge, or new perspective. • Create historical fiction drawing on sources.

Source: Reprinted from Hess, 2013. Adapted with permission.

The charts in these figures provide guidance to educators developing essential questions for unit and assessment planning. Each level of question is important in its own way, but in a competency-based model, the DOK 3- and DOK 4-type questions are the ones that truly allow students to demonstrate competency. Following are two examples of a DOK question related to Revolutionary America that contrast the difference in levels.

▸ **DOK 1:** What year did the Battle of Lexington and Concord occur? (This question is only asking a student to recall information.)

▸ **DOK 3:** Citing evidence and specific examples to support your argument, do you believe the colonists were right in declaring independence? (This question requires students to evaluate by citing evidence and developing a logical argument.)

Collaborative Action

Changing assessment practices is a process; it is not immediate. Despite the fact that many teachers recognize the way they assess growth is not truly capturing mastery, it is difficult to change something that's always been done a certain way. This is apparent during the early stages of a school's transformation to a competency-based assessment system, as teachers may still be grading students based on assessments designed previous to the start of the transformation. Grading might look different, but the assessments teachers use to determine grades may still be the same. These particular assessments never truly capture what a student knows, is able to do, or is able to transfer across subject areas, but then teachers' assessment literacy may not be developed enough early in the transformation process to build common summative assessments that allow teachers to assess students' competency. To truly transform assessment practices, grading and the assessments teachers use to determine proficiency will have to transform together. Very often, transformation in instruction follows.

A significant aha moment occurs for many educators making the shift to competency-based learning when they begin the detailed process of developing common summative assessments together—another reason why the PLC framework provides the critical foundational elements for success. Teacher teams work together to better understand what competency truly means and how they will determine it in students' work.

Collaborative teacher teams must decide specifically which competencies (there shouldn't be more than a couple) a performance assessment will assess (which is, again, what we want students to learn). Teachers should then identify those leverage standards that will allow students to get to competency. This is a very important process because it begins to focus the learning objectives within each grade level and helps focus the formative assessments teachers will use to determine an individual student's understanding along the way.

DuFour et al. (2016) stress the importance of common formative assessments in the work of teams. Common formative assessments, as well as the common summative assessments teacher teams develop, should begin with the end in mind. Teacher teams should begin by asking themselves the first of the four PLC critical questions: What is it we want students to know and be able to do (DuFour et al., 2016)? The second critical question frames the assessment piece of the competency puzzle: How will we know if they have learned it (DuFour et al., 2016)? It is imperative to develop assessments that truly capture what students have learned.

Executive director Dan French and the CCE have worked diligently with teachers and administrators in developing competency-based performance assessments that truly capture students' ability to demonstrate competency.

Practitioner Perspective
Dan French, Executive Director, Center for Collaborative Education

Moving toward a competency-based assessment system is first and foremost about returning teachers to the center of accountability in our schools, which is where they should be. A crucial shortcoming of the No Child Left Behind era, and the subsequent adoption of externally created and scored standardized tests, was that teachers were removed from the accountability equation. Those who had the most knowledge of students' understanding and skills, who were the designers of most assessments that students completed, and who were best positioned to make judgments about proficiency based on an entire body of a student's work have been left out of important decisions about students' academic growth.

Educators and policymakers are now realizing that we need new ways of assessment that better capture a broader range of student competencies. The Common Core State Standards promote an increased emphasis on higher-order thinking skills, while there is also a growing awareness of the importance of dispositions in nurturing reflective learners and the need to prepare graduates for an increasingly technological, global, and diverse world. The door has opened for a transformation of education accountability systems—one that is centered on competency-based, curriculum-embedded performance assessments that focus on real-world application of new knowledge, skills, and dispositions. This shift should empower teachers as the architects and drivers of the new system. Teachers should become the experts and leaders in creating, administering, and scoring high-quality, robust performance assessments, and ultimately in making proficiency determinations about their students.

Teachers as creators of student assessments is not unfamiliar territory. After all, teachers have always had to create formative and summative classroom assessments for their students. However, performance assessment systems introduce a new role for teachers.

continued ➡

Teachers need to create valid performance assessments that are aligned with the intended competencies and accurately measure whether students have mastered them. Teachers need to embed these valid performance tasks within the curriculum so that assessment becomes a seamless part of learning, and the tasks double as an assessment tool. Teachers, along with colleagues inside and outside their schools, need to score resulting student work reliably to ensure consistency within and across schools.

Given this fundamental shift, how do you empower teachers to take leadership roles to create and manage performance assessment systems? The answer lies in building a foundation of support for teachers that includes collaboration, a resource toolkit, and continual practice.

Collaborating

Teacher collaboration in PLCs drives the performance assessment system. In such a system, discipline-based and interdisciplinary grade-level teacher teams focus their time on the performance assessment cycle of design, validate, administer, score, and revise. Teachers gain practice in bringing curriculum units, lessons, and assessments, along with accompanying student work, to the table so teams can provide helpful feedback to improve assessment and student learning. In doing so, teachers learn that their craft improves through sharing their work. Of course, to accomplish this level of collaborative practice requires dedicated common planning time for teachers to engage in the work.

The Center for Collaborative Education facilitates Quality Performance Assessment (QPA) institutes to introduce teachers to performance-assessment literacy and protocols. In a focus group at the end of a yearlong QPA institute, one teacher noted the change in teacher collaboration as a result of introducing performance-assessment design and scoring of student work in her school:

> Teams have really bought into the process . . . taking student work and reflecting back to the assessment and then rubric and then asking, "Did we truly assess what we meant to assess?" The process gives teachers great feedback in reference to their teaching and whether or not they are reaching the students, and then how have they changed those rubrics or those assessments to then elicit the responses they really were looking for in their students. (Anonymous teacher, personal communication, New Hampshire Performance Assessment of Competency Education Tier 2 Focus Group, May 16, 2016)

Building a Toolkit

Much like anyone becoming proficient in new understandings and skills, teachers benefit from having a set of tools that provide guidance and structure in building a performance assessment system. For example, QPA's curriculum-planning template (Brown & Mednick, 2012) can assist teacher teams as they collaboratively create a high-quality performance task. The assessment validation checklist (Brown & Mednick, 2012) helps teams assess whether a task meets the varied requirements for being considered valid. The calibration protocol (Brown & Mednick, 2012) assists teams to learn the process of calibration and dialogue that leads to reliable scoring of student work. Protocols take into account the sensitivities that teachers may have in presenting their work, particularly within school cultures in which teachers are just starting to regularly share their work with colleagues.

Practicing

As with learning any new skill or knowledge, practice is key. Teachers need to gain experience in facilitating protocols and experiencing the entire cycle of task creation, validation, and scoring. As teachers accumulate experience, they can move toward becoming leaders in performance assessment, able to lead their colleagues in using protocols and other assessment tools. Developing a cadre of teacher leaders adept at performance assessment is the best means to building performance assessment capacity among the entire faculty. (D. French, personal communication, October 2016)

Validation

The collaborative teams' validation process is a crucial component of building performance assessments. Prior to administering an assessment, each team should have the opportunity to present its work to a different grade-level team. This allows for all-important feedback through another lens and is such an important part of collaborative teams' work. The validation of assessment promotes the cycle of continuous improvement critical to a PLC, and review of student work allows for teams to determine their growth based on results. These are all critical components of the PLC framework, and are only strengthened through the various processes teams undertake as they go through validation processes.

The CCE (2012) outlines the components a typical performance assessment validation process should entail as follows.

- Review of team norms
- Large-group presentation (by a small team) of materials and context explanation
- Independent, silent examination of materials by the whole team
- Clarifying questions from the whole team
- Completion of a validation checklist by the whole team to seek consensus on each item of the assessment
- The whole team sharing feedback from each section, with the presenter asking clarifying questions, providing information, and offering reflection
- Debriefing led by the meeting facilitator

The CCE (2012) tools in figures 5.6 and 5.7 (pages 112–117) can assist teams going through the validation process.

Assessment Information

Title of Assessment: _____   Date: _____

Grade and Subject: _____   Author: _____

Validation Team: _____

Quality Aligned Instruction

(Six to eight minutes ⏳)

1. ALIGNMENT

☐   Is clearly aligned to competencies and to specific content standards and habits.

☐   Is clearly aligned to 21st century skills.

☐   Is aligned to appropriate depth of knowledge to assess the standard. Identify and check the following assessed DOK levels. For example, an essay would mostly assess DOK 3, but some DOK 2 items might also be included. Check "most" for DOK 3 and "some" for DOK 2.

DOK 1: Recall; memorization; simple understanding of a word or phrase

☐ Most of the assessment	☐ Some of the assessment	☐ None of the assessment

DOK 2: Covers level 1 plus: paraphrase; summarize; interpret; infer; classify; organize; compare; and determine fact from fiction. There is a correct answer, but may involve multiple concepts.

☐ Most of the assessment	☐ Some of the assessment	☐ None of the assessment

DOK 3: Students must support their thinking by citing references from text or other sources. Students are asked to go beyond the text to analyze, generalize, or connect ideas. Requires deeper knowledge. Items may require abstract reasoning, inferences between and across readings, application of prior knowledge, or text support for an analytical judgment about a text.

☐ Most of the the assessment	☐ Some of the assessment	☐ None of the assessment

DOK 4: Requires higher-order thinking, including complex reasoning, planning, and developing of concepts. Usually applies to an extended task or project. Examples: evaluates several works by the same author; critiques an issue across time periods or researches a topic or issue from different perspectives; longer investigations or research projects.

☐ Most of the assessment	☐ Some of the assessment	☐ None of the assessment

☐   Assesses what is intended to be assessed—will elicit what the student knows and can do related to the chosen standards and benchmarks. Any scaffolding provided (such as a task broken into smaller steps or a graphic organizer to preplan a response) does not change what is actually being assessed.

☐   The assessment is scheduled appropriately in the year, with enough teaching time provided to allow all students to successfully complete it.

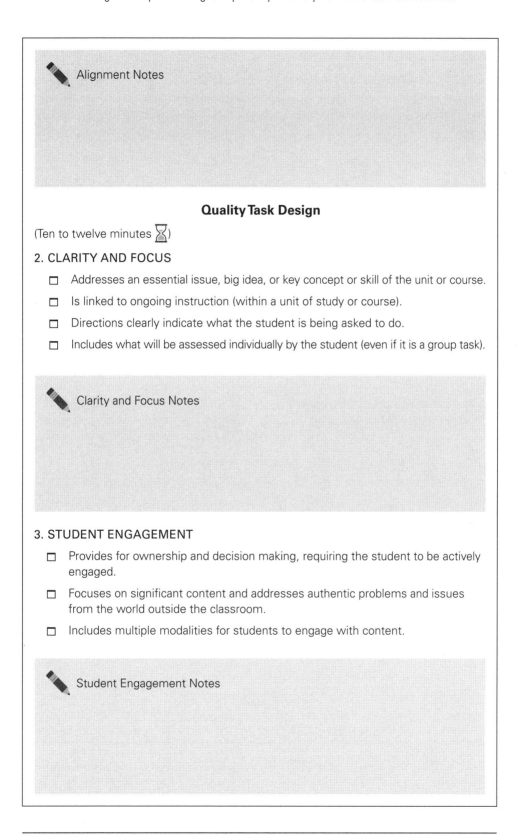

Alignment Notes

Quality Task Design

(Ten to twelve minutes ⧖)

2. CLARITY AND FOCUS

- ☐ Addresses an essential issue, big idea, or key concept or skill of the unit or course.
- ☐ Is linked to ongoing instruction (within a unit of study or course).
- ☐ Directions clearly indicate what the student is being asked to do.
- ☐ Includes what will be assessed individually by the student (even if it is a group task).

Clarity and Focus Notes

3. STUDENT ENGAGEMENT

- ☐ Provides for ownership and decision making, requiring the student to be actively engaged.
- ☐ Focuses on significant content and addresses authentic problems and issues from the world outside the classroom.
- ☐ Includes multiple modalities for students to engage with content.

Student Engagement Notes

Figure 5.6: Assessment validation checklist.

continued →

4. CRITERIA AND LEVELS

☐ Rubrics or scoring guides assess identified competencies and content standards.

☐ Exemplars or models illustrate expectations aligned to identified competencies and standards.

Criteria and Levels Notes

5. FAIRNESS

☐ The task is fair and unbiased in language and design.

☐ Rubric or scoring guide is clear.

☐ Material is familiar to students from identifiable cultural, gender, linguistic, and other groups.

☐ The task is free of stereotypes.

☐ All students have access to resources (such as Internet, calculators, spell check, and so on).

☐ Assessment conditions are the same for all students.

☐ The task can be reasonably completed under the specified conditions.

☐ Allows for accommodations for students with Iindividual Education Programs or 504 plans.

Fairness Notes

6. ADHERENCE TO PRINCIPLES OF UNIVERSAL DESIGN

- ☐ Instructions are free of wordiness and irrelevant information.
- ☐ Instructions are free of unusual words students may not understand.
- ☐ Format and layout conveys focus of expected tasks and products.
- ☐ Format clearly indicates what actual questions and prompts are.
- ☐ Questions are marked with graphic cues (bullets, numbers, and so on).
- ☐ Format is consistent.

Adherence to Principles of Universal Design Notes

Quality Data Analysis

(Eight to ten minutes ⧖)

(This section occurs only if student work is presented.)

7. STUDENT WORK ANALYSIS

- ☐ Student work sample demonstrates proficiency and mastery (evidence of DOK level 3 or 4 performance) of the assessed competency.
- ☐ If assessment is a common assessment or used for high-stakes decisions, student work can be scored reliably by all scorers using scoring guide and information provided.

Student Work Analysis Notes

Figure 5.6: Assessment validation checklist.

continued →

Validation Team Recommendation

(Eight to ten minutes ⏳)

☐ **Validation pending:** Please review feedback and make revisions.

☐ **Validation complete:** Please submit final edited version to team leader.

✏ Overall Feedback

Source: CCE, 2012. Adapted with permission.

*Visit **go.SolutionTree.com/PLCbooks** for a free reproducible version of this figure.*

Purpose

To ensure assessments have technical quality. This protocol can be used with performance assessments as well as traditional assessments. When we share our assessments with our colleagues, we are more likely to uncover our blind spots and assumptions.

Planning

- **Time:** Fifty to sixty minutes (First round will take more time as group develops familiarity with questions. More time is also required if student work is being reviewed with assessment.)

- **Group size:** Four or more

- **Roles:** Choose a facilitator, timekeeper, recorder, and reporter.

Setting Norms

- Honor our learning and be respectful of the work of the teacher and the student.

- Keep the conversation constructive; avoid judgmental language.

- Be appreciative of the facilitator's role and follow the guidelines and time constraints.

- Keep feedback crisp and to the point.

- Don't skip the debrief process.

Process

1. **Norms:** The facilitator reviews the protocol process, norms, and any additional questions or information if the assessment is being tuned. (two to five minutes)

2. **Presentation:** Presenter briefly walks through the materials with the group and explains the context of the assessment. (three to five minutes)

3. **Examination:** Group members silently examine the assessment materials. (seven to ten minutes)

4. **Clarifying questions:** The group asks any clarifying questions they have about the materials and process. (two to seven minutes; round one may require more time for clarification)

5. **Validation guide:** While the presenter silently takes notes, the facilitator leads groups through each section of the Validation Checklist and seeks consensus for each item. The facilitator reads each numbered item aloud and asks the group to consider whether the answer is yes or no and to be prepared to explain their choice. Once consensus is reached (80 percent agreement), the group moves on to the next numbered item. Times are specified for each section, and each section can be modified to meet the needs of the group, as long as seven minutes are left for the remaining steps of feedback and debrief. (twenty to thirty minutes)

6. **Feedback and reflection:** The team reads the feedback from each section. After hearing all of the feedback, the presenter may ask clarifying questions, provide further information, and offer reflections based on the feedback, but does not need to justify! The facilitator reminds the presenter to resist the tendency to justify. (eight to ten minutes)

7. **Debrief:** The facilitator leads the debrief (four minutes)
   - Did the team honor the norms at all times?
   - What went well? What could have gone better?
   - What are the implications of what we've learned for instruction?

Source: CCE, 2012. Used with permission.

Figure 5.7: Assessment validation protocol.

*Visit **go.SolutionTree.com/PLCbooks** for a free reproducible version of this figure.*

The Student's Role in Assessment

Students should self-assess their own learning in conjunction with a teacher's feedback. Rubrics play a crucial role in this process. (Visit **go.SolutionTree.com /PLCbooks** to access a sample student rubric.) Students should be able to honestly reflect on where they are in the learning process using a four-point rubric, and then compare this with the teacher's feedback. As Bramante and Colby (2012) note, "The achievement of a competency is communicated on an ongoing basis" (p. 71). Carol Ann Tomlinson and Tonya R. Moon (2013) describe assessment as the "compass for daily planning in a differentiated classroom" (p. 8). This compass provides the waypoints for next steps for both students and teachers and perfectly describes what assessment should be in a competency-based classroom.

Students should have some level of choice in assessment practices. In a competency-based, personalized model, teachers offer students various ways to demonstrate their learning; better yet, students can envision how they are going to demonstrate their understanding, presenting a proposal to the teacher and then co-creating the rubric that features expectations. Specifically, performance assessments should have multiple ways for students to demonstrate their understanding, with clear expectations outlined for each. In most schools, this component is still in its infancy.

> **Performance assessments should have multiple ways for students to demonstrate their understanding, with clear expectations outlined for each.**

If all students participate in a performance assessment at the same time, some individual students may be taking the assessment when they are not truly ready. Naturally, some are going to be ready before others. With the development of learning progressions (see chapter 3) that place students on their own learning continuums, students participate in performance assessments at any time, allowing for a very fluid environment for learning and assessment of learning.

Instructional Alignment

Teachers' increased assessment literacy has a powerful effect on instruction. As teachers engage in developing rigorous, high-quality performance assessments aligned with competencies, learning opportunities in the classroom evolve. If a performance assessment is at a DOK level 3, students must have opportunities to practice learning at this level. Once instructional practices change, students can better demonstrate their competency on summative assessments because higher DOK learning will be familiar to them. For example, in a performance assessment that requires students to compare various resources from print and media and develop an argument, students who have not had the opportunity to practice this type of transfer prior to being administered the assessment would understandably struggle. Teachers can build to higher-order assessment by facilitating opportunities for students to engage in these types of activities leading up to the summative assessment. This also provides formative data to teachers and students that can be used to strengthen the skills, knowledge, and dispositions necessary to prepare students for success.

The following section shows teachers a process and tool for building a common summative performance assessment.

Build Common Summative Performance Assessments

The CCE (2012) identifies the following five major steps in building a performance assessment.

1. Design common tasks.

2. Craft clear criteria and a rubric.

3. Administer the performance assessment and score student work.

4. Anchor assessments through exemplary work.

5. Refine the performance assessment and rubric.

Teams can use figure 5.8 to collaboratively develop summative performance assessments.

Unit:	Grade level:
Essential outcome: Students will be able to . . .	
Competencies: Leverage standards— Skills and dispositions—	
Essential questions to guide learning:	
Students will know (content) . . .	Students will be able to do (skills) . . .
Task summary:	Resources:

Figure 5.8: Performance assessment-planning template.   continued →

Rubric:	Possible accommodations:
Common performance assessment schedule or approximate time needed:	Formative assessment plan:
Plan for intervention and extension (after administration):	
Revisions to task (after administration):	

Source: Adapted from CCE, 2012; Hess, 2006; and McTighe & Wiggins, 2004.

*Visit **go.SolutionTree.com/PLCbooks** for a free reproducible version of this figure.*

The following sections detail this five-step process.

Designing the Task

When collaborative teams design a task, teachers begin by determining some important pieces of information. As teachers plan unit instruction, they must ask what it is that students should know and be able to do by the end (the first critical question of a PLC; DuFour et al., 2016) and what students should be able to do with that information. This is the competency the task will address, as well as the essential (or leverage) standards that fall under that competency. Within these essential standards, teachers include the skills and dispositions that a task will assess. Beginning the design process in this way allows teachers to focus their efforts on ensuring that all of their work is aligned with helping students meet the standards in an engaging way.

Teachers should discuss and record the skills and concepts they expect students to understand at the conclusion of the unit. This step helps teachers focus on areas in which it is important to develop formative assessments throughout the unit.

In a competency-based learning model, students have ownership of their learning. This recognition of student agency should be visible in performance assessments. Teachers should consider multiple and varied ways for students to demonstrate their understanding and competency.

The task summary should detail specifically what the task will entail; someone who is not familiar with the task should be able to understand what is expected. Task summaries should include directions for teachers and students and a time line for how long each specific portion of the assessment will take.

Teacher teams should consider the resources necessary for the task (videos, articles, books, and so on) that students will also need during the assessment. Teams and others should plan for possible accommodations as well. All students should have access to these accommodations; therefore, determining possible accommodations should include special educators, specialists, English learner instructors, and so on during development of the lesson plan.

Crafting Clear Criteria and a Rubric

One of the most difficult parts of building a well-developed, rigorous performance assessment is the creation of rubrics that assess what is intended. As the CCE (2012) explains, a *rubric* "describes the degree of quality, proficiency, and understanding along a continuum" (p. 65). Therefore, determining the expected criteria for competency through the development of a rubric prior to beginning the unit is imperative.

Brookhart (2013) describes performance-level indicators as "what one would observe in the work rather than the quality conclusions one would draw" (p. 26). Terms such as *proficient* provide feedback to a standard rather than a term like *good*. Teachers should keep performance-level indicators broad and general enough to allow students multiple pathways to demonstrate proficiency. If the performance-level descriptor is so narrow and confined that it limits the ability of teachers to effectively assess learning, it defeats the purpose of the rubric.

> **One of the most difficult parts of building a well-developed, rigorous performance assessment is the creation of rubrics that assess what is intended.**

In most competency-based learning environments, there are either four or five performance levels described in various ways: for example, *advanced*, *proficient*, *emerging*, and *limited*, or *advanced*, *beyond competent*, *competent*, *developing*, and *far from competent*. Teachers should separately assess (by standard) each component within a task, so we recommend that the number of actual competencies a task entails be limited to no more than two or three. Otherwise, what the teacher is truly attempting to have students demonstrate may become watered down.

Teachers first should determine what proficient looks like. This provides the basis for the rest of the four- or five-point rubric. It is always significantly easier to build rubrics using samples of real student work specific to a competency or standard. Teachers can then make determinations using actual evidence. However, if teams are at the very beginning of this process, they will not have student work. If this is the case, teams can go back to refine their rubrics based on what they learn from student work.

There is a dual benefit to developing high-quality rubrics. Not only do they provide clarity specific to the expectations for all teachers but, most important, they also provide structure and clarity for students to understand precisely what is expected of them as learners. Over time, students in a competency-based learning system will begin to look first at the rubric to better understand the expectations of a particular task.

Figure 5.9 shows an example of a rubric from Henry County Schools (n.d.b) in Georgia. This example demonstrates how each performance indicator is broken down into a learning progression.

Graduation Competency 1: Read closely to analyze and evaluate all forms of texts (such as complex literary and informational texts).				
Performance Indicator	**Emerging**	**Progressing**	**Competent**	**Exemplary**
a. Cite strong and thorough textual evidence to support an analysis of the text, including applicable primary or high school sources, and determining explicit and implicit meanings, such as inferences drawn from the text and where matters are uncertain.	Students select evidence but that evidence does not support analysis. Students paraphrase rather than cite. Students do not understand explicit or implicit meaning.	Students select evidence to support analysis but the cited evidence is not integrated. Students understand explicit but not implicit meaning.	Students construct support for analysis by citing integrated evidence from the text, including relevant supplementary sources. Students determine explicit and implicit meanings.	Students strengthen analysis through evaluation and selection of precisely integrated evidence, drawing from apt supplementary sources. Students articulate explicit and implicit meanings.

Source: Henry County Schools, n.d.b.

Figure 5.9: Competency rubric example.

As we discussed earlier in this chapter, teachers developing performance assessments gain great feedback in vertical teams when validating their work *prior to* administration. The feedback from vertical peers provides other perspectives, and allows a group of colleagues that have not been intimately involved in creating the performance assessment to look at the work through a different lens. Leaders should provide teachers with time to meet vertically to validate their performance assessments.

Administrating the Assessment

When students are ready to demonstrate proficiency, teachers administer the task according to the task summary. In a competency-based learning system, teachers determine student readiness using formative assessment data.

Typically, all students in a grade level take an assessment at the same time, with intervention and extension happening after the assessment. Ideally, a bank of assessments would be available, giving students choices in how they are going to demonstrate proficiency. When they are ready, students then take the assessment of their choice. We hope to see performance assessment administration evolve to the point that students are truly able to take the assessment when they are ready. This would require a great level of flexibility and responsive planning, but would be possible within a student-centered environment.

Anchoring Assessments Through Exemplary Work

The most powerful aspect of developing performance assessments is looking at student work together in a collaborative team. This process allows the teachers who created the assessment, along with another team of educators, to review the student work together in an inquiry process to determine whether they need to alter the assessment based on what the real student work is telling them. In essence, does the student work reflect what the team members intended when they built the assessment? Does the student work reflect competency?

Another important factor involved in looking at student work together is the process of identifying student work exemplars for future use with the assessment. This allows teachers to compare work samples to the rubric criteria to ensure comparability; this also allows teachers to *anchor* their assessments through student work samples that align with the team-created rubric.

> The most powerful aspect of developing performance assessments is looking at student work together in a collaborative team.

Another important outcome is the development of inter-rater reliability within and among teams. Inter-rater reliability is important in a competency-based learning model as it allows teachers to learn from each other and come to consensus about what defines each rubric level. In highly functioning collaborative teams, inter-rater reliability continues to develop to the point that when teachers assess student work, they bring this adjusted perspective to their individual classrooms.

Refining the Performance Assessment and Rubric

Teams should refine each performance assessment after administration. Don't be surprised to have major changes during this process, especially to the rubric. Many teams find that what they expect student work to look like is not the reality. This can occur due to unclear rubric language. Leaders should carve out time for teachers to revise the assessment soon after administration.

Through this ongoing process, teams continually refine assessments. It is uncommon for a team to use the exact same performance task more than once because, as part of the process of developing common summative assessments, teachers are always learning and making adjustments based not only on reflection of instruction in the classroom but also from the feedback on student work samples.

Deputy commissioner Paul Leather has been pivotal in New Hampshire's transition to a competency-based model of learning since the mid-1990s and has also been integral in the development of a first-in-the-nation assessment and accountability effort known as PACE (Performance Assessment of Competency Education).

Practitioner Perspective
Paul Leather, Deputy Commissioner, New Hampshire Department of Education

In March 2015, the U.S. Department of Education approved New Hampshire's PACE pilot in four New Hampshire school districts. The PACE pilot allows districts to reduce the level of standardized testing and replace tests with locally developed and managed assessments that are more integrated into a student's day-to-day work. The original four PACE-implementing districts—Sanborn Regional, Rochester, Epping, and Souhegan—have worked in partnership with the New Hampshire Department of Education (NHDOE) to develop the pilot that has been underway since 2015. Since that time, another four districts, Concord, Pittsfield, Monroe, and White Mountains School Administrative Unit 35, as well as two charters schools, Seacoast Charter School and the Virtual Learning Academy, have joined at the implementation level with ten other districts preparing to implement PACE, and more are joining each week.

A competency-based education system relies on a series of academic and 21st century learning targets that help connect content standards and critical skills leading to mastery of competencies. Competency-based education requires that educators and students develop methods to follow student progress and also that students have mastered key content and skills prior to moving to more complex knowledge and skills along defined learning trajectories. Competency-based education is best assessed through performance assessments, multistep demonstrations of both knowledge and skill at deep levels that result in products, exhibitions of learning, student reflection on that learning, and solutions to complex problems, all of which occur throughout a student's learning pathway. New Hampshire PACE brings together a coherent and comprehensive system of both local and common assessments that support competency education.

In order for PACE to be effective, it is necessary to build the capacity of educators. They must have deep levels of content knowledge, discipline-specific pedagogy, and assessment literacy to teach and assess a rigorous Common Core–aligned curriculum using complex performance tasks. To that end, New Hampshire has developed a fully networked approach to connect districts to one another and to target supports and expertise. Through a partnership with 2Revolutions, NHDOE provides the New Hampshire Network (www.education.nh.gov/networks), an information platform to facilitate virtual collaboration between and among stakeholders while at the same time seeding the transformation of structures, practices, and technology tools. More closely connected to the classroom, however, are fully embedded professional development strategies, such as the PLC framework. Schools have common learning planning times scheduled throughout each week of school, where educators examine student work, progress together, and review competencies, performance assessment design, and instructional practice, as well as develop their model of personalized learning supporting greater student agency. Such a design not only serves to enrich educator practice but also allows for multiple and intensive trials of improvement and innovation occurring throughout the year, rather than reliance on an annual improvement cycle, typical to public education. In 2017, another strategy emerged, supporting cohorts of teacher leaders in the development of common PACE tasks across the implementing districts and also in providing support in task implementation and scoring. This greater reliance on teacher leadership in the process only strengthens educator capacity so necessary for quality implementation.

Most important, the codirection and development of the PACE project, the intensive embedded professional learning and planning, and the development of teacher leaders in the process has resulted in a change of overall locus of control and ownership of the process as a whole. New Hampshire educators at every level will tell you that they own the process, that it is their assessment and accountability system, developed and maintained by them. Early results from 2015–2017 show that New Hampshire assessments are every bit as reliable and rigorous as statewide accountability assessments have been in both developing and predicting student learning. Because of these developments, it is fair to say that the emergence of New Hampshire PACE augurs a new era for education assessment and accountability for not just New Hampshire, but for the entire United States. (P. Leather, personal communication, October 2016)

Assessment of Skills and Dispositions

The critical competencies for success are evolving. Employers are looking for different skills than they did as recently as 2005. A National Association of Colleges and Employers (NACE; Adams, 2013) survey outlines the top four skills employers are looking for in an employee.

1. Ability to work in a team

2. Ability to make decisions and solve problems

3. Ability to plan, organize, and prioritize work

4. Ability to communicate verbally with people inside and outside an organization

This creates a certain sense of urgency in competency-based learning schools already separating the assessment of academics and behaviors in their classrooms, a major design principle of any competency-based learning system As we further embed opportunities for students to learn and grow within the competencies of communication, collaboration, creativity, and self-direction, we are helping to develop the skills and dispositions that will help them to be most successful in their careers and in college.

Although there are schools that have been focusing on these all-important competencies for many, many years, overall, the in-depth assessment of skills and dispositions is still a new concept. Despite the abundance of research depicting the true necessity of further developing the curriculum, instruction, and assessment of these crucial competencies, how to do it well remains a mystery to many educators.

Ron Ritchhart of Harvard University asks, "What if education were less about acquiring skills and knowledge and more about cultivating the dispositions and habits of mind that students will need for a lifetime of learning?" (as cited in Bellanca, 2015, pp. 58–59). Teachers in competency-based learning schools mindfully integrate these skill and disposition competencies into their curriculum, instruction, and assessment. But the process is one of trial and error, and students need to be integral in figuring out which skills to integrate within specific units of instruction or even in individual activities. The teacher role really becomes about recognizing opportunities to integrate the learning of skills and dispositions, and very importantly, pointing out times within the day to ask students questions about how they are metacognitively processing information or what is either inhibiting them from being successful within a disposition (self-direction, for example) or allowing them to be successful.

> **The teacher role really becomes about recognizing opportunities to integrate the learning of skills and dispositions, and very importantly, pointing out times within the day to ask students questions about how they are metacognitively processing information.**

There are multiple factors to consider when developing a rubric for skills and dispositions, such as communication, collaboration, creativity, and self-direction. In a competency-based learning system, teachers assess these dispositions using a body of evidence from students. This is important because the grade is based on multiple points of evidence, rather than just a point in time (the end of a trimester, for example). Rubrics should always accompany performance assessments. To begin, successful schools utilize a rubric specific to skills and dispositions for the entire group of students (for collaboration, for example). (Visit **go.SolutionTree.com/PLCbooks** to access a sample rubric.) Educators Arthur Costa and Bena Kallick (1995) propose that developmental rubrics representing continua of learning are the most appropriate way to assess for learning. This would include growth within skills and dispositions. A rubric for skills and dispositions should identify the indicators that will allow students to move forward. This is certainly in line with the idea of learning progressions guiding the learning for individual students. Each student will move at his or her own place along these continua, whether academic or nonacademic. The Essential Skills and Dispositions Frameworks (Lench, Fukuda, & Anderson, 2015) provide a research-based framework for teachers as they interpret skills such as communication, collaboration, creativity, and self-direction.

Student Self-Reflection

One of the most effective assessment practices in a competency-based learning system is student self-assessment; students determine where they are and create goals to help guide them. Teachers should not use honest student reflections summatively. This would potentially create an environment in which students self-assess higher than may be accurate for fear of getting a bad grade. When done in a safe environment—where consistent growth is applauded and modeled—students will honestly and accurately reflect on their learning.

Like so much of competency-based learning, there is no blue-print for teachers to reference when creating competency-friendly assessments. Teachers' learning will develop and their practices will evolve by starting somewhere and then committing to engage in a constant cycle of reflection to figure out what has worked and what needs refinement. This in itself is so incredibly valuable. Teachers model learning as an ongoing process for their students, and are guided by assessments that truly provide feedback and direction for further growth, the true purpose of assessment.

One of the most effective assessment practices in a competency-based learning system is student self-assessment; students determine where they are and create goals to help guide them.

Reflection Questions

Consider the following four reflection questions with your team.

1. There are many critical components to developing a high-quality performance assessment. Do you understand the various components of a performance assessment, including essential questions, DOK, and accessibility for all learners?

2. It is important to include various performance assessment cycle processes. Do your school teams participate in processes to validate performance assessments? Do you prioritize collaborative team time to engage in these processes?

3. Assessment should never be complete; teachers should continually iterate assessment based on feedback. Do you take time as a team to refine your assessments based on the feedback you receive from your colleagues and through student work?

4. Student ownership of learning is critical. Do you provide opportunities for students to determine how they can demonstrate their competency?

CHAPTER 6

Responding When Students Need Intervention and Extension

Providing students with individualized intervention and extension is an integral component of a competency-based learning system. This chapter focuses on schoolwide support structures related to the third and fourth critical questions of a PLC, What do we do if students don't learn it? and What do we do if students already know it (DuFour et al., 2016)? You will learn how in a competency-based learning school, individual teachers, collaborative teams, and the school as a whole respond when students need intervention or extension.

In many traditional U.S. schools, educators are beginning to identify structural elements keeping staff from meeting varied student needs. Brian Pickering, then principal of ConVal Regional High School in New Hampshire, shared with us an event within his school that was the impetus for change.

It all started in 2010, when Bailey, a senior at ConVal, went to the principal with a problem. The problem was straightforward; the solution, however, was not. Bailey needed help studying for an upcoming physics exam, but she played sports, so she couldn't stay after school to study, and she didn't have the same lunchtime as her physics teacher, and her teacher wasn't available before school. Bailey had tried, but she just couldn't find time to get the help she needed—and she wasn't alone. ConVal students were having trouble finding time for enrichment activities, extensions, mentoring, intervention and support, and social and emotional support.

What they needed, Brian realized, was a systemic personalized learning solution that fit into the school day. "I knew I couldn't support Bailey directly in physics, but it seemed crazy that we couldn't find time for this driven young woman to get the help she needed," he explained.

To find a solution, ConVal created a team of teachers, staff, parents, and students. Working together, they came up with the idea of a flexible block. They called it Teams in Academic Support Centers or TASC, and piloted the new system schoolwide during the 2011–2012 school year.

"It wasn't a study hall or an extra class. It wasn't an advisory or an after-school study session," said Brian, adding that it had all the benefits of each. The goal was for TASC to be a personalized, student-driven, directed, targeted block—a time for academic as well as social and emotional support.

This account from the principal illustrates what many schools experience as they make the transition to a more personalized approach to learning. A competency-based learning model provides opportunities within the school day for learners to have their individual needs met.

It is inevitable that schools shifting to a more personalized approach to learning and competency-based learning will begin to question, and then ultimately identify, ways students can receive intervention and extension opportunities above and beyond what teachers provide through whole-class instruction using standard curriculum and materials over and over again.

> **A competency-based learning model provides opportunities within the school day for learners to have their individual needs met.**

As DuFour, Eaker, and Many (2010) explain, when the staff in any school begin to dig into why they exist, philosophical conversations about their purpose as educators will become more focused. For example, if educators are asked if they believe students can learn at high levels, most—if not all—will agree with this notion, although there will inevitably be those who offer various excuses as to why certain students within the school may be unable to learn. This *aggressive minority* can derail the efforts of a well-intentioned staff unless the *silent majority* speaks up and offers its perspective on why it is imperative to stay the course in an attempt to better the learning experiences for all students.

The fourth design principal of competency-based learning states, "Students receive timely, differentiated support based on their individual learning needs" (Sturgis,

2015, p. 8). A competency-based learning school must have a model that allows students the timely intervention and support necessary to ensure mastery of content while students progress along their individual learning continuum.

Recognizing the need to change is typically a result of educators in a school coming to the realization that they are not providing students with the individualized support students need to be successful. Sometimes this is true of a cohort of students (students at risk, for example), but sometimes it is only true of smaller pockets of students throughout a school, such as a subset of an identified population (identified boys in mathematics). Despite the group's size, the evidence will be compelling enough to be the lever for change.

A competency-based learning school must have a model that allows students the timely intervention and support necessary to ensure mastery of content while students progress along their individual learning continuum.

Definitions
Intervention, Extension, and Enrichment

- **Intervention:** Small groups of students working with the teacher on content support, remediation, or proactive support

- **Extension:** Whole-class groups of students "going deeper" by doing work from within the curriculum that can't be covered during regular instruction

- **Enrichments:** Above-and-beyond activities outside the curriculum that expand students' experiences

---

This chapter describes how educators respond when students need intervention and extension. It discusses focusing on the why, setting the stage for scheduling, asking four questions to guide the scheduling process, beginning to build the schedule, understanding the tiers of intervention, extending the learning, including special education, transitioning to a new process, and supporting teachers during the process.

Focusing on the *Why* of the Intervention and Support

The traditional education system design does not provide students with necessary 21st century requisite skills, knowledge, and experiences. Our 21st century world today requires a very different skill set than the world we lived in at the turn of the century. And, according to the World Economic Forum (2016) publication *The 10 Skills You Need to Thrive in the Fourth Industrial Revolution*, we can expect more significant changes. Approximately 35 percent of the skills considered important in our workforce will change by 2020 (World Economic Forum, 2016). See table 6.1 for a comparison of the top-ten skills in 2015 and the top-ten skills anticipated in 2020.

Table 6.1: Top-Ten Skills Comparison—2015 and 2020

Top-Ten Skills in 2015	Top-Ten Skills in 2020
1. Complex problem solving	1. Complex problem solving
2. Ability to coordinate with others	2. Critical thinking
3. People management	3. Creativity
4. Critical thinking	4. People management
5. Negotiation	5. Ability to coordinate with others
6. Quality control	6. Emotional intelligence
7. Service orientation	7. Judgment and decision making
8. Judgment and decision making	8. Service orientation
9. Active listening	9. Negotiation
10. Creativity	10. Cognitive flexibility

Source: World Economic Forum, 2016.

Students must be able to proficiently demonstrate these skills to be successful in the world they will enter after graduation. The importance of a number of these skills is becoming more and more apparent. Our world increasingly values skills that require deeper thinking (complex problem solving and critical thinking, for example) and a competency-based learning environment can nurture these skills. Creativity, for example, jumps significantly (from ten to three), suggesting that identifying multiple solutions to a problem and thinking outside of the box are skills that are becoming more and more desirable to employers.

> **We have an obligation to ensure that our system meets not only the current needs of our world but also anticipates the needs of tomorrow's world.**

Our system is not preparing graduates for the world they will enter. Therefore, we have an obligation to ensure that our system meets not only the current needs of our world but also anticipates the needs of tomorrow's world. As Buffum et al. (2012) note, "Traditional school practices are in direct conflict with the formula for learning" (p. 9). Successful competency-based learning schools recognize that a time-based system is not going to provide the structures necessary for all students to receive the differentiated and personalized support they need to be successful.

If "potential dropouts can be predicted as early as first grade" (DuFour, 2015, p. 107), then we must not waste any time providing the intervention and support students need as soon as there is evidence that a student is struggling to learn a particular concept. Targeted, systematic interventions should be available for every student in a school as soon as he or she demonstrates a need, and the response must be immediate. Early intervention is imperative. The sooner interventions are available, the better.

Many high school graduates who go on to college are not prepared or do not make it further than their first year. According to ACT in 2013, over one-third of students entering college drop out within the first year (as cited in DuFour, 2015). Additionally, "more than one-third of students entering college require remedial courses" (Strong American Schools, 2008, as cited in DuFour, 2015, p. 107). Clearly, traditional teaching and learning methods are not adequately preparing today's students for the world they will enter.

Competency-based learning raises the bar on the learning we hold students accountable for. It creates a need to look at intervention and extension not simply as teacher-initiated activities but as integrated schoolwide responses that maximize all available resources.

Setting the Stage for Scheduling

Building a schedule to truly support student learning requires staff members to think critically about why their current schedule is set up the way it is, and then determine what support they absolutely must provide to students for each to progress. The key is to build an intervention and extension schedule that makes time accessible to all teachers who need to be involved with a particular group of students.

In elementary and middle school settings where specialists need to be available for each grade level, making time accessible can best be accomplished through a support and intervention schedule that does not overlap times for intervention throughout the day. For example, see the elementary school schedule shown in figure 6.1 (page 134). This allows the school to maximize any available human resources throughout the school, not just within a given grade level.

Schools should do their best to schedule grade-level intervention time so it does not conflict with another grade level's time. This is important because it allows grade levels to share human resources to support all learners in every grade. Instead of the five classroom teachers in a grade level being the only ones available during an intervention time, schools can access available human resources (paraprofessionals, specialists, and special educators) from other grade levels, potentially doubling support available, thus allowing for smaller group sizes.

	K	Grade 1	Grade 2	Grade 3	Grade 4	Grade 5
8:30–9:15 a.m.						
9:15–10:00 a.m.					**Support Block**	
10:00–10:45 a.m.	**Support Block**					
10:45–11:30 a.m.			**Support Block**			
11:30 a.m.–12:15 p.m.						
12:15–1:00 p.m.		**Support Block**				
1:00–1:45 p.m.						**Support Block**
1:45–2:30 p.m.				**Support Block**		
2:30–3:15 p.m.						

Figure 6.1: Sample elementary schedule for intervention and extension.

In a secondary setting where classes can include students of differing grades, it may be more advantageous to have the support period at the same time each day for all students. Develop a structure that allows teachers to schedule students for certain support and intervention opportunities, but that also provides students the opportunity to self-select opportunities for extension in their areas of interest. Each student's additional learning time will then consist of both intervention and extension over the course of a week. This ensures that student choice is part of each individual schedule, and each student also receives the support he or she needs. Find an example of a high school schedule in figure 6.2.

Advances in technology benefit educators as they revise schedules to improve student-support structures. What was once done by hand (literally, writing out schedules) can now be done with software that automatically assigns students to teachers depending on their individual needs for support, intervention, or extension.

Consider the sample high school schedule in figure 6.2. A grade-level team, such as the ninth-grade team, may choose to develop a support and intervention block schedule like the one in figure 6.3.

	Monday	Tuesday	Wednesday	Thursday	Friday
8:00–9:00 a.m.					
9:00–10:00 a.m.					
10:00–10:45 a.m.	**Support Block**	**Support Block**	**Support Block**	**Support Block**	**Support Block**
10:45–11:45 a.m.					
11:45 a.m.–12:15 p.m.					
12:15–1:15 p.m.					
1:15–2:15 p.m.					
2:15–3:15 p.m.					

Figure 6.2: Sample secondary intervention and extension schedule.

	Monday	Tuesday	Wednesday	Thursday	Friday
Mathematics	All students meet in homeroom with their advisor to plan the rest of their week.	Intervention	Intervention	Extension	Enrichment
English		Intervention	Enrichment	Intervention	Extension
Social studies		Enrichment	Intervention	Intervention	Extension
Science		Extension	Intervention	Enrichment	Intervention
Electives		Enrichment	Enrichment	Extension	Intervention

Figure 6.3: Sample grade 9 support block schedule.

One way successful schools coordinate such schedules is by building a schoolwide schedule collaboratively. This process should not include every staff member; instead, it should involve the school leadership team (DuFour et al., 2010). This team should be representative of the various subgroups within the school and include grade-level representatives, content representatives, specialists, and administrators. At a minimum, the leadership team should include both teachers and administrators.

Asking Four Questions to Guide Scheduling

Traditionally, administrators or counselors develop the schoolwide schedule, many times utilizing a previous year's schedule as the template. In a competency-based learning model, the leadership team starts from scratch (or close to it). Four questions help guide the process of building a schedule.

1. How was our current schedule created? Specifically, what is it built around?

2. What do we need within our schedule to help our students be most successful?

3. What are the current impediments to building a schedule that inhibit us from meeting our students' needs?

4. Where can our smaller collaborative team be flexible?

The leadership team should reflect on these four questions as they collaboratively build a schedule to best support learning for all students. Using these questions as a guide is imperative because they build a common understanding of why change is necessary. The teachers on the leadership team become advocates for the work, bringing the information back to their grade- or subject-level teams. In some cases, they are able to gather feedback during the process, resulting in even more buy-in from a greater number of staff within the school as the schedule is further developed based upon this feedback.

Let's take a look at each question in greater detail.

How Was Our Current Schedule Created? Specifically, What Is It Built Around?

Typically, when teachers are asked what their school schedule is built around, they respond with nonacademic reasons for time blocks during a school day. Lunch, band, and recess are all examples of times during the day that schedules may have traditionally been built around. Schools might also have considered human resources when designing schedules, especially in situations where schools share staff members across grade levels or even between buildings. These factors impede a school's ability to offer necessary support at times when the support would be most effective.

This first question is crucial because it explores the traditional basis for most schools' scheduling. This allows leadership team members to develop a common understanding that will help during the difficult conversations ahead (specifically, question four).

What Do We Need Within Our Schedule to Help Our Students Be Most Successful?

This second question generates a tremendous amount of positive discussion because it focuses on a topic intrinsic to teachers' reason for being: how to help students. Some teams approach this question by asking, "If we were teaching in a perfect world, what would our schedule include?"

Invariably, as a team discusses this question, the necessity for collaborative team time and focused support time for all students becomes the priority. With these two items as the starting point, teams can move on to what is inhibiting them from successfully incorporating collaborative time and focused support time within their daily schedule.

What Are the Current Impediments to Building a Schedule That Inhibit Us From Meeting Our Students' Needs?

The third question allows all leadership team members to share hurdles to developing a schedule that allows teachers to effectively support all students. There will be many reasons, ranging from the obvious that all experience (lunch, contracted prep time, and so on) to the individual complaints ("I can't work well with so and so"). Importantly, it gives all school groups a representative voice. Effective leadership teams record the answers for all team members to see in preparation for answering the next question.

Where Can Our Collaborative Team Be Flexible?

The purpose of the last question is to begin to shift the collaborative team's thinking from problems to solutions. Each team member is responsible for beginning to solve problems specific to his or her smaller collaborative group (grade level, subject, and so on). Answering this fourth question is an important step because, in many schools and at many grade levels, teachers are doing things a certain way *because it is the way it's always been done*. Once prompted to think about the reasoning, the potential for change becomes real. Additionally, when collaborative leadership team members hear from their colleagues about scheduling, they experience subtle encouragement to abandon rigid thinking, which makes way for different approaches.

Beginning to Build the Schedule

Once the leadership team has answered the four questions, it is ready to tackle creating the schedule. The following questions should guide team discussion as members plan for how their school will provide opportunities for support and extension within the daily schedule.

1. How will we determine the learning targets and progressions for each competency?

2. How will we determine the intervention and extension each student will receive in our school?

3. How will we monitor each student's growth and learning?

4. How will we maximize existing human resources?

It is imperative that the leadership team understands each of these questions before beginning the planning process. The first three questions are specific to collaborative teams planning academic structures. The last question allows teachers to think about the human resources aspect of providing focused intervention and extension.

Let's delve into these questions a bit deeper.

How Will We Determine the Learning Targets and Progressions for Each Competency?

Each competency must have learning progressions that outline the targets a student must reach to ultimately be proficient within that competency. Teachers must be clear about what is expected within each competency in a unit of instruction. In K–12 competency-based learning districts, this learning progression truly diverges from a traditional time-based system. Instead, it focuses on each student and his or her place along the learning continuum of each competency.

Admittedly, a dichotomy exists within most public schools transitioning to competency-based learning systems. As Bramante and Colby (2012) outline, our schools are based on seat time rather than competency. Schools in the process of transitioning are doing so within the confines of a time-based system. Regardless of the constraints that may exist in any school—competency based or not—teams must be clear on the essential knowledge and skills that students must be proficient in. Otherwise, how will the team determine which students need intervention and support?

How Will We Determine the Intervention and Extension Each Student Will Receive in Our School?

Teachers must decide which assessment data will determine the intervention and extension they provide to students. Chapter 5 outlined the need to not only develop summative performance assessments that determine competency but also to include formative assessments along the way that allow teachers to determine where students are in their learning on an ongoing basis. As Buffum et al. (2012) note:

> While individual teachers are constantly gathering evidence in their own classrooms, collaborative teams of teachers plan frequent, *common* formative assessments as part of their instructional cycle, and use this information to respond collectively to the needs of *all* their students. (p. 57)

This is an integral component of a successful approach to intervention. The team must not only plan the assessments but also utilize the information collectively to implement focused student supports.

How Will We Monitor Each Student's Growth and Learning?

In a competency-based learning system, a body of evidence is necessary to make a determination about each student's demonstration of competency. For that reason, teachers must provide multiple opportunities for students to demonstrate competency. Summative assessment data determines competency, but the formative information leading up to the summative assessment is crucial for identifying the need for timely and effective support for struggling students. Conversely, if a student has already demonstrated mastery, that student should be able to continue along his or her learning progression, extending and deepening his or her learning. Buffum et al. (2012) outline the importance of convergent assessment in the overall approach to monitoring student growth. This concept applies in a competency-based learning system as well.

How Will We Maximize Existing Human Resources?

Schools must examine all of their available human resources and then develop a schedule that allows staff to maximize each. Many elementary- and middle-level competency-based learning schools develop master schedules in which the Tier 2 intervention and extension time does not overlap (see figure 6.1, page 134). At an elementary school, for example, this means each day has a dedicated block of time for each grade level for reteaching and enriching that does not overlap.

This is important so elementary and middle schools can begin to allocate additional human resources to a team during this block of time. A grade level is flooded with human resources during this time, maximizing the skill and expertise of case managers, paraprofessionals, reading specialists, and other specialists, all in addition to classroom teachers. Students with greater needs have the opportunity to work in smaller groups, sometimes even in groups as small two or three students.

In a high school setting where the support period is at the same time for all students, specialists may choose to work with a specific grade level or support a specific content area on different days of the weekly schedule. This strategy maximizes

> The collective responsibility of all teachers for all students will slowly begin to ingrain itself throughout the school.

resources while giving students choice and voice in how they build their support and intervention schedule each week.

The collective responsibility of all teachers for all students will slowly begin to ingrain itself throughout the school. A teacher who once only thought about the students in her own class will accept responsibility for the growth and success of students in her entire grade level. The paraprofessional assigned to a specific grade level will work across grade levels, and his maximized schedule allows him to support students throughout the day, regardless of the grade level.

Understanding the Tiers of Intervention

Response to intervention is a multitiered system of support (MTSS). As we discussed earlier, it includes three tiers represented as an inverted pyramid (Buffum et al., 2012): Tier 1, Tier 2, and Tier 3.

Tier 1

All students have access to Tier 1 instruction. Competency-based learning model schools meet each student where he or she is along the learning progression within Tier 1, but most schools are not there yet; they are still confined to a grade-level system. Because of this, it is imperative that all students receive instruction in grade-level competencies and standards. This is non-negotiable. Historically, many students with greater needs were pulled from class during vital learning opportunities, depriving them of learning they need to continue to move forward, creating an even wider gap. In a competency-based learning system, all students should have access to Tier 1 instruction—both those needing support and those demonstrating readiness for deeper extension.

Tier 2

In a competency-based learning system, educators should create and define Tier 2 time for every student within the school so that each receives instruction specific to his or her place along a learning continuum. During Tier 2, students who have not met the targets receive focused intervention. Once those students demonstrate mastery of the intended targets, the system should be fluid enough to allow them to begin to work on something else. In some cases, when a student is still not demonstrating expected mastery or progress, educators may need to intensify the intervention.

There are many benefits to including time for Tier 2 in the schedule. All teachers are mutually accountable for student success and working interdependently to meet the needs of all learners within the grade level or subject area. Each block of time for support is flooded with human resources, allowing students to be organized into smaller groups for more focused support for the students who need it most.

In schools most successful at providing ongoing opportunities for reteaching and relearning, the staff work together to determine the most qualified resource to work with a particular student, and they ensure that person is available to provide support and intervention during a prescribed time (D'Agostino & Murphy, 2004; Vaughn, Gersten, & Chard, 2000, as cited in Buffum, Mattos, & Weber, 2010).

Additionally, Buffum et al. (2012) outline the following five characteristics of effective intervention.

1. **Research based:** Proven to work and allows collected data to demonstrate growth

2. **Directive:** Not optional (Instead, plan interventions and provide remediation based on collected data.)

3. **Correctly administered:** Trained professionals deemed most effective to work with particular students and their needs

4. **Targeted:** Precisely planned interventions (If it is too broad, it is likely to be unsuccessful. Teams must dig into the data to identify exactly where a student may be struggling, then plan interventions that will provide the remediation necessary for that student's success.)

5. **Timely:** Promptly responding to student needs (Assessment should be ongoing and groupings flexible to allow opportunities for students to receive the support they need, when they need it. Teams meeting on an ongoing basis can build regrouping into their weekly or biweekly meetings.)

Tier 3

The purpose for instituting extended support systems in schools "is to close achievement gaps, not widen them" (Buffum et al., 2012, p. 177). In this vein, it is necessary for some students to receive an even greater degree of support—but not at any expense. Students accessing even greater levels of intervention should receive what they need with the understanding that this should not, by any means, replace the core curriculum (Tier 1). The additional tiers of support provide students with the individualized and focused intervention necessary for them to be successful. The goal is for no student to need Tier 3 intervention.

Extending the Learning

The intent of any school is to ensure all students are learning at high levels. A major team focus is on those students not demonstrating competency as they plan Tiers 2 and 3 groupings. But there is another whole cohort of students who can access personalized learning opportunities during this time as well.

In a competency-based learning system, students who demonstrate competency in specific areas should have the opportunity to extend their learning. During Tier 2, students who prove their competency should engage in activities that will challenge them as learners. A competency-based learning model, by nature, meets each student where he or she is, and provides the time, guidance, and support that allows each student to continue along his or her learning progression.

> In a competency-based learning system, students who demonstrate competency in specific areas should have the opportunity to extend their learning.

As Buffum et al. (2012) acknowledge, it is important for collaborative teams to identify how they will provide enrichment and extension for students who have already demonstrated mastery. These students should not become the helper or another teacher. Students must have rigorous opportunities to extend their learning by engaging in activities that require a deeper DOK.

Including Special Education

Like any other students in a competency-based learning model, students with special needs should access the available individualized learning supports. In many cases, a student's case manager would actually provide this support, but this isn't a requirement. For example, if a school's reading specialist is clearly the most qualified individual to provide intervention to students specific to reading, then the identified student should receive this support from the reading specialist.

A learning support system is a necessary component of a competency-based learning system, but it does not replace the need for the three-tiered system. In a National Center for Learning Disabilities (n.d.) blog post, the editors state, "CBE [competency-based education] doesn't replace RTI or MTSS. In fact, a framework like MTSS can help make sure each student is making progress and meeting competencies at a reasonable pace." Essentially, a competency-based learning model, when implemented with fidelity, provides equity and access for all learners. Expectations are high for all, and a teachers' responsibility is to provide the support, structure, feedback, and guidance to allow each student to progress.

Kathleen Murphy has worked in urban, suburban, and rural districts supporting students as a special education case manager and a special education coordinator. Kathleen has worked in two districts transitioning to a competency-based learning environment.

Practitioner's Perspective
Kathleen Murphy, K–12 Special Education Coordinator, Allenstown School District, New Hampshire

Competency-based learning calls for all students to receive a personalized system for learning tailored to their individual needs. In the field of special education, we have been charged with this task since the inception of IDEA [Individuals With Disabilities Education Improvement Act of 2004]. The development and implementation of a student's individualized education plan strongly correlates to the way in which we must look at all learners in competency-based learning, on progressions of skill development, and with a strong emphasis on personalization. In a competency-based setting, students with educational disabilities are given an individualized pathway for instruction in addition to their special education goals, accommodations, and services.

As a special education teacher in a competency-based elementary school, I was able to use the framework for competency-based learning to empower my work of designing curriculum specifically tailored to the students. The notion that all students no longer should be assessed in the same manner revitalized my practice and allowed for greater levels of participation by my students in their regular education settings. I worked as a member of the grade-level and special education teams to review student achievement data. This gave me the opportunity to determine the best ways for students to receive high-quality instruction and demonstrate their understanding. No longer restricted in how they could demonstrate their learning, students had opportunities to showcase their learning in a way that could be tailored to their strengths and interests. As a special educator, I worked to help students understand their strengths and provided curriculum and assessments that built upon those strengths while also challenging them to push their thinking and work with content to a higher level. In addition to addressing competencies at the Tier 1 level, I was able to identify specific areas of weaknesses and provide timely and targeted assistance in a Tier 2 approach for these students. I felt more confident in my ability to identify areas of weaknesses because my use of competencies allowed me to look at curriculum and standards at a deeper level. In turn, this made Tier 2 instruction more successful for students. After analyzing progress-monitoring data, the team may determine that a student needs a more significant level of intervention, and Tier 3 support is provided.

In my current role as a special education administrator, I support a comprehensive team approach to develop IEPs that meet the individual needs of the student in addition to providing ways in which the team can support a student through progressions within the curriculum. The value of the special education team lies in the expertise of each individual member and the ways in which he or she can contribute to enhance the overall learning of each student. For example, an occupational therapist may provide insight and strategies to assist a student in visual tracking tasks that were impacting his or her ability to read

continued →

fluently. The specialist shares this insight with the team, and the team looks for ways to embed this skill or provide direct instruction when appropriate, which assists the student in achieving reading competencies and meeting targeted IEP goals in the areas of reading fluency and visual tracking. The power of the special education team to work as a highly functioning team within a PLC will always benefit the student.

Competency-based education empowers educators to think differently about their curriculum and opens doors for creativity and collaboration among school-based groups to support the development of all students. (K. Murphy, personal communication, September 2016)

Transitioning to a New Process

Schools transitioning to a competency-based learning model must first embrace the school's mission and vision (DuFour et al., 2016). If this vision encompasses a learning-for-all mindset, then the staff must determine what will allow them to support all learners in their building. It begins with recognizing the current system is not providing each student with what he or she needs to be most successful.

In many traditional schools, time is not yet allotted for reteaching and extension within the school day. There are numerous reasons why "it just won't be possible" to do something like that "in this school." But it is possible. It is just a matter of staff working together to figure out how to start and what commitments to make. Once the process begins, teachers identify ways to improve their model of support and extension and (hopefully) make those necessary changes.

With so much evidence pointing to why schools must change, doesn't it seem obvious that changes need to be made? It is not that easy, though, and Buffum et al. (2010) outline four major reasons schools won't move forward in this crucial work.

1. Schools view RTI as a way to qualify students for special education.

2. Schools do RTI because they feel they have to do at least enough to avoid punitive effects.

3. Schools implement RTI simply to raise test scores, only focusing on the bubble students they can move into the proficient category to help their school's overall scores.

4. Some schools will not take the responsibility and exert the effort to look deeply within themselves and their own practices and consider what they might change. Instead, these schools place blame on everyone but themselves and continue to do things the same exact way that they've always done them.

This work takes time. Any school implementing a multi-tiered system of support in its building will inevitably run into an implementation dip, most likely within the first six months (Fullan, 2001). Unfortunately, many schools will look at this dip as an opportunity to go back to their old ways, rather than as a temporary hurdle. Teachers will also be very tempted to go back to old ways; however, as teachers continue to work collaboratively and move forward in their practices (and within the process), student performance will reflect their commitment to change.

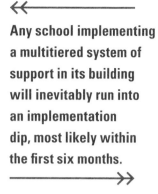

Any school implementing a multitiered system of support in its building will inevitably run into an implementation dip, most likely within the first six months.

Supporting Teachers

This chapter discusses how implementing a competency-based learning model in a school requires a change in thinking specific to how we support students. Also very important, it requires a change in how schools support teachers. As schools transform their model of education for students, they must also transform the models of support in place for teachers.

As schools transform their model of education for students, they must also transform the models of support in place for teachers.

Here are three effective ways to provide support to teachers to adequately prepare them to support students.

1. Ensure time exists within the teachers' daily schedule and school professional development calendar for collaboration. The master schedule should allow for as much collaboration time as possible. The work we ask teachers to do is difficult. They must have time to do it well.

2. Rethink the use of the phrase *staff meeting*. Traditional staff meetings are unnecessary. Memos or emails can address administrative issues. Instead, this time should be for the horizontal or vertical teaming that allows staff members the opportunity to work with each other to create assessments, review student data, or plan interventions.

3. Embed agile professional development. The days of the one-and-done professional development model are over. Professional development must mirror what teachers try to create for students in classrooms. It must reflect the five components of an effective intervention model: (1) research based, (2) directive, (3) correctly administered (by trained professionals), (4) targeted, and (5) timely (Buffum et al., 2012), plus it must be differentiated. Different teachers need support in different areas. The model should be fluid enough to allow teachers to identify potential areas for growth, and they should receive the resources

necessary to progress in their learning. Figure 6.4 (page 146) shows the necessary components of professional development in a competency-based learning system.

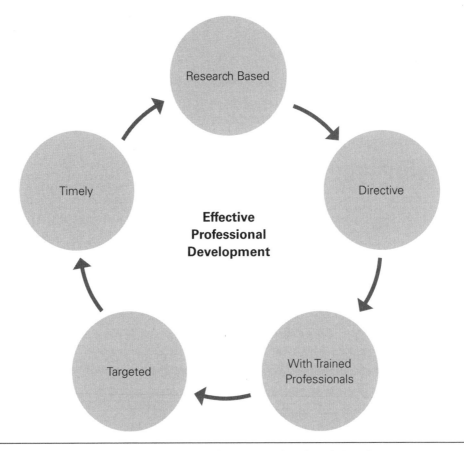

Figure 6.4: Integral components of effective professional development.

Implementing a competency-based learning system requires a high level of differentiation in the school's instruction and assessment practices. It is therefore necessary to build structures within the school schedule to support this work. These structures are necessary for both students and teachers, and if done collaboratively, provide the foundation for teachers to meet each student where he or she is and the support necessary for the student's continued progress along an individual learning continuum.

Reflection Questions

Consider the following four reflection questions with your team.

1. Schedules traditionally inhibit innovation in schools due to fixed components. How could our schedule evolve to allow for a more

collaborative approach to meeting the needs of all learners? How involved are teachers in developing the master schedule?

2.   Time for support and extension embedded within the school day is necessary. Do you allocate time to provide opportunities for individualized support or extension to ensure each student moves forward in his or her learning progression? Is this available for all students every day?

3.   Analysis of student growth should be consistent and inform next steps for all students. Do you have processes in place that allow you to monitor each student in your school? Do collaborative teams review these data regularly and make instructional changes based on them?

4.   Human resources must support student learning in new and creative ways. Do all staff members participate in providing students support and opportunities for extension in your school? Are students working with the teachers who best support their learning (not necessarily their homeroom teacher) based on available data?

CHAPTER 7

Sustaining the Change Process

A well-known quote on change by playwright George Bernard Shaw states, "Progress is impossible without change, and those who cannot change their minds cannot change anything." Change can be a particularly difficult task to undertake in a school setting, an environment often entrenched in traditions, policies, and deeply rooted beliefs and values. Now that we have introduced competency-based learning and how it connects to the four essential questions of a PLC (DuFour et al., 2016), it is time to shift our focus to how to make the change from traditional to competency-based learning. Schools must start by analyzing the change process itself in the context of the work ahead. This chapter focuses on change management in the school setting. Readers will learn how to sustain the change process as they begin to evolve from a traditional to a competency-based learning system.

Building the Case for Change

There comes a point when every leader is faced with the opportunity and need for change in order to ensure the survival of the organization. For some, the opportunity presents itself before change is needed, but for others, it comes too late, if it comes at all. Imagine what it would have been like to be the CEO of a U.S. home entertainment rental chain in 1997. With the declining cost of VCRs in the 1980s, the 1990s saw a sharp revenue increase in the home entertainment business. Mom-and-pop movie and video game rental stores appeared on every corner in America, fighting for sales with national chain stores that could offer the same service with better selection at a lower price point. In the late 1980s and early 1990s, home entertainment rental stores offered American consumers the opportunity to bring the movie experience into their living rooms, adding convenience to their lives and lowering their cost to provide their families the full movie experience.

The home entertainment rental model was simple: stock as many movie and video game titles as could physically fit in the store and make them available for single or multiday rentals to customers. As the 1990s wore on, these stores got larger and larger. Many started stocking multiple copies of recent releases only to sell them used to customers later when demand for the titles subsided. That CEO seemed to have a business model built to last.

Around 2000 or about five years before that peak, a new technology would ultimately threaten the way home entertainment rental chains operate. The Internet was an opportunity for the change CEOs and small-business owners needed to embrace to ensure the survival of their businesses. But the CEOs and small-business owners didn't capitalize on the opportunity. In the early 2000s, home entertainment business people saw the Internet as simply a novelty for computer programmers to share files, data, and images. It would be another five years before the Internet had the capability to stream video media on a massive scale, and this ultimately would become the game changer for the entire home entertainment rental industry. By then, other smaller start-up companies who invested early in the Internet put the rental companies out of business for good, replacing the rental model with one built on streaming and on-demand availability of media content to consumers right from their Internet device. Derek Khanna (2013) summarized the dilemma that these companies faced as byproducts of dynamic competition. Khanna wrote, "The ups and downs of winners and losers in the market is evidence of dynamic competition—exactly what the free market empowers. The failure of a leading market power and the rise of a new market power with a different market model, that consumers seem to prefer, is evidence of the market working. Consumers win when companies rise and fall and new market models compete with old market models."

The CEO should have recognized the need for change earlier, but didn't. By the time the CEO was ready to adjust the model, others had already taken away the market share.

Similar to the home entertainment rental industry, the music industry also encountered its own need for change in the late 1990s and early 2000s. It was then that the Internet began breeding peer-to-peer file-sharing networks that allowed consumers to easily share music files with others. Fear quickly broke out in the music industry as the prospect that consumers wouldn't have to pay for their music started to become a reality. Before these file-sharing networks could gain ground in the industry however, record labels brought them to court over copyright infringement and were all but disbanded. This result gave major music industry leaders the ability to capitalize on the Internet to change their business models to promote the long-term health and sustainability of their organizations.

Competency-based learning has the potential to do for the education industry what the Internet did for the entertainment and music industries. In today's society, there exists a huge disconnect between how employers and secondary schools define college and career readiness. Schools are steeped in tradition, much like the antiquated video rental store from the 1990s. The need for change is strong with schools, but leading a school through the change process is not easy. A school leader's journey to help his or her school make the shift from traditional to competency-based learning will be filled with ups and downs. It will require leaders to display grit, determination, and resilience. It is a significant shift for teachers, students, and parents alike. It is messy. No matter how much advance planning and preparation a staff completes in anticipation of the change, many will feel a sense of, as Rick DuFour describes in his professional development work, building the plane while flying it in those first few years of implementation. To best capitalize on the opportunity that competency-based learning presents, school leaders must develop the capacity to operate in the face of adversity, stay true to their ideals and to the model, and trust that teachers will stand with them so that together they will face the challenges that lie ahead and find a way to work through them as a school community. To be successful, school leaders need a change-management model to help them sustain the change process from traditional to competency-based learning in their schools.

> **Competency-based learning has the potential to do for the education industry what the Internet did for the entertainment and music industries.**

Learning From Penguins

Since the mid 1990s, the business world turned to the change-management model John P. Kotter (1996) first developed at Harvard Business School. The model is based on an eight-step process that school leaders can use as a framework to help build a successful plan for change management in their own schools. John P. Kotter and Holger Rathgeber (2005) explain their change-management process in a fable about a colony of penguins who must decide how to respond when they discover their iceberg is melting. In the fable, it is the initial work of one penguin scout who made the important realization that life as the colony knew it was about to change. He began the process to make others aware of the problem and developed a plan to help the colony move forward from this potential threat. As one might imagine, not all in the colony took the news well. The fable is a microcosm of how individuals react in the face of change and the change process. Kotter and Rathgeber (2005) outline eight steps to successful change management, shown in figure 7.1.

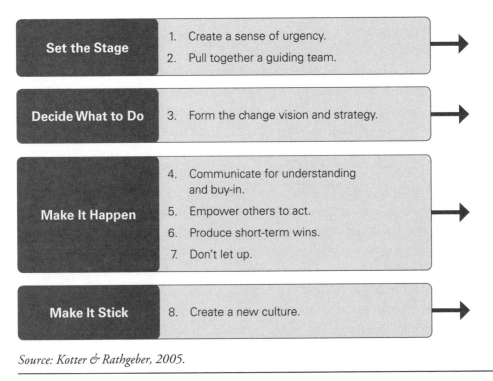

Source: Kotter & Rathgeber, 2005.

Figure 7.1: Eight steps for successful change management.

Let's examine the eight steps of successful change management.

Step 1: Create a Sense of Urgency

To initiate the shift from traditional to competency-based learning, school leaders must first focus their efforts on helping all school stakeholders (teachers, students, parents, and policymakers) recognize the need for the shift and why it cannot wait. There is a growing movement toward competency-based learning models in all schools. What started in small states (like New Hampshire and Iowa) as policy recommendations to develop proficiency and competency-based learning high school curricula has quickly become a disruptor to the entire K–20 education system—with the same significance and magnitude the assembly line had to the manufacturing industry at the turn of the 20th century and the peer-to-peer file sharing networks had to the music industry at the close of the 20th century. According to a 2016 International Association for K–12 Online Learning (iNACOL) report, all but five states in the United States had at least some level of policy in place at the state level to support competency-based learning.

Clayton M. Christensen (n.d.) defines *disruptive innovation* as "a process by which a product or service takes root initially in simple applications at the bottom of a market and then relentlessly moves up market, eventually displacing established competitors." Michelle R. Weise and Clayton M. Christensen (2014) explain why competency-based learning has become such a disruptor for the education system, particularly for higher education:

> In business, companies tend to innovate faster than their customers' needs evolve. Most end up producing products or services that are too sophisticated, too expensive, or too complicated for many customers in their market. They pursue these sustaining innovations because this is what has historically helped them succeed: by charging the highest prices to their most demanding and sophisticated customers, companies achieve greater profitability. Inevitably, though, they overshoot the performance needs of their customers and, at the same time, unwittingly open the door to disruptive innovations at the bottom of the market. A disruptive innovation gains traction by initially offering simpler, more affordable, and more convenient products and services to nonconsumers, people for whom the alternative is nothing at all. (p. 1)

According to Robert Kelchen (2015), as the cost of education continues to rise both in public and private K–12 schools, colleges, and universities, many are turning to competency-based learning models to streamline operations, restructure programming and services, and ultimately provide a more personalized and customizable product at a lower cost to consumers (students). Schools that don't recognize the strength of this movement may become obsolete (or close) in just a short amount of time, the same way that the home entertainment rental industry went bankrupt.

iNACOL (n.d.) believes so strongly in competency-based learning and its power to transform learning it has become a major focus. Since at least 2005, iNACOL promoted competency-based learning as a catalyst for new learning models and used it to transform its national policy. The following iNACOL (n.d.) initiatives pave the way for schools to move to a competency-based learning model.

- ▸ Replacing seat time with competency-based learning systems
- ▸ Redesigning accountability to support competency-based learning
- ▸ Improving access to educational opportunities and multiple pathways
- ▸ Providing fair and adequate funding
- ▸ Modernizing human capital systems to support next-generation educators
- ▸ Improving technology infrastructure and increasing broadband access

- ▶ Shifting educational learning content to digital and open educational resources (OERs)

- ▶ Providing good governance of student data to ensure privacy and security

- ▶ Ensuring quality in blended and online learning with a focus on outcomes

In December 2015, President Barack Obama signed the Every Student Succeeds Act (ESSA), legislation to replace the No Child Left Behind Act (NCLB, 2002). ESSA creates opportunities for states to develop personalized learning models that hold all students to high academic standards and prepare all students for success in college and careers. States quickly responded by developing better policies and programs to support competency-based learning work in schools and districts.

At its Center for Policy Advocacy, iNACOL (n.d.) has developed several state recommendations in response to ESSA. These recommendations mirror some of the same strategies discussed throughout this book.

> Create innovation zones to create room in state policy for school districts to innovate and implement new learning models.

> Convene a competency-based education task force to identify barriers and opportunities, and to provide a feedback loop.

> Provide flexibility to school districts to allow students to earn credits on demonstrated mastery.

> Launch pilot programs and planning grants to support personalized, competency-based learning models.

> Create policies that enable multiple pathways to earning credits and to graduation.

> Ensure mastery by implementing proficiency-based diplomas.

> Redesign systems of assessments to support student-centered learning.

> Create next generation accountability models focused on enabling continuous improvement.

> Build local capacity to transform education, connecting districts with research and experts, technical assistance, specialized training and peer learning networks. (iNACOL, n.d.)

Now is the time for schools to become part of this movement. As the ancient Chinese proverb suggests, "The best time to plant a tree was twenty years ago. The second best time is now." See also *Responding to the Every Student Succeeds Act With the PLC at Work Process* (DuFour, Reeves, & DuFour, 2018).

Step 2: Pull Together the Guiding Team

Two of the most popular ways for schools to implement change is by way of a top-down approach or a ground-up approach. With a *top-down* approach, the vision or direction for change work comes from above—from policymakers, the school district office, or the school leader's office. Stakeholders (in this case, teachers, students, and parents) generally have little to say about the *what* or *why* of the change, but are often included in the *how* of the change. This approach often yields a faster implementation time line, but it can be difficult to create buy-in from stakeholders to sustain the change beyond the initial phases.

In contrast, a *ground-up* approach often starts with individual classroom teachers or teacher teams implementing a change, and that change spreads to larger teacher groups until it becomes a schoolwide or systemwide initiative. This approach has an advantage over a top-down approach because it cultivates a high degree of buy-in from stakeholders. However, it comes at a cost, with two major disadvantages compared to the top-down approach. First, this type of approach to change takes a considerable amount of time, very likely far exceeding the time line for the top-down model. The second disadvantage is a result of the extended implementation time line; it can produce a high degree of variability from teacher to teacher, classroom to classroom, and grade level to grade level as it expands unless there is an oversight committee to prevent such discrepancies.

The best approach for a competency-based learning school reform initiative is actually a hybrid of the top-down and ground-up approaches. Such a model would start with a school or district developing a vision or strategic plan for the shift to a competency-based learning model. In that strategic plan, the school or district should commit to implementing the change over the next several years. That work could include the following.

- ▶ **Policy and procedure revisions:** Review and update existing school or district policies and procedures to best fit the competency-based learning philosophy.

- ▶ **Financial commitments:** Prepare for potential funding issues that may arise as a result of the shifts in personnel, supply, and technology needs.

- ▶ **Professional development:** Commit to provide training necessary for existing and new staff over several years.

After making these initial commitments, the school or district should form a guiding team to oversee the scope and sequence of the entire change process. Kotter and Rathgeber (2005) note that the guiding team is a powerful group that should possess the following qualities: "leadership skills, credibility, communications ability, authority, analytical skills, and a sense of urgency" (p. 130). While the makeup of every team will be different, there are a few personality types to consider when selecting team members (see figure 7.2).

Figure 7.2: Guiding team members' personality types.

Let's take a closer look at the various personality types to consider for your school or district guiding team.

Smart Leaders

Smart leaders are staff members who have built a positive reputation in the school community for their leadership skills, authority, and credibility. They may be new to the school or district, or they may come from the existing ranks. Some of the best smart leaders on a guiding team are not administrators but rather teacher leaders. Richard DuFour and Michael Fullan (2013) support this claim:

> Sustaining systemic improvement, however, relies less on the brilliance of a charismatic leader and more on the task of creating dispersed, widely shared leadership that supports an organizational system and culture that enables people throughout the organization to succeed at what they are being asked to do. (p. 64)

These are often teachers who play (or have played) an important leadership role for the school, such as a team leader, schoolwide committee chair, or project manager for a project or initiative. Teacher leaders bring a high degree of credibility to the team and also help foster buy-in from all stakeholders as the change process moves forward.

Data Hounds

Data hounds are individuals in a school or school district who are the local experts at all aspects of data collection, data management, and data reporting. They are generally classroom teachers, team leaders, or curriculum coordinators who have historically managed large amounts of classroom data or data for their team or school. Data hounds will need access to professionals skilled with database organization and management as this will become an important resource for the data hounds as the work develops. The data hounds play an important role for the guiding team by helping the members identify the data and data-collection techniques to monitor the progress and effectiveness of the shift to competency-based learning.

Public Relations Masterminds

The public relations masterminds will assume responsibility for communication of the *how*, *when*, and *what* of the change process. The *how* should include multiple communication vehicles. In addition to the standard newsletter, newspaper articles, and parent information events, give consideration and attention to various forms of social media, a popular way for teachers, students, parents, and community members to receive information and engage in dialogue regarding the change process. Public relations masterminds use their skill sets to determine the best time (or the *when*) to release information as well as what information to release. Putting out too little on a topic (the *what*) leads people to make assumptions, but putting out too much information all at once can become overwhelming. The public relations masterminds find the delicate balance between these two extremes.

Go-Getters

The go-getters balance a guiding team by ensuring that a sense of urgency is brought to the work. Go-getters can be teachers, parents, students, or administrators comfortable operating in the change environment. They understand that not all aspects of the plan are ironed out prior to implementation, and they are comfortable working in a messy environment through a transition process. Go-getters are easily identifiable because they historically are the early adopters in school and district initiatives. They are typically the first to volunteer to be on committees or study groups. A go-getter's primary responsibility on the team is to manage the time line for change and ensure work is not getting stalled or diverted along the way.

In the following practitioner perspective, a superintendent shares some of the strategies he employed to shepherd his Michigan school district through the change-management process as it transitioned to a competency-based learning model.

Practitioner Perspective:
David M. Richards, Superintendent, Fraser Public Schools, Michigan

At Fraser Public Schools in Macomb County, Michigan, the primary goal of our district strategic plan is to develop a school system that allows students to "move on when ready." Meaning, as a student demonstrates mastery in a content area, he or she is able to gain access to the next level of resources regardless of the amount of time required to demonstrate proficiency.

When we began this process, our leadership team and staff spent a great deal of time talking through our *why* and establishing our shared belief that this level of change was critical to our sustainability and success going forward. In the beginning stages of this process, we spent purposeful energy talking through our mission (What is our purpose?) and our vision (What is our desired state we seek to become?). As we developed our common language and belief system in what we believed the new model of our school district needed to be, it became evident that we needed to build a shared vision among our staff, board of education, parents, students, and community leaders.

As our district's learning environment continues to go through this transformation, our leaders are faced with the challenge of managing the transition and tending to the personal and professional needs of the staff. One critical factor that has supported our work has been the realization that in order for there to be a new beginning, there has to be an end (Bridges, 2009). Meaning, in order for our staff to adjust their instructional strategies and practices, we need to have a purposeful end to many of the current practices. We refer to this as *organized abandonment*. What is it we can stop doing in order to begin doing the new work? By remaining aware of the need to discontinue certain work, it has allowed us to keep a focus on leveraging our time and resources on the right work and at the right time. This focus has also allowed us to remain cognizant of the human side of the transition process.

Throughout the change process, as leaders, we need to be mindful of the human impact the change is having on staff. We are asking them to move away from what has defined their successful careers as master teachers and shift to a new model of learning where they are facilitators and coauthors of student academic progressions. As staff go through this process, we need to care for their emotional needs as they begin to take instructional risks, integrate technology, reimagine their daily routine, and begin transforming their role. In many ways, we are requiring staff to experience the five stages of grief, which over the years in my own professional practice I have come to define as (1) denial—"This too shall pass," (2) anger—"What was wrong with what we were doing?" (3) bargaining—"Is there any way I can keep doing what I was doing?" (4) depression—"I miss the good ol' days," and (5) acceptance—"This is inevitable." As such, being quick to listen to their concerns and being empathetic to what they are experiencing provides much-needed support in the change process.

One example of how our leadership team responded to the human side of the transformation was in the purposeful professional development we provided throughout the journey. Teachers were made aware of the training opportunities available with the expectation that our building principals and central office staff would be modeling the instructional strategies and learning we would expect from our teachers. The new expectations for high-impact teaching strategies (Smith, Chavez, & Seaman, 2012) were modeled for staff by administrators prior to being implemented in our classrooms. By doing so, staff concerns de-escalated, knowing our transformation process would not be done within a *gotcha* environment. The result was an increased confidence in the change process and our redesign efforts. (D. M. Richards, personal communication, October 2016)

Step 3: Form the Change Vision and Strategy

To foster buy-in, create a sense of urgency for change, and make that future a reality for all stakeholders. The guiding team must spend time building the case for competency-based learning and how shifting to this philosophy will be different from staying the course with the traditional school model. DuFour and Fullan (2013) write, "Visions of what the system can become someday must be converted into specific steps that can be taken today to generate forward momentum" (p. 66). They go on to state, "The long journey must be broken down into immediate, doable steps. Vague generalities must be redefined into specific indicators to clarify how people throughout the organization can monitor their progress" (p. 66).

Applying DuFour and Fullan's (2013) argument to the competency-based learning strategic planning process, an effective change vision and strategy should answer the following three key questions.

1. What are the limitations in the current school model that a shift to a competency-based learning model will address?

2. With what time line will we implement the change?

3. What outcomes will we use to measure the effectiveness of the change?

Using a protocol can help the team focus and refine its vision and strategic planning phase work. In 2002, the National School Reform Faculty (NSRF), Harmony Education Center, published a particularly helpful protocol for schools engaging in the shift to competency-based learning. For team use in the early planning stages of a reform initiative, future protocol (also known as back to the future) is structured similarly to NSRF's tuning protocol, which teams can use as a structure to review student work. Through a series of prompts, the future protocol (NSRF, 2002) can help the team meet the following goals:

> › To expand and clarify the vision of what a group or individual is really trying to accomplish

> › To identify opportunities and avenues for focused improvement
>
> › To guide purposeful actions and reduce wasted efforts (p. 1)

One of the biggest reasons a school is unsuccessful in a shift to competency-based learning happens at this critical strategic planning and vision step because the school or guiding team does not take the time to outline a clear vision and detailed strategy for that future reality, leaving too much to interpretation. As a result, later in the change process, the team sometimes makes concessions and compromises with stakeholders that take the school off its intended course. This happens in schools that don't clearly outline their future reality only to find that policymakers do not enact a specific enough policy to make the new model enforceable, or schools that do not take the time to fully explain the new future reality to staff only to find staff trying to continue to operate in the same manner they did prior to the change process. The strategic planning process is integral to the success of the entire implementation plan.

Step 4: Communicate for Understanding and Buy-In

We argue that communication is the edge of a sword by which a leader will live or die. Mastering the art of effective communication is a delicate balance of patience and attention to detail. Communicate too little and people will draw conclusions from their own assumptions. Communicate too much and it can become overwhelming for people, diverting or detracting from the school's change-management work. There exists between these two extremes a very narrow window that represents an appropriate amount of communication, and it is up to the leader and the guiding team to identify it and use it to their advantage to advance their work. In the shift from a traditional to a competency-based learning model in a school or district, it is essential that as many stakeholders as possible understand and accept the vision and change strategy.

Earlier in this chapter, we discussed the need for a guiding team member dedicated to overseeing the public relations and communication strategies for the change process. This public relations mastermind cannot work alone, but rather will work with guiding team members and key stakeholders in the school community to implement a comprehensive communications plan. When developing this plan, the first questions to consider are, What messages need to get to stakeholders? At what points during the change-management process should those messages be delivered?

Answering these questions is an opportunity to think about the information stakeholders require to accept the vision and strategy for the shift from traditional to competency-based learning. Not all information needs to be released at the onset of the change process. Rather, it may be helpful to stagger the information over a longer period of time. Here is an example of how this could be done (see figure 7.3).

Month	Communication Focus
September	Help stakeholders understand what competency is, how to develop competencies for each course or grade level, and how competencies connect to each other as part of a K–12 learning progression.
November	Help stakeholders understand how teachers use the DOK concept to develop rubrics to assess student work.
January	Help stakeholders understand how teachers develop and implement performance tasks to measure student learning and how these tasks differ from more traditional assessments.
March	Help stakeholders understand how a criterion-referenced grading system with rubrics differs from a percentage-based grading system.
May	Help stakeholders understand the bigger picture of how grading and reporting in a competency-based learning model will look as a student moves through the K–12 system and ultimately to higher education or a career.

Figure 7.3: Sample first-year competency-based learning implementation communication plan.

In this example, note that the guiding team identifies a specific theme for each two-month period. Stakeholders need to understand these critical topics or themes to accept the vision and strategic plan. From this outline, the public relations mastermind could begin to develop the specific communications strategies for each theme.

Another question when developing a communication plan is this: How should the messages be delivered to stakeholders? As noted earlier in this chapter, communication strategies should not only include a variety of media—from traditional press releases and newsletter articles to information nights and coffee-hour discussions—but also through a strong presence with various forms of social media. The public relations mastermind and the guiding team should pay special attention to how their community stakeholders like to receive information, and which media will generate the most stakeholder engagement and dialogue.

The last question to answer is, What steps will we take to ensure that stakeholders are receiving and interpreting messages correctly? This is perhaps the most critical question a school leader or guiding team must consider when developing a change-management plan for competency-based learning implementation. How to answer this question may differ greatly from school to school or district to district based on the resources available, but steps must be taken to collect data and build a strategy to act if messages are not having the desired impact.

Step 5: Empower Others to Act

Earlier in this chapter when introducing how to form a guiding team, we discussed the advantages and disadvantages of the top-down and ground-up approaches to systemic change. We believe that a hybrid of that model or one that empowers others to act and be part of the change process is best. Kotter and Rathgeber (2005) note this as a critical part of the change-management process, suggesting that school leaders and the guiding team need to "remove as many barriers as possible so that those who want to make the vision a reality can do so" (p. 131). DuFour and Fullan (2013) introduce the *loose-tight dilemma* that many school leaders will face when trying to find ways to empower others to act. They write, "The challenge at all levels of the system is to navigate this apparent dichotomy and find the appropriate balance between tight and loose, between assertiveness and autonomy" (p. 33).

One of the easiest ways for a school leader to accomplish this step is to identify the early adopters and go-getters on their staff ready to implement aspects of the competency-based learning model earlier than their peers, give them some guardrails to operate within, and then step to the side and let them innovate with a pilot-program initiative.

Pilot programs help school leaders develop trust and support for the change process while providing an opportunity to collect some early data to support the change. This can go a long way toward silencing some critics of the work. DuFour and Fullan (2013) write, "Effective change involves developing an engaging process that draws people into something that the vast majority of people find worthwhile while the number of skeptics becomes smaller and smaller" (p. 33). In small schools, a pilot could be limited to individual teachers, small teacher groups, or a grade-level team. Larger schools and districts could implement a pilot competency-based learning model using a school-within-a-school approach or opt to just put one or a handful of schools on such a program.

Step 6: Produce Short-Term Wins

Undoubtedly, the shift from a traditional to a competency-based learning model will take years of careful planning and implementation. The journey of this shift may outlast some of the stakeholders. When starting this work, school leaders run the risk of some stakeholders dismissing it as a fad or a new initiative that won't last. To keep everyone laser focused on the long-term goals and products, school leaders must build in opportunities to produce and celebrate short-term wins along the journey. As DuFour and Fullan (2013) note, "Small wins translate long-range goals that many in the organization may dismiss as unrealistic into doable, short-term tasks that people recognize they can accomplish. Each incremental step forward helps build momentum for the change" (p. 74).

These small wins do not have to be significant events or milestones. Kotter and Rathgeber (2005) refer to them simply as "visible, unambiguous successes" (p. 131). Here are some examples of short-term successes that schools shifting to competency-based learning may celebrate along the way.

▸ Celebrate reaching staff consensus on schoolwide procedures, practices, or organizational structures that will support competency-based learning work.

▸ Celebrate the development and adoption of common competency statements from course to course or grade level to grade level.

▸ Celebrate the development and adoption of common course-based and grade-level-specific rubrics and performance tasks.

▸ Celebrate short-term wins with student data.

▸ Celebrate the individual teachers and collaborative teams that practice innovative classroom instruction and assessment techniques.

Step 7: Don't Let Up

School leaders committed to making long-lasting changes in their schools press harder and faster, and they are relentless in their pursuit to initiate and support the change process with resilience and determination. They demonstrate *resolute leadership*, a phrase DuFour and Fullan (2013) define as "leaders with the collective efficacy that enables them to persist in the face of problems, plateaus, and paradoxes" (p. 77). Resolute leaders don't let up; they maintain their laser-like focus on obtaining the guiding team's vision for the future reality during the vision and strategic planning process. These leaders don't let others divert their attention or sideline them from staying the course. One of the biggest threats to the resolute leader is the *blocker*—the stakeholder who is looking to thwart, divert, or slow down the change process. School leaders may find many types of blockers in their efforts to foster a competency-based learning culture. Following are just a few examples of the common blocker types.

> **School leaders committed to making long-lasting changes in their schools press harder and faster, and they are relentless in their pursuit to initiate and support the change process with resilience and determination.**

The *overworked-teacher blocker* is one who attempts to negatively impact change-process momentum by claiming that the competency-based learning model is too much work and he or she does not have the time to do it successfully. These blockers often suggest they need more training or time to process the training they already received. In team meetings, instead of rolling up their sleeves and engaging in teamwork, they look for opportunities to divert the meeting's focus to a discussion of why the team should do the work at all. When asked to complete a task, they argue that they don't have the time to do it because they have to attend to their other job responsibilities. Overworked-teacher blockers often have a difficult time working in a collaborative environment and feel uncomfortable with the additional layer of accountability from team members that environment fosters. These blockers would much prefer to go back to the traditional system where they could be left alone to instruct and assess students as they see fit—with little or no accountability for how they go about it. School leaders can overcome the tactics of overworked-teacher blockers by practicing resolute leadership and continuing to hold them accountable to their team and to the work of the school.

The *concerned-for-their-child's-transcript parents* are blockers who are uncomfortable with any school structure that looks fundamentally different from the structure they experienced when they attended school. They question any school change that might impact their children's high school transcript because it may impact their child's postsecondary plans. This can include changes at the elementary and middle school level as well as the high school level. These blockers firmly believe colleges and universities approach admissions the same way they did when the parent applied many years ago. They also believe the best way to cultivate college readiness is to raise students in a culture that promotes behaviorism and adherence to the rules as a compliance tool. The best way for a school leader to overcome these blockers is to develop trust and working relationships with them. The school leader should also help these blockers understand that in an effective competency-based learning model, colleges and universities will not receive different information but rather more enhanced information than they have historically.

The *guinea-pig student blocker* is a student who believes that any school change should wait until after he or she graduates because the student does not want to be a guinea pig in a large scientific experiment. These blockers firmly believe that any change may negatively impact their educational experience if it is tied to reporting grades. They are often fueled by their parents, who often share their viewpoint on the potential impact the change may ultimately have on their ability to get into the college of their choice. Students who know how to *play the game of school* in a traditional points-accumulation model may be apprehensive to move to a competency-based learning model where their ability to display good academic behaviors may not correlate to good grades. Guinea-pig student blockers can often be the easiest group of blockers for a school leader to work with if the school leader builds in opportunities for students to have choice and voice in their learning—one of the hallmarks of an effective personalized learning model like competency-based learning.

When faced with these and any other host of blockers, effective and resolute school leaders don't get discouraged. They continue to work toward engaging stakeholders in the change process, looking for continuous improvement with a focus on innovation. The PLC framework is an important component of meeting and sustaining any successful change-management or sustainability plan to move a school from a traditional to a competency-based learning model.

Step 8: Create a New Culture

Since the mid-1980s and for a variety of reasons, the American education system has left many veteran teachers skeptical or, at the very least, hesitant to embrace change. Too often, a new administrator brings some new ideas to the school, which then lead to new initiatives, new programs, and ultimately a new direction and focus. Douglas Reeves (2010) refers to this phenomenon as *initiative fatigue*, and goes on to suggest that it occurs when teachers get tired of starting new initiatives without ever finishing the ones they spent time developing from the previous years. A school leader doesn't want competency-based learning to be the latest fad or trend. While it will take time to develop, the ultimate success of the competency-based learning model will occur when the philosophy becomes ingrained in the fabric of the school culture. As Kotter and Rathgeber (2005) suggest, the final step in the change-management process is to create a new culture where stakeholders "hold on to the new ways of behaving, and make sure they succeed, until they become strong enough to replace old traditions" (p. 131).

If constructed correctly, the vision and strategic planning document will help foster what DuFour and Fullan (2013) refer to as *systemness*, or "when large numbers of people at all levels identify and commit to the larger system," adding that it manifests in the following way:

> When a shared mindset is evident through common language and the knowledge of what is working and why, when large numbers of people can both walk the talk and talk the walk—these are all signs that people realize that there is a system at work and that they and others *are* the system. (p. 77)

Educators in successful competency-based learning schools come to realize that the competency-based learning model isn't something on their plate, it *is* their plate. Competency-based learning provides the foundation on which educators base all their work. The collaborative teams within the PLC become the structure by which they engage in the work. With this approach, the professional mindset of staff is so laser focused on student learning they oftentimes find it difficult to leave their school for another school that does not have the competency-based learning philosophy. It can be hard to go back.

When appropriate, school leaders should look for opportunities to start new traditions that support the competency-based learning philosophy. Popular among many competency-based learning high schools is minimizing (but not removing) the role class rank plays in the school culture. Traditionally, the top-ranked students in a class speak at graduation. A better tradition might be to invite interested students (those who want to be considered for the honor of speaking at graduation) to submit a speech in advance for a jury of students and staff to judge blindly. The best speeches could be chosen for graduation. This new tradition works to minimize an old tradition (comparing students to each other) and instead promotes a competency-based learning philosophy by suggesting that the best speeches, when judged against a standard, will be chosen for the ultimate exhibition of student work—the honor of speaking at graduation. The message is subtle, but the new tradition aligns with the new philosophy. That is how school leaders can use traditions to slowly ingrain the competency-based learning philosophy into the very fabric and culture of the school.

Reflection Questions

Consider the following eight reflection questions with your team.

1. What are some specific things that we can do to create a sense of urgency in your school for the need to move to a competency-based learning philosophy?

2. Who must be members of your guiding team to manage the change process?

3. What must be a part of your change vision? What strategies might be needed to help your guiding team operate effectively?

4. What are the most effective means of communicating to promote understanding of competency-based learning and buy-in for change?

5. How will you empower others to act?

6. What are some short-term wins your guiding team should focus on to support the change process?

7. When the going gets rough, what can you do to help your guiding team stay true to the change process and not let up?

8. How will we know when competency-based learning has become part of your school culture and not just a new initiative or fad?

CHAPTER 8

Using a School-Design Rubric to Assess Where Your School Is in Its Competency Journey

A s we have stressed throughout this book, moving a school from a traditional to a competency-based model is a journey, not an event. This journey has multiple entry points and can look different from school to school and district to district. At the beginning of the journey, it can look both overwhelming and daunting to school leaders and teachers, leaving them with critical questions such as, Where do we start? Is there a correct order to what we need to do and how we need to do it? How will we know when we have arrived at our destination? Will we ever be finished? It can get frustrating to all involved because there are no universal answers to any of these questions that apply to every school setting. This chapter focuses on thinking ahead. It examines developing an action plan to assess where a school is and where staff want to go on their competency-based learning journey. Remember, there will be areas of strength and areas for growth in every school.

> ←
>
> **Moving a school from a traditional to a competency-based model is a journey, not an event. This journey has multiple entry points and can look different from school to school and district to district.**
>
> ⟶

The intent of the rubric in this chapter is to assist teams in identifying areas of strength and necessary growth to allow teams to plan for their next steps together.

There is a strong correlation between the PLC process and competency-based learning. We believe very strongly that the most effective way to implement competency-based learning at a high level is through the PLC at Work model, but this does not preclude a school that is not a PLC from implementing competency-based learning; rather, it provides a starting point.

To aid in implementation and to help school leaders and teachers address these and many other questions that will likely arise during the journey, we developed a tool that schools can use called the competency-based learning school-design rubric. Think of this rubric as a road map. While this road map doesn't tell a school exactly how to get to the destination or where the nearest rest stop is, it does give schools insight into some of the critical junctures and ultimately the scope and sequence of the work ahead as well as what the work will look like as the school moves from an initiating to a high-performing level. This rubric will fill the same need for school leaders that rubrics fill for students. Brookhart (2013) stresses the importance of rubrics for students, stating:

> Rubrics are important because they clarify for students the qualities their work should have. This point is often expressed in terms of students understanding the learning target and criteria for success. For this reason, rubrics help teachers teach, they help coordinate instruction and assessment, and they help students learn. (p. 11)

For the school leader, this rubric clarifies the qualities that a competency-based school should have. It will help school leaders and designers develop their strategic plans for the work and coordinate the various aspects of the implementation. Ultimately, this rubric will help the school sustain its work as competency-based learning moves from a new initiative to becoming part of the culture of the school.

The competency-based learning school-design rubric is based on Sturgis's (2015) five-part definition of competency-based learning introduced at the beginning of this book.

1. Students advance upon demonstrated mastery.

2. Competencies include explicit, measurable, transferable learning objectives that empower students.

3. Assessment is meaningful and a positive learning experience for students.

4. Students receive timely, differentiated support based on their individual learning needs.

5. Learning outcomes emphasize competencies that include application and creation of knowledge, along with the development of important skills and dispositions.

Each of these parts is a competency-based learning design principle that the rubric expands on. For each principle, the rubric identifies what a K–12 school should look like at the initiating, developing, and high-performing levels. At the initiating level, a school is just starting the conversations for its journey from traditional to competency-based learning. As the school begins to adopt policies, procedures, and organizational and support structures to support the work, it moves to the developing level. When these policies, procedures, and structures are fine-tuned and standardized so that they infiltrate all aspects of school functions and operational structures, the school has moved to the performing level.

We now spend some time exploring each of the design principles for this rubric.

Principle 1: Students Move When Ready

In the current education system, we confine ourselves to measuring student learning over the course of a set period of time. In secondary schools and colleges, learning is quantified by credit hours, and these credit hours become the unit of measure used when students transition from one school to another or when employers review transcripts to gain insight into whether or not a prospective employee has obtained the necessary skills to be deemed career ready. Competency-based learning schools have moved away from the long-held belief that learning outcomes are time-bound and instead accept the idea that standards are the true measure of learning. With carefully crafted assessments that are tied to these standards and rubrics, competency-based learning schools can measure to what degree students have mastered a concept or skill. These schools have structures whereby students can advance academically upon demonstration of mastery regardless of grade level. Throughout the learning process, educators monitor the pace and progress of each student as they are challenged at their appropriate level. Students in competency-based learning schools cannot simply test out of a particular skill or course by taking one assessment. Students must produce a sufficient body of evidence from multiple measures in order to be deemed proficient.

As a school starts on its competency-based learning journey, at the onset it likely has policies in place that support standards-referenced grading and student advancement, which happens at the end of a grade level or course. Bound completely by a school calendar with strict academic terms, student learning opportunities in these schools are primarily driven and monitored by clearly defined grading terms (quarters or trimesters) and the start and end times of the school day in each grade level or course. These time-bound measures are often arbitrary, dividing a school year into smaller, equal parts. In secondary schools, it is not uncommon for grades to be calculated by averaging these quarter or trimester grades. The practice of averaging averages to get more averages in commonplace in computing overall course grades. For initiating-level competency-based learning schools, advancement happens at the end of a grade level or course when students have produced sufficient evidence to be deemed proficient based on grade level or course standards for that particular time period.

As a competency-based learning school moves to a developing level, the school is still dependent on a school-year time structure but new policies allow teachers to meet students where they are by allowing them to access the curriculum that is before or beyond grade level as needed. Teachers have the ability to manage personalized classrooms with clear academic levels, and they can group and regroup students so that they can access units that are before or beyond the grade-level curriculum. Within the existing school calendar, the school has several opportunities for students to advance along their own continuum of learning upon demonstrated mastery through blended and online learning. At the elementary level, this happens through multiage classrooms and at the secondary level, through extended learning opportunities such as apprenticeships, community service, independent study, internships, performing groups, college courses, private instruction, and extended learning opportunities.

The highest-performing competency-based learning schools have removed time as a barrier or a measurement of student learning. They have developed policies that provide students with multiple and varied opportunities to advance upon demonstrated mastery any time, any place, any way, and at any pace, unbound by a school calendar or clock. They allow students to advance beyond the school that they are in to the next level. At the elementary level, policies support multiage groupings of students and at the secondary level, extensions to higher education when students are ready based on their own learning progression. In these schools, students effectively monitor and self-assess their pace and progress through their learning. The school has a mechanism to track student pace and progress by way of a personalized learning plan. The school has an established quality-control system with clearly defined levels of proficiency that are used to determine when students are ready to move on with teacher input. See figure 8.1.

Design Principle 1: Students Move When Ready			
Big Ideas: • Policy language supports a model where students advance academically upon demonstration of mastery—regardless of grade level. • Teachers monitor the pace and progress of students as they are challenged at their appropriate level. • Students must produce sufficient evidence in order to be deemed proficient.	Notes:		
	SCALE		
Indicator	**Performing** **School meets all characteristics in Developing and improves by . . .**	**Developing** **School meets all characteristics in Initiating and improves by . . .**	**Initiating** **School characteristics include . . .**
Policy Language	Policies provide students with multiple and varied opportunities to advance on demonstrated mastery any time, any place, any way, and at any pace, unbound by a school calendar or clock. They allow students to advance beyond the school that they are in to the next level. At the elementary level, policies support multiage groupings of students and at the secondary level, extensions to higher education when students are ready based on their own learning progression.	Policies allow teachers to meet students where they are by allowing them to access the curriculum that is before or beyond grade level as needed.	Policies support standards-referenced grading and student advancement, which happens at the end of a grade level or course.

Figure 8.1: Rubric for competency-based learning school-design principle 1.   continued ➜

Monitoring of Pace and Progress	The student effectively monitors and self-assesses his or her pace and progress. A mechanism exists for the school to track student pace and progress, such as a personalized learning plan.	Teachers have the ability to manage personalized classrooms with clear academic levels. They can group and regroup students so that they can access units that are before or beyond the grade-level curriculum as needed.	The school calendar drives student learning opportunities and monitoring by the school calendar and the start and end times of the school day in each grade level or course.
Evidence of Proficiency	The school has an established quality-control system with clearly defined levels of proficiency that teachers use to determine when students are ready to move on with teacher input.	Within the existing school calendar, the school has several opportunities for students to advance along their own continuum of learning upon demonstrated mastery through blended and online learning. At the elementary level, this happens through multiage classrooms and at the secondary level, through extended learning opportunities such as apprenticeships, community service, independent study, internships, performing groups, college courses, private instruction, and extended learning opportunities.	Students advance at the end of a grade level or course when they have produced sufficient evidence to be deemed proficient based on grade-level or course standards.

Principle 2: Competencies Include Explicit, Measurable, Transferable Learning Objectives That Empower Students

A cook would tell you that a superior dish starts with quality ingredients. You can't have a praiseworthy chicken soup without fresh vegetables and quality meat. You can't prepare a great New England lobster roll without the freshest of seafood and bread. As discussed in chapter 3, competencies provide the backbone and foundation for a competency-based learning system. Competencies act as the quality ingredients that will lead to a tasty dish.

Competencies act as the quality ingredients that will lead to a tasty dish.

In competency-based schools, there exists an extensive framework of standards, learning progressions, and competencies, aligned with national, state, and local frameworks, that have been mapped K–12 as a continuum of learning progressions and include both academic skills that are transferable across content areas as well as habits of learning behaviors. Students in these schools know exactly where they are and what they need to do next because the school or school district has established clear transitional and graduation competencies that articulate what it means to be ready for the next level. At all levels in the K–12 system, competencies have a high level of cognitive demand and are applicable to real-life situations because they require an understanding of relationships among theories, principles, and concepts. Through these competencies, students are expected to have a deep understanding of content as well as application of knowledge to a variety of settings by promoting complex connections through creating, analyzing, designing, proving, developing, and formulating.

At the highest level, effective competency-based learning schools leverage the power of teacher collaboration to calibrate competencies across subject areas and grade levels throughout the school or school system to ensure a common understanding of proficiency by looking at student work. Collaborative teams are laser focused on calibration. As DuFour, Eaker, and Many (2006) write, "Professional learning communities create an intensive focus on learning by clarifying exactly what students are to learn and by monitoring each student's learning on a timely basis" (p. 43). Collaborative teams in effective competency-based learning schools answer the first two critical questions of a PLC: What do we want our students to learn and be able to do, and how will we know when each student has learned it (DuFour et al., 2016)? We do this by looking at how the subject area or grade level fits into the larger scope and sequence of the system's established K–12 learning progressions and competencies.

This alignment and awareness for system thinking is what best separates developing from high-performing competency-based learning schools. See figure 8.2.

Design Principle 2: Competencies Include Explicit, Measurable, Transferable Learning Objectives That Empower Students			
Big Ideas: • There is a framework of standards, learning progressions, and competencies aligned with national, state, or local frameworks. • Competencies have a high level of cognitive demand and rigor. • There is a system to calibrate the competencies across grade levels and content areas to ensure a common understanding of proficiency.	**Notes:**		
Indicator	**SCALE**		
	Performing School meets all characteristics in Developing and improves by . . .	**Developing** School meets all characteristics in Initiating and improves by . . .	**Initiating** School characteristics include . . .
Framework of Standards and Competencies	Competencies are applicable to real-life situations and require an understanding of relationships among theories, principles, and concepts.	The school has expanded the framework of standards to include competencies with performance assessments and include both academic skills that are transferable across content areas as well as habits of learning behaviors. These are mapped K–12 as a continuum of learning progressions based on the standards so that students know exactly where they are and what they need to do next. The school district has established clear transitional and graduation competencies that articulate what it means to be ready for the next level.	The school has developed a framework of standards that are aligned with national, state, and local frameworks in the school and are limited to scope and sequence of the textbook, program, or resource.

Cognitive Demand	The cognitive demand of the competencies is high—they require students to have a deep understanding of content as well as application of knowledge to a variety of settings by promoting complex connections through creating, analyzing, designing, proving, developing, and formulating.	The cognitive demand of the competencies is medium—they ask students to show what they know in limited ways through identifying, defining, constructing, summarizing, displaying, listing, or recognizing. Teachers occasionally ask students to create conceptual connections and exhibit a level of understanding that is beyond the stated facts or literal interpretation through reasoning, planning, interpreting, hypothesizing, investigating, and explaining.	The cognitive demand of the competencies is low—they ask for routine or rote thinking, and require basic recall of information, facts, definitions, and other similar simple tasks and procedures.
System of Calibration	In collaborative teams, teachers regularly engage in the calibration of the competencies across grade levels and content areas to ensure a common understanding of proficiency by looking at student work.	Standards-referenced grading makes it clear what students know and how they are progressing. Teachers have a shared understanding of proficiency by grade level and course by looking at student work.	The competencies are very specific to the facts in the content. The school has selected a taxonomy to have common language about depth of knowledge and has started a process to identify the competencies for each grade level, content area, and course.

Figure 8.2: Rubric for competency-based learning school-design principle 2.

Principle 3: Assessment Is Meaningful

Assessment and grading are often held up as two hallmarks of tradition in schools today. If a school is to become truly effective at competency-based learning, it must be willing to look at its traditions with an open mind and be willing to make adjustments and changes as needed to make its assessment and grading practices amenable to a philosophy where students are judged with a body of evidence against a standard and not against each other. Many schools that attempt to move from traditional to competency-based learning stumble at this design principle if they try to compromise with their stakeholders by maintaining some of the traditional assessment and grading practices that have been proven to be obsolete in best preparing students to be successful in the 21st century.

In high-performing competency-based learning schools, assessment practices make extensive use of quality performance assessments and allow teachers to assess skills or concepts in a variety of ways. The CCE (2012) identifies several essential questions that quality performance assessments raise for curriculum and instruction:

> What content is most important? What do we want learners to be able to do with their learning? What evidence will show that students really understand and can apply learned content? How good is 'good enough'? What can we do to improve performance? (p. ii)

Teachers in highly effective competency-based learning schools regularly use quality performance assessments as the primary type of assessment with students to demonstrate mastery and indicate when students are proficient.

If a school is to become truly effective at competency-based learning, it must be willing to look at its traditions with an open mind and be willing to make adjustments and changes as needed.

All stakeholders in high-performing competency-based learning schools, from teachers and school leaders to students to parents, share a common belief that grades are about what students learn, not what they earn. This philosophy promotes the ideal that in order for teachers to make a judgment on student learning they must first collect a vast body of evidence from students. Grading is not a game where teachers arbitrarily award points to students but rather a professional exercise in judging evidence from student work against set criteria as outlined in a rubric. Teachers grade all assessments against these well-defined rubrics that they have developed, calibrated, and refined through collaborative team work.

The hallmark for high-performing competency-based learning schools in this particular design principle is that in PLCs, their teacher teams regularly calibrate their instruction, grading, and assessment practices to develop a common understanding of proficiency. The PLC framework allows teams to work interdependently and hold individual members of the team accountable for the work. As an added layer, these high-performing competency-based learning schools have established schoolwide or districtwide systems to hold all teachers accountable for the effective use of the common grading and assessment practices and expectations. See figure 8.3.

Design Principle 3: Assessment Is Meaningful			
Big Ideas: • Assessment practices make extensive use of quality performance assessment and allow teachers to assess skills or concepts in a variety of ways. • Grades are about what students learn, not what they earn. • Teachers regularly calibrate their instruction, grading, and assessment practices to develop a common understanding of proficiency.	**Notes:**		
Indicator	**SCALE**		
	Performing **School meets all characteristics in Developing and improves by . . .**	**Developing** **School meets all characteristics in Initiating and improves by . . .**	**Initiating** **School characteristics include . . .**
Assessment Practices	The use of quality performance assessments is widespread among all teachers and is the primary type of assessment they use with students to demonstrate mastery. Just-in-time assessments indicate when students are proficient. The school has developed the capacity for project-based learning or other ways for students to demonstrate knowledge at the highest level.	In addition to traditional assessment measures, teachers in the school make extensive use of formative assessment and some use of performance assessments—multistep assignments with clear criteria, expectations, and processes that measure how well a student transfers knowledge and applies complex skills to create or refine an original product. Students have choice about how to demonstrate their learning.	Although linked to specific competencies, assessment practices are still very traditional—predominantly paper-and-pencil tests and quizzes with no schoolwide systemic attempt to control the depth of knowledge level. Few assessments are graded against a well-defined rubric and little to no common understanding exists among teachers on what proficiency means.

Figure 8.3: Rubric for competency-based learning school-design principle 3.

continued →

Grading Practices	All assessments are graded against well-defined rubrics. The school has established a system to hold all teachers accountable for the effective use of the common grading expectations. Teachers hold each other accountable as members of a collaborative team.	Most assessments are graded against a well-defined rubric. The school has established a common set of competency-friendly grading practices. Practices include separation of formative and summative assessments, use of a rubric scale, elimination of quarter averages, and promotion of reassessment without penalty.	Few assessments are graded against a well-defined rubric. Grading practices differ greatly from teacher to teacher and grade level to grade level.
System of Calibration	Teachers collaborate regularly in teams to calibrate assessments and to use the data from them to align instruction and make greater revisions of the curriculum as well as monitor the pace and progress of individual students.	Teachers regularly collaborate to develop and calibrate these performance assessments against learning progressions by reviewing student work and monitoring the pace and progress of individual students. Teachers are beginning to align their instructional strategies with performance assessments.	Little to no common understanding exists among teachers of different grade levels and content areas on what proficiency means.

Principle 4: Students Receive Differentiated Support

Schools need comprehensive schoolwide structures to systemically address both the third and fourth critical questions of a PLC: What will we do if students haven't learned it, and what will we do if students already know it (DuFour et al., 2016)? Mattos and Buffum (2015) acknowledge two universal truths in education that teachers and schools must consider as they seek to answer these PLC questions: "Every student does not learn the same way" (p. 1) and "Every student does not develop at the same speed" (p. 2). Schools that are just beginning their competency-based learning journey recognize these truths but often have limited structures in place to ensure that all students receive regular, timely, differentiated support based on their individual learning needs. Most of the structures are limited to students who are identified for a special learning plan by way of a 504, IEP, or English learner (EL) identification or to students who are available only at certain times of the day such as lunch, before school, or after school when these structures are made available to students.

As schools continue on their competency-based learning journey, they begin to develop more comprehensive structures to ensure that *all* students, regardless of whether or not they are identified in some way, receive regular, timely, differentiated support based on their individual learning needs. These structures are offered regardless of whether or not the student is identified in some way and are scheduled in such a way so that all students can access them without conflicts in their schedule. Many schools do this by incorporating a flexible grouping time into their grade-level or schoolwide schedule where they can provide reteaching, intervention, and enrichment to students.

> **As schools continue on their competency-based learning journey, they begin to develop more comprehensive structures to ensure that *all* students, regardless of whether or not they are identified in some way, receive regular, timely, differentiated support based on their individual learning needs.**

High-performing competency-based learning schools expand upon and unify their support structure strategies, making them part of a comprehensive support structure system that can ensure that students who are not making progress receive regular, timely, differentiated support based on their individual learning needs at the time of their learning. It is not uncommon in these schools for educators who share the same students, including teachers, special educators, guidance counselors, administrators, and other specialists, to collaborate regularly in teams on these personalized, differentiated support structures for students.

In competency-based learning schools, collaborative teams need to play a critical role in monitoring these student support structures. In schools that are just beginning this work, teachers often work individually to monitor the pace and progress of their students and make instructional adjustments as necessary. As schools begin to expand on their work, teachers, through their collaborative team structure, begin to develop a shared understanding of what the typical pace and progress of a student should be throughout his or her learning and use it to monitor individual students. As schools reach the highest level of performance as a competency-based learning school there exist schoolwide systems driven by collaborative teams that monitor the individual pace and progress of students throughout their learning. School leaders use the information collected on pace and progress to help develop personalized professional development plans for teachers to improve instruction. See figure 8.4, page 180.

Design Principle 4: Students Receive Differentiated Support			
Big Ideas: • Structures exist to ensure that all students have access to and receive regular, timely, differentiated support. • There are systems to monitor the pace and progress of individual students throughout their learning.	**Notes:**		
Indicator	**SCALE**		
	Performing **School meets all characteristics in Developing and improves by . . .**	**Developing** **School meets all characteristics in Initiating and improves by . . .**	**Initiating** **School characteristics include . . .**
Support Structures	The school has a comprehensive support structure to ensure that students who are not making progress receive regular, timely, differentiated support based on their individual learning needs at the time of their learning. Professionals who share the same students, including teachers, special educators, guidance counselors, administrators, and other specialists, collaborate regularly as teams on these personalized, differentiated support structures for students.	The school has some structures in place to ensure that all students receive regular, timely, differentiated support based on their individual learning needs. These structures are offered regardless of whether or not the student is identified in some way and are scheduled in such a way so that all students can access them without conflicts in their schedule (such as a flexible learning period that all students can access).	The school has limited structures in place to ensure that all students receive regular, timely, differentiated support based on their individual learning needs. Most of the structures are limited, either to identified students (IEP, EL, 504, and so on) who require them for an education plan or to students who are available only at certain times of the day when these structures are made available in the schedule (such as lunch or after school).

| Monitoring Structures | Teams monitor the individual pace and progress of students throughout their learning. School leaders use the information collected on pace and progress to help develop personalized professional development plans for teachers to improve instruction. | Teachers have a shared understanding of what the typical pace and progress of students should be throughout their learning and use it to monitor individual students. | Teachers work individually to monitor the pace and progress of their students and make instructional adjustments as necessary. Specialists are included as necessary. |

Figure 8.4: Rubric for competency-based learning school-design principle 4.

Principle 5: Learning Outcomes Measure Both Academic Skills and Dispositions

One of the prevailing philosophies in competency-based learning schools is that academic grades must be pure, based on learning outcomes from academic skills in order to accurately report out on what a student knows and is able to do. *Academic dispositions*, the behaviors associated with learning such as effort, time management, and participation, are also important; teachers clearly define and articulate these dispositions, but they are completely separated when reported as grades. Students are held accountable for both academic skill learning outcomes and dispositions that have been identified for each grade level and course in the school or school system. Both learning outcomes and dispositions are designed so that demonstration of mastery includes application of skills and knowledge. Assessment of these skills and dispositions is ongoing, as multiple and varied opportunities exist for each. Expanded learning opportunities, including those that take place outside of the classroom and school setting, as a way for students to personalize how they will demonstrate mastery of lifelong learning skills based on their needs and life experiences in order to help them be college and career ready.

To build up to this ideal, schools that are just starting their competency-based learning journey have established learning outcomes that measure application and creation of knowledge as well as the development of important skills and dispositions. These dispositions, however, are often not defined by just one specific rubric and are typically only assessed at certain times during the year, making student ownership limited. When reported as grades, learning outcomes and dispositions are often blended together, making it impossible to interpret grades as a true measure of what a student has mastered and at what level for a particular academic learning outcome.

As schools advance their work and move to a developing level for this design principle, rubrics clearly define and articulate student expectations for dispositions and provide more opportunity for student growth. Teachers in these competency-based learning schools assess these dispositions on a regular and ongoing basis, throughout a unit, course, or grade level. Teachers and the school use data collected through these assessments to determine a student's college and career readiness. When it comes to the reporting of grades, developing competency-based learning schools have created systems and structures to allow progress toward mastery of both learning outcomes that measure application and creation of knowledge and dispositions to be completely separated when reported as grades.

As competency-based learning schools move to the highest-performing level, instruction and assessment of skills and dispositions becomes ongoing, with students being guided along their own learning progression within these competencies. In these schools, students receive ample opportunities for reflection and growth throughout the learning process. Student self-reflection is a regular part of the assessment process and students take active ownership in their growth related to these noncurricular cognitive competencies. Both learning outcomes and dispositions appear as separate grades on both report cards and transcripts. See figure 8.5.

Design Principle 5: Learning Outcomes Measure Both Academic Skills and Dispositions	
Big Ideas:	Notes:
• Both learning outcomes and dispositions are designed so that demonstration of mastery includes application of skills and knowledge. Multiple and varied opportunities exist to assess both learning outcomes and dispositions. • Teachers completely separate learning outcomes and dispositions when they report grades. Expanded learning opportunities provide a way for students to personalize how they will demonstrate mastery of lifelong learning skills based on their needs and life experiences in order to help them be college and career ready.	

Indicator	SCALE		
	Performing School meets all characteristics in Developing and improves by . . .	**Developing** School meets all characteristics in Initiating and improves by . . .	**Initiating** School characteristics include . . .
Learning Outcome and Disposition Design	Instruction and assessment of skills and dispositions are ongoing, with students being guided along their own learning progression within these competencies. Students receive ample opportunities for reflection and growth. Student self-reflection is a regular part of the assessment process and students take active ownership in their growth related to these noncurricular cognitive competencies.	Student expectations for dispositions are clearly defined by rubrics that provide more opportunity for growth. Teachers assess these dispositions on a regular and ongoing basis. The school uses collected data to determine a student's college and career readiness.	Learning outcomes measure application and creation of knowledge as well as the development of important skills and dispositions. The dispositions are not defined by one specific rubric and are only assessed at certain times during the year, making student ownership limited.
Separation of Learning Outcomes and Disposition Grades	Both learning outcomes and dispositions appear as separate grades on both report cards and transcripts.	Progress toward mastery of both learning outcomes that measure application and creation of knowledge and dispositions are completely separated when reported as grades.	Learning outcomes and dispositions are blended together when reported as grades.

Figure 8.5: Rubric for competency-based learning school-design principle 5.

How the Rubric Can Help Build Your School's Journey

We reminded readers at the beginning of this chapter that moving a school from a traditional to a competency-based structure is a journey that has multiple entry points and can look different from school to school and district to district. The best way to start your journey is to first use the competency-based learning school-design rubric for self-reflection. In an effort to develop an implementation plan for competency-based learning, school leaders should encourage their stakeholders (educators, students, parents, and community leaders) to take a deep dive with this tool to answer these important questions (see figure 8.6).

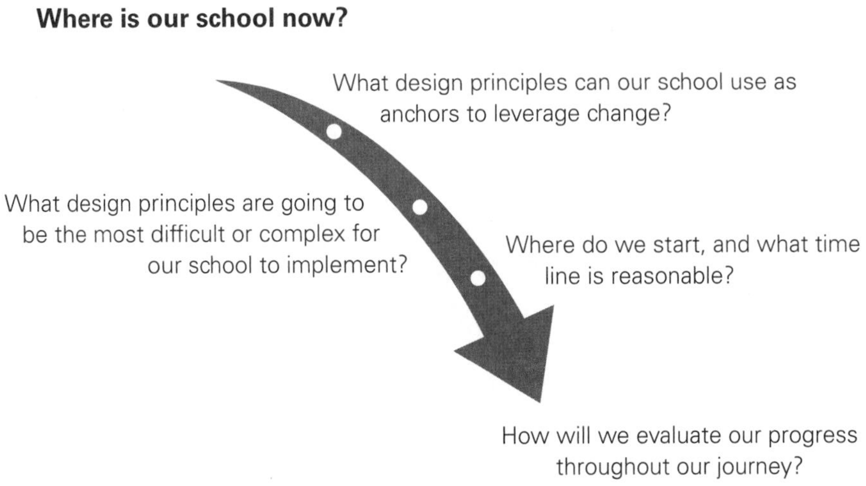

Where is our school now?

What design principles can our school use as anchors to leverage change?

What design principles are going to be the most difficult or complex for our school to implement?

Where do we start, and what time line is reasonable?

How will we evaluate our progress throughout our journey?

Figure 8.6: Critical questions for stakeholders when starting competency-based learning.

Where Is Our School Now?

Identifying a starting point for the work is critical. It will set the tone and the pace for the implementation plan that will need to be developed to move the school from where it is to where it wants to be. Using this rubric for self-reflection will help stakeholders take inventory of what resources it has available to help through the transition and what foundational work has been done (or needs to be done) to support the new competency-based learning structure. For example, through a self-assessment process a school may determine that its teachers do not have enough of an understanding of depth of knowledge to be able to assess the cognitive demand of the school's standards framework, one of the components of an initiating-level school with the first competency-based learning design principle. A different school may discover that its teachers do not have enough of an understanding of rubrics and rubric-based grading to be able to start to implement the assessment design principle, and time may need to be spent developing this prerequisite knowledge. This rubric will help schools find their starting point, an important part of the journey.

What Design Principles Can Our School Use as Anchors to Leverage Change?

There are many ways to enter the competency-based learning journey, but knowing which way to enter in order to leverage support with stakeholders is critical. During the self-reflection process as school leaders work with stakeholders to identify where the school is and where it wants to go, it may become apparent that some design principles will be easier for the school to implement than others. This could happen for a variety of reasons. First, the school may already be doing specific elements of that design principle, either as a whole school or through a smaller program or pilot. Second, teachers in the school may already have ample prerequisite knowledge necessary to implement one of the design principles sooner than another. Third, the school may simply have a structure or climate that might be more conducive to implementing one design principle over another. Whatever the case may be, it is critical for a school to identify which principles can be anchored to leverage change.

Many schools think there is a linear pattern to the work and the design principles are listed in the order that they must be completed: develop robust competencies, reform assessment and grading, create differentiated support structures, separate academics and dispositions, and then develop a move-when-ready structure. While this order is one way to approach the work, it is not the only way. Some schools use a backward design approach and start with discussions on grading and reporting, recognizing that when teachers see that grading and reporting will change, it will force a change in philosophy for both the way teachers approach assessment (and then instruction) and also create the need for the development of a robust system of competencies. Some schools start simply with the move-when-ready discussion, starting with a clean slate and working with stakeholders to identify how such an approach could increase personalization for students through choice and voice, and knowing that when stakeholders get excited about this idea it will lead to the need to discuss other design principles. Understanding which design principles can help a school make gains putting competency-based learning into practice is a critical step in the competency-based learning implementation journey.

What Design Principles Are Going to Be Most Difficult or Complex for Our School to Implement?

This question runs parallel to the previous one. Through the self-reflection process a school must determine which design principles it can use to leverage change because they will be easier to implement, but it must also identify the principles that will be the most difficult to enact. Schools will need to spend time identifying tools, resources, and strategies to overcome this challenge.

Many schools that are new to this work struggle with the final design principle, the move-when-ready one. This principle requires a substantial amount of redesign to the very foundational structure of schools. This can include how the school organizes students into grade levels or courses, how it is staffed, and its pending patterns and priorities. If the school needs to get clearance from a reluctant governing body to make any of these changes, this design principle could become a challenge. For this school, additional time will need to be spent to create buy-in among those elected officials. Other schools may find the grading and reporting discussion is the most difficult (part of design principle 3). If the school has historically done well on traditional measures of school success, stakeholders may be reluctant to change—reminiscent of the "if it isn't broken don't fix it!" mentality. This is especially true in affluent communities, where college acceptance and graduation rates are high and the school community generally believes that its school is already high performing, even though it may not be using the best measures to make such a bold statement. With either of these examples, it is essential for a school to know at the onset of the journey which design principles are going to require additional effort to implement so that an appropriate set of strategies can be built into the plan.

Where Do We Start, and What Time Line Is Reasonable?

Competency-based learning cannot be implemented overnight, but depending on where a school enters the journey and where it wants to go, implementation time lines will vary greatly from school to school and district to district. At the onset of the journey the school must identify what its time line will be for the work. This rubric can provide great insight into answering that question. In our experience, a time line of three to five years is typical for this work. Anything fewer than three years is often too rushed and leads to gaps in the implementation, and any longer can make it difficult to force the implementation to stick and become a part of the culture of the school community. Many schools face a fair amount of turnover with staff, but a three- to five-year window may be enough to keep the key people for the implementation in place, including both school leaders and other governing bodies.

Here is an example of a four-year implementation time line developed for a traditional secondary school that rated itself at the initiating phase to help implement the second design principle on meaningful assessment.

> ▸ **Year 1:** Train staff on developing rubric-based QPAs and using competency-friendly grading practices. Develop, validate, administer, validate using student work, and refine one QPA over the course of one school year.

▸ **Year 2:** Expect all teachers to implement at least three QPAs during the year. Expect that all assignments and QPAs are graded using rubrics but that a final grade is still reported on the one hundred–point scale. Encourage staff to implement competency-friendly grading practices in their classrooms.

▸ **Year 3:** Expect collaborative teams to develop additional QPAs in each grade level and content area, calibrating their rubrics and assignments with their team. Implement common schoolwide grading practices such as a rubric scale, separation of academics from academic behaviors, and reassessment for all.

▸ **Year 4:** Expect that all assessments that measure competency are performance assessments and that they are made available to students when they are ready to show what they know. Ensure that all teachers are using the same common grading practices from grade level to grade level and course to course in the school. Expand on the choices that students have to demonstrate evidence of their learning. Calibrate all work through the work of collaborative teams.

How Will We Evaluate Our Progress Throughout Our Journey?

At the onset of the journey, the school must establish an evaluation plan to gauge the success of its implementation. This plan will become critical in the "selling" of the plan to stakeholders, and ultimately to creating buy-in and need for the work ahead. The evaluation plan should be specific: at the end of a three- to five-year period it should evaluate how changes in student achievement, instructional practices, assessment practices, and grading practices contributed to the competency-based learning structure. It should include to what degree professional development impacted and supported the work. It should rate to what extent student agency factored into the work. Finally, it should include how the professional learning community structure supported all of the work. During the strategic planning process, it may be helpful for the school to set goals for itself to guide its work and ultimately evaluate its success in implementing competency-based learning. Here are a few sample goals that a school may adopt for the work.

▸ Within three years, our school will implement a flexible period in the school day that will be used for reteaching, intervention, and enrichment. All students will access this time for this purpose on a regular basis and data will be kept to track how often students made effective use of this time, how often teachers assigned students to specific places during this time, and what impact the time had on student learning.

▸ Within five years, our school will eliminate the credit hour system for tracking what courses students have completed and instead move to a model where students will receive credit for courses based on whether or not they master each of the competencies for those courses.

▸ Within two years, our school will implement a system whereby reassessment will be encouraged and expected by all teachers to be carried out for all students for any assessment for which a student earns less than a proficient rating. The school will track data on how often reassessment is done and how often a student grade changes (and what that change is).

Goals such as the ones identified above will help a school stay focused on its implementation time line but will also provide valuable data to be used later when it is time to evaluate the success of the implementation with stakeholders.

Top-Five List for Successful Transition to Competency-Based Learning

A
t the beginning of this book, we suggested that our American education system is broken. Many educators are currently using temporary fixes as we hobble along until we can devise a better solution. We went on to claim that in our efforts to hold people accountable and uphold the ideals of a free and appropriate education for all, our society has lost sight of what the real purpose of schools *should* be: learning for all, whatever it takes (DuFour et al., 2016). As a solution to this problem, we introduced a learning-centered philosophy and approach to education called competency-based learning. We walked you through what you need to know about this philosophy in order to effectively lead your school through a transition from traditional to competency-based learning. We provided you with a road map so you can chart your own school or district's journey. As you begin your journey, we offer you these final pieces of advice and words of wisdom, in the form of a top-five list.

5. **Include all stakeholders in the work:** As a school leader, you will need buy-in and commitment from all school stakeholders, including teachers, students, parents, and community members, in order to make competency-based learning an integral part of your school culture.

4.   **Be a prophet of research:** As you start this journey, there will be many who try to resort to a more traditional philosophy or practice because that is what they know or are comfortable with. Don't let them challenge the work with their traditional views. Be a prophet of research, and bring research into the discussion whenever possible.

3.   **Don't compromise the model:** Too often, schools make concessions and compromises with stakeholders who are not ready to accept the competency-based learning philosophy. Be true to the model and stay the course; don't let the model get watered down or misdirected by a compromise that doesn't fit the school's beliefs, but also recognize where some concessions might be made.

2.   **Keep student learning at the center:** The hallmark of the competency-based learning philosophy is increased student learning. Repeat phrases like *grades are about what students learn, not what they earn* and as DuFour et al. (2016) say, *learning for all, whatever it takes.* When teams get derailed from their work, remind them to focus on students, not adult issues. Above all, keep students at the center of all your school does.

1.   **Start today:** No amount of planning will ever completely prepare your school to be successful on this journey, but you don't have to have all of the answers before your school begins. Start your school's journey today, even if you start slow. Doing something will be better than doing nothing. Your students deserve it. Your teachers deserve it. You deserve it.

Safe travels.

APPENDIX

Competency-Based Learning School-Design Rubric

Design Principle 1: Students Move When Ready			
Big Ideas: • Policy language supports a model where students advance academically upon demonstration of mastery—regardless of grade level. • Teachers monitor the pace and progress of students as they are challenged at their appropriate level. • Students must produce sufficient evidence in order to be deemed proficient.	Notes:		

Indicator	SCALE		
	Performing **School meets all characteristics in Developing and improves by . . .**	**Developing** **School meets all characteristics in Initiating and improves by . . .**	**Initiating** **School characteristics include . . .**
Policy Language	Policies provide students with multiple and varied opportunities to advance on demonstrated mastery any time, any place, any way, and at any pace, unbound by a school calendar or clock. They allow students to advance beyond the school that they are in to the next level. At the elementary level, policies support multiage groupings of students and at the secondary level, extensions to higher education when students are ready based on their own learning progression.	Policies allow teachers to meet students where they are by allowing them to access the curriculum that is before or beyond grade level as needed.	Policies support standards-referenced grading and student advancement, which happens at the end of a grade level or course.

page 1 of 10

Monitoring of Pace and Progress	The student effectively monitors and self-assesses his or her pace and progress. A mechanism exists for the school to track student pace and progress, such as a personalized learning plan.	Teachers have the ability to manage personalized classrooms with clear academic levels. They can group and regroup students so that they can access units that are before or beyond the grade-level curriculum as needed.	The school calendar drives student learning opportunities and monitoring by the school calendar and the start and end times of the school day in each grade level or course.
Evidence of Proficiency	The school has an established quality-control system with clearly defined levels of proficiency that teachers use to determine when students are ready to move on with teacher input.	Within the existing school calendar, the school has several opportunities for students to advance along their own continuum of learning upon demonstrated mastery through blended and online learning. At the elementary level, this happens through multiage classrooms and at the secondary level, through extended learning opportunities such as apprenticeships, community service, independent study, internships, performing groups, college courses, private instruction, and extended learning opportunities.	Students advance at the end of a grade level or course when they have produced sufficient evidence to be deemed proficient based on grade-level or course standards.

Design Principle 2: Competencies Include Explicit, Measurable, Transferable Learning Objectives That Empower Students

Big Ideas:	Notes:
• There is a framework of standards, learning progressions, and competencies aligned with national, state, or local frameworks. • Competencies have a high level of cognitive demand and rigor. • There is a system to calibrate the competencies across grade levels and content areas to ensure a common understanding of proficiency.	

Indicator	SCALE		
	Performing School meets all characteristics in Developing and improves by . . .	**Developing** School meets all characteristics in Initiating and improves by . . .	**Initiating** School characteristics include . . .
Framework of Standards and Competencies	Competencies are applicable to real-life situations and require an understanding of relationships among theories, principles, and concepts.	The school has expanded the framework of standards to include competencies with performance assessments and include both academic skills that are transferable across content areas as well as habits of learning behaviors. These are mapped K–12 as a continuum of learning progressions based on the standards so that students know exactly where they are and what they need to do next. The school district has established clear transitional and graduation competencies that articulate what it means to be ready for the next level.	The school has developed a framework of standards that are aligned with national, state, and local frameworks in the school and are limited to scope and sequence of the textbook, program, or resource.

page 3 of 10

Cognitive Demand	The cognitive demand of the competencies is high—they require students to have a deep understanding of content as well as application of knowledge to a variety of settings by promoting complex connections through creating, analyzing, designing, proving, developing, and formulating.	The cognitive demand of the competencies is medium—they ask students to show what they know in limited ways through identifying, defining, constructing, sum-marizing, displaying, listing, or recognizing. Teachers occasionally ask students to create conceptual connec-tions and exhibit a level of understanding that is beyond the stated facts or literal interpretation through reasoning, planning, interpreting, hypoth-esizing, investigating, and explaining.	The cognitive demand of the competencies is low—they ask for routine or rote thinking, and require basic recall of information, facts, definitions, and other similar simple tasks and procedures.
System of Calibration	In collaborative teams, teachers regularly engage in the calibration of the competencies across grade levels and content areas to ensure a common understanding of proficiency by looking at student work.	Standards-referenced grading makes it clear what students know and how they are progressing. Teachers have a shared understanding of proficiency by grade level and course by looking at student work.	The competencies are very specific to the facts in the content. The school has selected a taxonomy to have common language about depth of knowledge and has started a process to identify the competencies for each grade level, content area, and course.

Design Principle 3: Assessment Is Meaningful			
Big Ideas: • Assessment practices make extensive use of quality performance assessment and allow teachers to assess skills or concepts in a variety of ways. • Grades are about what students learn, not what they earn. • Teachers regularly calibrate their instruction, grading, and assessment practices to develop a common understanding of proficiency.	Notes:		

Indicator	SCALE		
	Performing **School meets all characteristics in Developing and improves by . . .**	**Developing** **School meets all characteristics in Initiating and improves by . . .**	**Initiating** **School characteristics include . . .**
Assessment Practices	The use of quality performance assessments is widespread among all teachers and is the primary type of assessment they use with students to demonstrate mastery. Just-in-time assessments indicate when students are proficient. The school has developed the capacity for project-based learning or other ways for students to demonstrate knowledge at the highest level.	In addition to traditional assessment measures, teachers in the school make extensive use of formative assessment and some use of performance assessments— multistep assignments with clear criteria, expectations, and processes that measure how well a student transfers knowledge and applies complex skills to create or refine an original product. Students have choice about how to demonstrate their learning.	Although linked to specific competencies, assessment practices are still very traditional— predominantly paper-and-pencil tests and quizzes with no schoolwide systemic attempt to control the depth of knowledge level. Few assessments are graded against a well-defined rubric and little to no common understanding exists among teachers on what proficiency means.

Grading Practices	All assessments are graded against well-defined rubrics. The school has established a system to hold all teachers accountable for the effective use of the common grading expectations. Teachers hold each other accountable as members of a collaborative team.	Most assessments are graded against a well-defined rubric. The school has established a common set of competency-friendly grading practices. Practices include separation of formative and summative assessments, use of a rubric scale, elimination of quarter averages, and promotion of reassessment without penalty.	Few assessments are graded against a well-defined rubric. Grading practices differ greatly from teacher to teacher and grade level to grade level.
System of Calibration	Teachers collaborate regularly in teams to calibrate assessments and to use the data from them to align instruction and make greater revisions of the curriculum as well as monitor the pace and progress of individual students.	Teachers regularly collaborate to develop and calibrate these performance assessments against learning progressions by reviewing student work and monitoring the pace and progress of individual students. Teachers are beginning to align their instructional strategies with performance assessments.	Little to no common understanding exists among teachers of different grade levels and content areas on what proficiency means.

Design Principle 4: Students Receive Differentiated Support		

Big Ideas:

- Structures exist to ensure that all students have access to and receive regular, timely, differentiated support.
- There are systems to monitor the pace and progress of individual students throughout their learning.

Notes:

Indicator	SCALE		
	Performing **School meets all characteristics in Developing and improves by . . .**	**Developing** **School meets all characteristics in Initiating and improves by . . .**	**Initiating** **School characteristics include . . .**
Support Structures	The school has a comprehensive support structure to ensure that students who are not making progress receive regular, timely, differentiated support based on their individual learning needs at the time of their learning. Professionals who share the same students, including teachers, special educators, guidance counselors, administrators, and other specialists, collaborate regularly as teams on these personalized, differentiated support structures for students.	The school has some structures in place to ensure that all students receive regular, timely, differentiated support based on their individual learning needs. These structures are offered regardless of whether or not the student is identified in some way and are scheduled in such a way so that all students can access them without conflicts in their schedule (such as a flexible learning period that all students can access).	The school has limited structures in place to ensure that all students receive regular timely, differentiated support based on their individual learning needs. Most of the structures are limited, either to identified students (IEP, EL, 504, and so on) who require them for an education plan or to students who are available only at certain times of the day when these structures are made available in the schedule (such as lunch or after school).

Monitoring Structures	Teams monitor the individual pace and progress of students throughout their learning. School leaders use the information collected on pace and progress to help develop personalized professional development plans for teachers to improve instruction.	Teachers have a shared understanding of what the typical pace and progress of students should be throughout their learning and use it to monitor individual students.	Teachers work individually to monitor the pace and progress of their students and make instructional adjustments as necessary. Specialists are included as necessary.

Design Principle 5: Learning Outcomes Measure Both Academic Skills and Dispositions			
Big Ideas: • Both learning outcomes and dispositions are designed so that demonstration of mastery includes application of skills and knowledge. Multiple and varied opportunities exist to assess both learning outcomes and dispositions. • Teachers completely separate learning outcomes and dispositions when they report grades. • Expanded learning opportunities provide a way for students to personalize how they will demonstrate mastery of lifelong learning skills based on their needs and life experiences in order to help them be college and career ready.	Notes:		

Indicator	SCALE		
	Performing **School meets all characteristics in Developing and improves by . . .**	**Developing** **School meets all characteristics in Initiating and improves by . . .**	**Initiating** **School characteristics include . . .**
Learning Outcome and Disposition Design	Instruction and assessment of skills and dispositions are ongoing, with students being guided along their own learning progression within these competencies. Students receive ample opportunities for reflection and growth. Student self-reflection is a regular part of the assessment process and students take active ownership in their growth related to these noncurricular cognitive competencies.	Student expectations for dispositions are clearly defined by rubrics that provide more opportunity for growth. Teachers assess these dispositions on a regular and ongoing basis. The school uses collected data to determine a student's college and career readiness.	Learning outcomes measure application and creation of knowledge as well as the development of important skills and dispositions. The dispositions are not defined by one specific rubric and are only assessed at certain times during the year, making student ownership limited.

Separation of Learning Outcomes and Disposition Grades	Both learning outcomes and dispositions appear as separate grades on both report cards and transcripts.	Progress toward mastery of both learning outcomes that measure application and creation of knowledge and dispositions are completely separated when reported as grades.	Learning outcomes and dispositions are blended together when reported as grades.

REFERENCES AND RESOURCES

7th grade social studies competency template: Basic course information. (n.d.). Accessed at https://docs.google.com/document/edit?hgd=1&id=1n9zz4VghWJYThtBdTVtU0z 7mVJpVmwx2qtCO36JTrvo on February 8, 2017.

Achieve. (2015). *The role of learning progressions in competency-based pathways*. Washington, DC: Author.

ACT. (2013). *2012 retention/completion summary tables*. Accessed at www.act.org /research/policymakers/pdf/12retain_trends.pdf on August 19, 2013.

Adams, S. (2013, October 11). The 10 skills employers most want in 20-something employees. *Forbes*. Accessed at www.forbes.com/sites/susanadams/2013/10/11/the-10 -skills-employers-most-want-in-20-something-employees/#29c591df752d on September 22, 2016.

Ainsworth, L. (2003). *Power standards: Identifying the standards that matter most*. Englewood, CO: Advanced Learning Press.

Ainsworth, L., & Viegut, D. (2006). *Common formative assessments: How to connect standards-based instruction and assessment*. Thousand Oaks, CA: Corwin Press.

Aungst, G. (2014, September 4). *Using Webb's depth of knowledge to increase rigor* [Blog post]. Accessed at www.edutopia.org/blog/webbs-depth-knowledge-increase-rigor -gerald-aungst on January 24, 2017.

Bailey, K., & Jakicic, C. (2012). *Common formative assessment: A toolkit for Professional Learning Communities at Work*. Bloomington, IN: Solution Tree Press.

Bellanca, J. A. (Ed.). (2015). *Deeper learning: Beyond 21st century skills*. Bloomington, IN: Solution Tree Press.

Bloom, B. S. (1956). *Taxonomy of educational objectives: The classification of educational goals*. New York: David McKay.

Bramante, F., & Colby, R. (2012). *Off the clock: Moving education from time to competency*. Thousand Oaks, CA: Corwin Press.

Bridges, W. (2009). *Managing transitions: Making the most of change* (3rd ed.). Philadelphia: Da Capo Press.

Bristow, S., & Patrick, S. (2014). *An international study in competency education: Postcards from abroad*. Vienna, VA: International Association for K–12 Online Learning.

Brookhart, S. M. (2013). *How to create and use rubrics for formative assessment and grading.* Alexandria, VA: Association for Supervision and Curriculum Development.

Brown, C., & Mednick, A. (2012). *Quality performance assessment*: *A guide for schools and districts.* Boston: Center for Collaborative Education. Accessed at www.ode.state.or.us /wma/teachlearn/testing/resources/qpa_guide_oregon.pdf on February 8, 2017.

Bruner, J. S. (1960). *The process of education.* Cambridge, MA: Harvard University Press.

Buck Institute for Education. (n.d.a). *What is project based learning (PBL)?* Accessed at www. bie.org/about/what_pbl on June 15, 2017.

Buck Institute for Education. (n.d.b). *Why project based learning (PBL)?* Accessed at www.bie.org/about/why_pbl on September 22, 2016.

Buffum, A., Mattos, M., & Weber, C. (2010). The why behind RtI. *Educational Leadership,* *68*(2), 10–16.

Buffum, A., Mattos, M., & Weber, C. (2012). *Simplifying response to intervention*: *Four essential guiding principles.* Bloomington, IN: Solution Tree Press.

Burke, K. (2010). *Balanced assessment: From formative to summative.* Bloomington, IN: Solution Tree Press.

Calkins, L. (2017). *Units of study—Writing.* Accessed at www.heinemann.com/unitsofstudy /writing/default.aspx on February 8, 2017.

Center for Collaborative Education. (2012). *Quality performance assessment*: *A guide for schools and districts.* Boston: Author. Accessed at www.ode.state.or.us/wma /teachlearn/testing/resources/qpa_guide_oregon.pdf on February 8, 2017.

Christensen, C. M. (n.d.). *Disruptive innovation.* Accessed at www.claytonchristensen.com /key-concepts on June 7, 2017.

Colby, R. (2017). *Competency-based education: A new architecture for K–12 schooling.* Cambridge, MA: Harvard Education Press.

Common Core State Standards Initiative. (n.d.a). *About the standards.* Accessed at www.corestandards.org/about-the-standards on February 8, 2017.

Common Core State Standards Initiative. (n.d.b). *Development process.* Accessed at www .corestandards.org/about-the-standards/development-process on August 29, 2016.

Conzemius, A. E., & O'Neill, J. (2014). *The handbook for SMART school teams: Revitalizing best practices for collaboration* (2nd ed.). Bloomington, IN: Solution Tree Press.

Costa, A., & Kallick, B. (1995). Assessment in the learning organization: Shifting the paradigm. Alexandria, VA: Association for Supervision and Curriculum Development.

D'Agostino, J. V., & Murphy, J. A. (2004). A meta-analysis of reading recovery in United States schools. *Educational Evaluation and Policy Analysis, 26*(1), 23–38.

Darling-Hammond, L., & Adamson, F. (2014). *Beyond the bubble test: How performance assessments support 21st century learning.* San Francisco: Jossey-Bass.

Dewey, J. (1897). *My pedagogic creed.* Accessed at http://dewey.pragmatism.org/creed.htm on June 15, 2017.

DuFour, R. (2015). *In praise of American educators*: *And how they can become even better.* Bloomington, IN: Solution Tree Press.

DuFour, R., DuFour, R., Eaker, R., & Many, T. W. (2006). *Learning by doing: A handbook for Professional Learning Communities at Work* (1st ed.). Bloomington, IN: Solution Tree Press.

DuFour, R., DuFour, R., Eaker, R., & Many, T. W. (2010). *Learning by doing: A handbook for Professional Learning Communities at Work* (2nd ed.). Bloomington, IN: Solution Tree Press.

DuFour, R., DuFour, R., Eaker, R., Many, T. W., & Mattos, M. (2016). *Learning by doing: A handbook for Professional Learning Communities at Work* (3rd ed.). Bloomington, IN: Solution Tree Press.

DuFour, R., & Fullan, M. (2013). *Cultures built to last: Systemic PLCs at Work*. Bloomington, IN: Solution Tree Press.

DuFour, R., Reeves, D., & DuFour, R. (2018). *Responding to the Every Student Succeeds Act With the PLC at Work Process*. Bloomington, IN: Solution Tree Press.

Epping School District. (2013). *Epping School District competencies for learning*. Accessed at www.sau14.org/ESD%20Competencies%20for%20Learning%20-%20July%202013.pdf on August 19, 2016.

Every Student Succeeds Act of 2015, Pub. L. No. 114–95, 20 U.S.C. § 1177 (2015).

Fullan, M. (2001). *Leading in a culture of change*. San Francisco: Jossey-Bass.

Gobble, T., Onuscheck, M., Reibel, A. R., & Twadell, E. (2016). *Proficiency-based assessment: Process, not product*. Bloomington, IN: Solution Tree Press.

Gray, A. (2016). *The 10 skills you need to thrive in the Fourth Industrial Revolution*. Accessed at www.weforum.org/agenda/2016/01/the-10-skills-you-need-to-thrive-in-the-fourth-industrial-revolution on August 3, 2016.

Guskey, T. R. (Ed.). (2009). *Practical solutions for serious problems in standards-based grading*. Thousand Oaks, CA: Corwin Press.

Henry County Schools. (n.d.a). *Competency-based learning introduction*. Accessed at http://schoolwires.henry.k12.ga.us/Page/84942 on February 8, 2017.

Henry County Schools. (n.d.b) *Cross-curricular graduation competencies*. Accessed at http://schoolwires.henry.k12.ga.us/site/handlers/filedownload.ashx?moduleinstanceid=106366&dataid=128172&FileName=Four%20Cs%20Graduation%20Competencies%20Perf%20Indicators%20and%20Scoring%20Criteria.pdf on June 15, 2017.

Henry County Schools. (n.d.c). *Elementary science graduation competencies*. Accessed at http://schoolwires.henry.k12.ga.us/cms/lib08/GA01000549/Centricity/Domain/64/Elementary%20Science%20Competencies.pdf on February 8, 2017.

Heritage, M. (2008). *Learning progressions: Supporting instruction and formative assessment*. Washington, DC: Council of Chief State School Officers.

Hess, K. K. (2006). *Performance assessment-planning template*. Dover, NH: Center for Assessment.

Hess, K. K. (2010). Using learning progressions to monitor progress across grades. *Science and Children, 47*(6), 57–61.

Hess, K. K. (2012). *Learning progressions in K–8 classrooms: How progress maps can influence classroom practice and perceptions and help teachers make more informed instructional decisions in support of struggling learners* (Synthesis report 87). Minneapolis: University of Minnesota, National Center on Educational Outcomes.

Hess, K. (2013). *Linking research with practice: A local assessment toolkit to guide school leaders.* Underhill, VT: Educational Research in Action.

Horn, M. B., & Staker, H. (2015). *Blended: Using disruptive innovation to improve schools.* San Francisco: Jossey-Bass.

Individuals With Disabilities Education Improvement Act of 2004, Pub. L. No. 108-446 § 300.115 (2004).

International Association for K–12 Online Learning. (2016, April). *iNACOL's policy priorities.* Accessed at www.inacol.org/our-work/inacol-center-for-policy-advocacy on October 30, 2016.

International Association for K–12 Online Learning. (n.d.). *A snapshot of K–12 competency education state policy across the United States.* Accessed at www.competencyworks.org /wp-content/uploads/2012/05/2016-Snapshot-of-CBE-State-Policytimestamp.png on June 7, 2017.

Kelchen, R. (2015). *The landscape of competency-based education: Enrollments, demographics, and affordability.* Washington, DC: American Enterprise Institute Center on Higher Education Reform.

Khanna, D. (2013). *A look back at how the content industry almost killed Blockbuster and Netflix (and the VCR).* Accessed at https://techcrunch.com/2013/12/27/how-the -content-industry-almost-killed-blockbuster-and-netflix on June 7, 2017.

Kotter, J. P. (1996). *Leading change.* Boston: Harvard Business School Press.

Kotter, J. P., & Rathgeber, H. (2005). *Our iceberg is melting: Changing and succeeding under any conditions.* New York: Portfolio.

Lench, S., Fukuda, E., & Anderson, R. (2015). *Essential skills and dispositions: Developmental frameworks for collaboration, creativity, communication, and self-direction.* Lexington, KY: Center for Innovation in Education at the University of Kentucky.

Maine Department of Education. (2008). *Summary of the reorganization law.* Accessed at www.maine.gov/education/reorg/lawsummary.html on June 27, 2017.

Maine Department of Education. (2013). *Design criteria chart.* Accessed at https://www1. maine.gov/doe/proficiency/standards/Design%20Criteria%20Chart%20Defining%20 Performance%20Indicators.pdf on September 21, 2017.

Marzano, R. (2003). *What works in schools: Translating research into action.* Alexandria, VA: Association for Supervision and Curriculum Development.

Marzano, R. J., & Haystead, M. W. (2008). *Making standards useful in the classroom.* Alexandria, VA: Association for Supervision and Curriculum Development.

Mattos, M., & Buffum, A. (Eds.). (2015). *It's about time: Planning interventions and extensions in secondary school.* Bloomington, IN: Solution Tree Press.

McTighe, J., & Wiggins, G. (2004). *The understanding by design professional development workbook.* Alexandria, VA: Association for Supervision and Curriculum Development.

McTighe, J., & Wiggins, G. (2013). *Essential questions: Opening doors to student understanding.* Alexandria, VA: Association for Supervision and Curriculum Development.

Mosher, F. (2011). *The role of learning progressions in standards-based education reform.* Accessed at http://repository.upenn.edu/cgi/viewcontent.cgi?article=1010&context =cpre_policybriefs on June 15, 2017.

Moss, C. M., & Brookhart, S. M. (2012). *Learning targets: Helping students aim for understanding in today's lesson.* Alexandria, VA: Association for Supervision and Curriculum Development.

National Center for Learning Disabilities. (n.d.). *Competency-based education: Frequently asked questions* [Blog post]. Accessed at www.ncld.org/archives/blog/competency -based-education-frequently-asked-questions on April 14, 2017.

National Governors Association Center for Best Practices & Council of Chief State School Officers. (2010a). *Common Core State Standards for English language arts and literacy in history/social studies, science, and technical subjects.* Washington, DC: Authors. Accessed at www.corestandards.org/assets/CCSSI_ELA%20Standards.pdf on September 5, 2017.

National Governors Association Center for Best Practices & Council of Chief State School Officers. (2010b). *Common Core State Standards for mathematics.* Washington, DC: Authors. Accessed at www.corestandards.org/assets/CCSSI_Math%20Standards .pdf on September 5, 2017.

National School Reform Faculty. (2002). *Future protocol a.k.a. back to the future.* Accessed at www.nsrfharmony.org/system/files/protocols/future.pdf on July 5, 2016.

New Hampshire Department of Education. (n.d.). *New Hampshire Common Core State Standards–aligned mathematics model graduation competencies.* Accessed at www .education.nh.gov/innovations/hs_redesign/documents/model_math_competencies .pdf on February 8, 2017.

New Hampshire Department of Education. (2010). *Competency validation rubric.* Accessed at www.education.nh.gov/innovations/hs_redesign/documents/validation _rubric.pdf on September 12, 2016.

New Hampshire Department of Education. (2013). *State model competencies.* Accessed at www.education.nh.gov/innovations/hs_redesign/competencies.htm on June 15, 2017.

New Hampshire Department of Education. (2014). *New Hampshire work-study practices*: *Rationale for work-study practices—June 2014.* Accessed at www.education.nh.gov /innovations/hs_redesign/documents/nhsbea-approved-final.pdf on October 30, 2016.

No Child Left Behind Act of 2001, Pub. L. No. 107–110, 20 U.S.C. § 6319 (2002).

O'Connor, K. (2009). *How to grade for learning, K–12* (3rd ed.). Thousand Oaks, CA: Corwin Press.

Perkins, D. N. (2009). *Making learning whole: How seven principles of teaching can transform education.* San Francisco: Jossey-Bass.

Popham, W. J. (2007). All about accountability: The lowdown on learning progressions. *Educational Leadership, 64*(7), 83–84.

Popham, W. J. (2008). *Transformative assessment.* Alexandria, VA: Association for Supervision and Curriculum Development.

Reeves, D. (2010). *Transforming professional development into student results.* Alexandria, VA: Association for Supervision and Curriculum Development.

Rochester School Department. (n.d.). *Rochester School District competency-based learning grade 3 parent information sheet*: *Competency statements.* Accessed at www.rochesterschools .com/competencies/CompetencyStatements_Grade3.pdf on February 8, 2017.

Sergiovanni, T. J. (2007). *Perspectives on school leadership*: *Taking another look* (Monograph no. 16). Camberwell, Victoria, Australia: Australian Council for Educational Research, Australian Principals Centre. Accessed at http://research.acer.edu.au/cgi /viewcontent.cgi?article=1015&context=apc_monographs on September 1, 2016.

Silva, E., White, T., & Toch, T. (2015). *The Carnegie Unit: A century-old standard in a changing education landscape.* Stanford, CA: Carnegie Foundation for the Advancement of Teaching.

Smith, S. K., Chavez, A. M., & Seaman, G. W. (2012). *Teacher as architect: Instructional design and delivery for the modern teacher.* Las Vegas, NV: Modern Teacher Press.

Souhegan High School. (n.d.). *Program of studies 2016–2017.* Accessed at http://sau39 .org/cms/lib07/NH01912488/Centricity/Domain/8/Program%20of%20Studies %2016-17.pdf on August 18, 2016.

Stiggins, R. (2005). From formative assessment to assessment for learning: A path to success in standards-based schools. *Phi Delta Kappan, 87*(4), 324–328.

Strong American Schools. (2008). *Diploma to nowhere.* Washington, DC: Author. Accessed at www.broadeducation.org/asset/1128-diploma%20to %20nowhere.pdf on April 8, 2015.

Sturgis, C. (2015). *Implementing competency education in K–12 systems: Insights from local leaders.* Vienna, VA: International Association for K–12 Online Learning, Texas Education Agency. (2010). *Texas Essential Knowledge and Skills for English Language Arts and Reading, Subchapter A. Elementary.* Accessed at http://ritter.tea.state.tx.us/rules/tac /chapter110/ch110a.html#110.16 on January 17, 2017.

Tomlinson, C. A., & Moon, T. R. (2013). *Assessment and student success in a differentiated classroom.* Alexandria, VA: Association for Supervision and Curriculum Development.

Vatterott, C. (2015). *Rethinking grading: Meaningful assessment for standards-based learning.* Alexandria, VA: Association for Supervision and Curriculum Development.

Vaughn, S., Gersten, R., & Chard, D. J. (2000). The underlying message in LD intervention research: Findings from research syntheses. *Exceptional Children, 67,* 99–114.

Webb, N. L. (2005). *Web alignment tool.* Wisconsin Center of Educational Research. University of Wisconsin-Madison. Accessed at http://static.pdesas.org/content /documents/M1-Slide_19_DOK_Wheel_Slide.pdf on June 15, 2017.

Weise, M. R., & Christensen, C. M. (2014). *Hire education: Mastery, modularization, and the workforce revolution.* Lexington, MA: Clayton Christensen Institute for Disruptive Innovation.

Wiggins, G., & McTighe, J. (1998). *Understanding by design.* Alexandria, VA: Association for Supervision and Curriculum Development.

Wiggins, G., & McTighe, J. (2005). *Understanding by design* (2nd ed.). Alexandria, VA: Association for Supervision and Curriculum Development.

World Economic Forum. (2016). *Future of jobs report: Employment, skills, and strategy for the fourth industrial revolution.* Geneva, Switzerland: Author.

Wormeli, R. (2006). *Fair isn't always equal: Assessing and grading in the differentiated classroom.* Portland, ME: Stenhouse.

INDEX

A

academic behavior versus learning evidence, 73–75, 83–84

academic skills and dispositions, 181–183

Achieve, 50

acquisition, 49

ACT, 133

Adamson, F., 38

Ainsworth, L., 35

à la carte models, 11

application, 49

assessments

    See also performance assessments

    convergent, 139

    formative (*for* learning), 7, 16, 38, 79–80, 94–95, 109

    meaningful, 14–18

    Quality Performance Assessment (QPA), 14–15

    reassessments, 17, 84–85, 95

    relationship between grades and, 79–81

    role of, 175–178

    student's self-, 117–118

    summative (*of* learning), 7, 16, 38, 80–81, 94, 109, 119–124

B

backward design, 24, 78, 94

Bailey, K., 94, 95

Blended (Horn and Staker), 41

blended learning, 10–11

bottom-up approach, 55

blockers

    concerned-for-their-child's-transcript parent, 164

    guinea-pig student, 164

    overworked-teacher, 163–164

Bloom's taxonomy, 95–107

Bramante, F., 8–9, 35, 46, 117

Brookhart, S. M., 78, 81, 121, 168

Bruner, J., 45–46

Buck Institute for Education, 64

Buffum, A., 39–40, 132, 138–139, 141, 142, 144, 178

C

Calkins, L., 42

Carnegie, A., 8

Carnegie unit, 8–9

Center for Collaborative Education (CCE), 14–15, 38, 89, 111–117, 119, 121, 176

change

    case for, 149–151

    celebrate short-term wins, 162–163

    communicating, 160–161

    culture for, 165–166

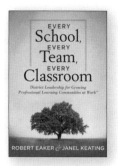

Every School, Every Team, Every Classroom
Robert Eaker and Janel Keating
The PLC journey begins with a dedication to ensuring the learning of every student. Using many examples and reproducible tools, the authors explain the need to focus on creating simultaneous top-down *and* bottom-up leadership. Learn how to grow PLCs by encouraging innovation at every level.
BKF534

Learning by Doing, Third Edition
Richard DuFour, Rebecca DuFour, Robert Eaker, Thomas W. Many, and Mike Mattos
Discover how to transform your school or district into a high-performing PLC. The third edition of this comprehensive action guide offers new strategies for addressing critical PLC topics, including hiring and retaining new staff, creating team-developed common formative assessments, and more.
BKF746

School Improvement for All
Sharon V. Kramer and Sarah Schuhl
Discover how to use *School Improvement for All* to drive sustained school improvement and increase student achievement in your PLC. Each chapter includes space for teacher teams to determine next action steps and a list of questions to help bring greater focus to improvement efforts.
BKF770

Transforming School Culture [Second Edition]
Anthony Muhammad
The second edition of this best-selling resource delivers powerful, new insight into the four types of educators and how to work with each group to create thriving schools. The book also includes Dr. Muhammad's latest research and a new chapter of frequently asked questions.
BKF793

Solution Tree | Press

a division of

Solution Tree

Visit SolutionTree.com or call 800.733.6786 to order.

"Tremendous, tremendous, tremendous!

The speaker made me do some very deep internal reflection about the **PLC process** and the personal responsibility I have in making the school improvement process work **for ALL kids**."

—Marc Rodriguez, teacher effectiveness coach,
Denver Public Schools, Colorado

PD Services

Our experts draw from decades of research and their own experiences to bring you practical strategies for building and sustaining a high-performing PLC. You can choose from a range of customizable services, from a one-day overview to a multiyear process.

Book your PLC PD today!
888.763.9045

Solution Tree